SYSTEMS OF HOUSING SUPPLY AND HOUSING PRODUCTION IN EUROPE

Systems of Housing Supply and Housing Production in Europe
A comparison of the United Kingdom, the Netherlands and Germany

ANDREW GOLLAND
Centre for Comparative Housing Research
School of the Built Environment
De Montfort University, Leicester

LONDON AND NEW YORK

First published 1998 by Ashgate Publishing

Reissued 2018 by Routledge
2 Park Square, Milton Park, Abingdon, Oxon, OX14 4RN
711 Third Avenue, New York, NY 10017, USA

Routledge is an imprint of the Taylor & Francis Group, an informa business

Copyright © Andrew Golland 1998

All rights reserved. No part of this book may be reprinted or reproduced or utilised in any form or by any electronic, mechanical, or other means, now known or hereafter invented, including photocopying and recording, or in any information storage or retrieval system, without permission in writing from the publishers.

Notice:
Product or corporate names may be trademarks or registered trademarks, and are used only for identification and explanation without intent to infringe.

Publisher's Note
The publisher has gone to great lengths to ensure the quality of this reprint but points out that some imperfections in the original copies may be apparent.

Disclaimer
The publisher has made every effort to trace copyright holders and welcomes correspondence from those they have been unable to contact.

A Library of Congress record exists under LC control number: 98073403

ISBN 13: 978-1-138-34547-8 (hbk)
ISBN 13: 978-1-138-34549-2 (pbk)
ISBN 13: 978-0-429-43785-4 (ebk)

Contents

Figures and tables vi

Preface and acknowledgments xi

1 Introduction 1

2 Theory and method in comparative analysis 18

3 Systems of housing supply: between policy and process 44

4 Structure and agencies in housing supply 97

5 Housing production and housing systems: a statistical analysis 140

6 Conclusions 190

Bibliography and references 201

Figures and tables

Figure	1.1	Dwellings constructed per 1000 inhabitants	6
Figure	1.2	Housing production in the United Kingdom	7
Figure	1.3	Housing production in the Netherlands	8
Figure	1.4	Housing production in Germany	9
Figure	2.1	The political system	25
Figure	2.2	Elements of the system of housing supply	28
Figure	2.3	Structure and systems: conceptual framework	37
Figure	2.4	The measurement of housing outcomes	41
Figure	2.5	A philosophy of method	42
Figure	3.1	Housing investment as a percentage of GDP and GFCF	47
Figure	3.2	Housing production in Germany: first and second Förderungswege	52
Figure	3.3	Housing production in the Netherlands: Sector A and B housing	54
Table	3.1	Synthesis of production policy issues	56
Figure	3.4	Supply and ownership of land for housing development	57

Table	3.2	Synthesis of land policy issues	62
Figure	3.5	Development plans and land values	68
Table	3.3	Synthesis of planning policy issues	70
Figure	3.6	Land allocation and land availability	72
Table	3.4	Synthesis of land supply issues	76
Figure	3.7	Modes of infrastructure provision for housing development: the United Kingdom	79
Figure	3.8	Modes of infrastructure provision for housing development: the Netherlands	80
Figure	3.9	Modes of infrastructure provision for housing development: Germany	80
Table	3.5	Synthesis of issues relating to infrastructure provision	83
Figure	3.10	Housing supply by volume house builders in the United Kingdom	85
Figure	3.11	The building process in the Dutch market sector	87
Table	3.6	Synthesis of the building process	90
Figure	3.12	The role of state and market in housing supply	96
Figure	4.1	Linkages in housing supply in the Netherlands	106
Figure	4.2	British governments, 1970-1993	111
Figure	4.3	Dutch governments, 1970-1992	119
Figure	4.4	German governments, 1970-1993	126
Figure	4.5	The macroeconomies of the United Kingdom, the Netherlands and Germany	133
Table	5.1	Housing production: total output	142
Table	5.2	Net household increase	143

Table	5.3	Decreases in the housing stock	144
Table	5.4	Housing stock and households	145
Figure	5.1	Total housing production, household increase and housing stock decrease in the United Kingdom	147
Figure	5.2	Total housing production, household increase and housing stock decrease in the Netherlands	147
Figure	5.3	Total housing production, household increase and housing stock decrease in Germany	148
Figure	5.4	Housing suppliers, housing finance and housing tenure in the United Kingdom	151
Figure	5.5	Housing suppliers, housing finance and housing tenure in the Netherlands	152
Figure	5.6	Housing suppliers, housing finance and housing tenure in Germany	153
Table	5.5	Housing production in the United Kingdom	154
Table	5.6	Housing production in the Netherlands	155
Table	5.7	Housing production in Germany	156
Table	5.8	Nominal and real house prices in the United Kingdom, the Netherlands and Germany	162
Table	5.9	Nominal and real land plot prices in the United Kingdom, the Netherlands and Germany	163
Table	5.10	Nominal and real building costs per dwelling in the United Kingdom, the Netherlands and Germany	165
Table	5.11	House prices, land prices and building costs: data sources and definitions	167
Figure	5.7	Private sector housing production and profit in the United Kingdom	169
Figure	5.8	Private sector housing production and profit in the United Kingdom	169

Figure	5.9	Private sector housing production and profit in the Netherlands	171
Figure	5.10	Private sector housing production and profit in the Netherlands	172
Figure	5.11	Private sector housing production and profit in Germany	173
Figure	5.12	Private sector housing production and profit in Germany	174
Table	5.12	Unemployment in the United Kingdom, the Netherlands and Germany	177
Table	5.13	GDP per head in the United Kingdom, the Netherlands and Germany	178
Figure	5.13	Social sector housing production and unemployment in the United Kingdom	179
Figure	5.14	Social sector housing production and unemployment in the United Kingdom	180
Figure	5.15	Social sector housing production and unemployment in the Netherlands	181
Figure	5.16	Social sector housing production and unemployment in the Netherlands	182
Figure	5.17	Social sector housing production and unemployment in Germany	183
Figure	5.18	Social sector housing production and unemployment in Germany	184
Figure	5.19	Social sector housing production and GDP in the United Kingdom	185
Figure	5.20	Social sector housing production and GDP in the United Kingdom	186
Figure	5.21	Social sector housing production and GDP in the Netherlands	187

Figure	5.22	Social sector housing production and GDP in the Netherlands	187
Figure	5.23	Social sector housing production and GDP in Germany	188
Figure	5.24	Social sector housing production and GDP in Germany	188

Preface and acknowledgments

The investigation of European systems of housing supply springs from an interest in both the house building and land supply process, as well as from a desire to look further at the links between social science methods and housing. Coming from a land management perspective, I was initially interested in the potential application of economic theory for housing supply and how a number of frameworks might help to explain housing outcomes. Having taken the comparative direction however, I found the initial way to be a difficult route. In bringing together all the important facets which make up housing systems, it was necessary to utilise a more holistic framework drawing on a range of social science methods. In doing this, I believe that I am in good company although I have, throughout the book, attempted to clarify where I differ, or concur, with other researchers in the field.

Assisting me with my PhD dissertation, from which this book emanates, have been my two supervisors, Professor Michael Oxley and Norma Carter, also of the Department of Land Management. They have greatly encouraged me in the social science method and have ensured that sufficient financial means have been available to make visits abroad to the respective countries where I have learnt first hand about planning, land and housing policies. To them, I express my gratitude. The establishment of a Centre for Comparative Housing Research in 1995 under the direction of Professor Oxley, has proven to be a great incentive for the furthering and completion of this work. During the time of writing, comparative research has been carried out for The British Council, The Joseph Rowntree Foundation and the Royal Institution of Chartered Surveyors. In addition, several research projects on housing markets and housing need in the local and regional area have been carried out. This experience has assisted me in balancing the analysis of the different countries.

The countries which are compared in the book are the United Kingdom, the Netherlands and Germany. There is a scientific rationale for choosing this framework, which is given in the Introduction. However, no scientific 'experiment' can be carried out without the necessary components and instruments. It is thus important to state that of all the European countries, these three provide a reasonably good range of comparable data on housing supply and land markets. This does not mean that the findings of the research are foolproof; more that the statistical work can at least be challenged in the future. Another pragmatic reason for choosing these three countries is related to language skills, where some personal experience has been helpful. In addition, there have been several researchers in the other countries, who have always been very willing to assist, not only with the specific texts, but also in explaining more generally about the individual housing systems. In these respects, I would like to thank in particular Dr Peter Boelhouwer and Drs Marjolein Spaans of the OTB Research Institute at the University of Delft, and also Dr Thomas Hafner of the Städtebauliches Institut, University of Stuttgart. These individuals have always been especially prepared to discuss comparative issues, or organise visits for me in the Netherlands and Germany. This has been of great assistance.

The results, findings and outcomes from the broader comparative research programme are provided in a number of places including this book. Elsewhere, the reader is referred to articles by the author including Golland (1996;1994) and Spaans et al (1996). The first of these articles emanated from the European Network for Housing Research's Young Housing Researchers Conference held in Vienna in 1995. This was organised by a colleague from the Centre of Comparative Housing Research, Jacqueline Smith, and which proved to be a very useful forum for all in the transition stage to full PhD status. Otherwise, a number of papers were disseminated at academic and policy seminars and forums over the past four or five years. Despite these opportunities, the challenge of keeping apace with European housing policy developments has been considerable. Many European countries, rightly, or wrongly, have moved further in favour of market solutions since the mid 1990s and another book is no doubt needed to deal with the very latest developments. However, convergence is a slow process, and considerable differences do still exist between European housing systems. It is hoped that this book, as a free-standing study, can illuminate these differences fully, and show what happens in housing supply under different political and economic circumstances.

There are many individuals and organisations to whom I owe my thanks. Of great importance has been the funding from the Polytechnic and University Funding Council, and my thanks are to Professor Brian Field, formerly Head of the School of the Built Environment, for his continued support of the housing research focus at the University. In addition, there are colleagues at the Centre for Comparative Housing Research whom I should like to thank. In particular, Dr Tim Brown and Dr Peter King who have assisted at various points along the way with methodological and theoretical issues. In assembling the comparative information, I have been greatly assisted by a number of individuals at housing and planning ministries. Particular thanks go to Mr Rob Ligterink and Drs Matthé van Oostrum at the Dutch Ministry of Housing, Mr Lentes at the German Ministry for Planning, Housing and Urban Development and Mr Rob Ellison at the Department of the Environment. Many interviews have taken place and I should like to thank, amongst others, the following for helping with the substantive issues: Professor H. Dieterich of the University of Dortmund, Dr B. Needham of the University of

Nijmegen, Professor H. Priemus of OTB, Technical University of Delft, Mr N. Rietdijk of the Netherlands Building Federation and Mr J. Vermeer of the Province of South Holland.

Finally, I owe a great debt of gratitude to all my family who have assisted along the way. To my mother and father, who ultimately set me on housing route. To my wife, who now has me lined up for some DIY on our own 'housing system' and to the children who have amused themselves during innumerable weekend hours without my attendance.

1 Introduction

1.1 Housing supply and housing production: aims of the study

This book is a response to contemporary questions about the relationship between different systems of housing supply and the production outcomes which ensue. It is a study of three European countries: the United Kingdom, the Netherlands and Germany, which will be compared and contrasted in terms of housing production policies, land policies and physical planning systems. The book attempts to show how differences in aspects of public policy and levels of private sector provision bring about changes in the volume and tenure of new housing production over time.

Since the early 1970s, there have been significant changes in the way European housing has been supplied. Invariably the focus of research is on the extent to which systems are converging, and hence bringing about similar results or outcomes. At other times, theory suggests that housing systems are so inhibited by institutional structures or restrained by cultural norms that convergence or harmonisation cannot easily be foreseen. These factors are problems not only for policy makers and practitioners, but also for theorists and those concerned with comparative methodology. The book recognises the difficulties involved in comparing countries and attempts to use a framework and a selection of three case studies which highlight the most relevant contemporary aspects of new housing production. The aims of the study are primarily twofold:

> To improve understanding of the way in which European systems of housing supply function and hence to explain better production outcomes.

> To identify different theoretical and methodological approaches to comparing housing systems and to consider their efficacy in the light of an empirical investigation.

1.2 Contemporary policy issues and historical research approaches: towards a hypothesis

A main purpose in writing this book is to identify a meaningful hypothesis associated with systems of housing supply and test it against housing production outcomes. To find a useful hypothetical standpoint means initially reviewing existing and previous approaches to comparing and analysing housing systems.

Studies of housing systems often begin with very general hypotheses which are applied across a broad number of countries. The research of Burns and Grebler (1977), for example, sought to explain, or link 'outcomes', which were primarily levels of investment in housing, with levels of economic development experienced by different countries, both 'developed' and 'developing'. Their hypothesis suggested that levels of investment were linked closely with levels of economic development. This was largely proven, but where the spread of countries considered was so broad that political, institutional and historical factors could be easily underplayed in discussing general differences of outcome. Other advocates of the general or broad hypothesis include Donnison and Ungerson (1982) who developed the thesis that:

> housing policies and the housing markets of industrial society are converging - irrespective of party-political, ideological or institutional circumstances (Schmidt, 1989, p.84).

This hypothesis could be explained in terms of the 'logic of industrialism' (ibid) and the robustness of the convergence theory was empirically tested on housing outcomes for a number of industrialised countries. An important finding is that housing outcomes are not wholly explained by a convergence in macroeconomic performance; levels of owner-occupation, for example, are not strongly correlated with levels of economic development. There is no 'logic of industrialisation' which pre-determines housing outcomes. Schmidt found that the 'housing policies of industrialised nations have diverged, not converged'; that 'housing policy and housing market processes must primarily be understood in terms of the organisation of the policy-making and implementing systems'; and that:

> this does not mean....that economic and demographic factors lack significance. Rather they provide background factors which set the stage, so to speak, and beyond which institutional and ideological factors seem to play an increasingly important part (Schmidt, 1989, p.98).

Schmidt's findings are important for this and other contemporary comparative studies in that his rejection of convergence has since caused researchers and policy analysts to demand a closer examination of the individual nature and structure of housing systems. The new direction has been prescribed in no small part by those giving greater emphasis to the political economy and cultural context of European housing systems. In many interesting cases (Barlow and Duncan, 1994; Ambrose and Barlow, 1987), the focus has been on housing supply and housing production. Work in this area provides many important reference points for the determinants of housing production (Ambrose and Barlow, 1987, p.111) and the frameworks for comparing housing systems (Barlow and Duncan, 1994, p.40).

Barlow and Duncan's (ibid) main contribution to comparative methodology can be seen to lie in the emphasis they give to the construction of a robust and meaningful analytical framework. They use the idea of 'regime type(s) in welfare capitalism' to compare and contrast housing systems and outcomes. 'Regime types' are 'liberal welfare states', 'corporatist welfare states', 'social democratic welfare states' and 'rudimentary welfare states'. This framework derives from the work of Epsing-Andersen (1990) who examined social policy and labour markets in several European countries. The methodology of Barlow and Duncan involves examining housing provision in the context of Epsing-Andersen's work. This draws on the assumption that Britain, France and Sweden are respectively, good examples of 'liberal' 'corporatist' and 'social-democratic' countries. The framework then becomes relevant for exploring the significance of different levels of state regulation and intervention in housing systems.

In respect of method, Barlow and Duncan's (1994) work is worthy of further comment; their emphasis on the selection of 'extreme' country cases is important for highlighting the particular consequences of different levels of government intervention: Britain, France and Sweden are the country examples. Their thesis is that there is a need to overcome the assumption that 'markets' are 'good' whilst 'governments' are 'bad' (Barlow and Duncan, 1994, p.xi); moreover, the conclusion should consider what matters is the 'market-state mix' (Barlow and Duncan, 1994).

This is an interesting conclusion, although one which still demands more attention to explaining how the differences come about. Alternatively, a more mechanistic approach can be adopted. Such is the methodology used in a recent and wide ranging research project of the German Housing Ministry (B.M.Bau, 1993). This is a study of the operation of land markets in housing and commercial property supply. It considers five countries, of which Britain, the Netherlands and Germany are three, (France and Italy being the other two). The study proceeds on the basis of a pro-forma analysis of specific issues; for example 'procedure for planning permission', 'role of development plans, 'compulsory acquisition', 'infrastructure provision', etc. These aspects are linked in a strong conclusion, which states that:

> Simple property-market systems function better than complicated ones...a simple system is demonstrated by the property market systems of the Netherlands and Britain...this is...all the more surprising...since these two countries represent very different property systems. The system in the Netherlands is dominated chiefly by the influence of the public sector, whereas the British system is shaped more significantly than anywhere by market forces (B.M.Bau, 1993, p.xxxii).

Such an analysis undoubtedly appeals for a much more rigorous examination of the apparent paradoxes evidenced in housing systems and their outcomes.

There is additional literature associated with the German Housing Ministry study (B.M.Bau, 1993), although the associated work is not so directly analytical. Related work on housing and land markets is contained in Williams and Wood (1994), (The United Kingdom), Needham et al, (1993) (The Netherlands) and Dieterich et al, (1993) (Germany). They begin from the viewpoint that there should be some common goals or expectations of land supply systems, which include a 'sufficient supply of property' (Needham et al, 1993, p.210), in 'appropriate' locations and at 'appropriate' prices. These seem reasonable expectations, although there are some comparative difficulties with the framework adopted. As Oxley (1995) has highlighted in a review of the works, there is an attempt to draw conclusions 'having regard to issues of economic efficiency and social equity' which are 'notoriously difficult to appraise'. The methodological emphasis is in practice on 'very detailed, tightly structured descriptions' (ibid) and the texts are 'much stronger on information than evaluation'.

The associated Housing Ministry report (B.M.Bau, 1993) has greater utility for comparative analysis. This is above all because its conclusions suggest the idea that there can be systems which are very different but which can still produce similar outcomes. This can occur because, although there may be very differing roles for the state in housing supply, systems nevertheless function in a similar way, and hence bring about similar results.

From this standpoint it has become possible to establish a hypothesis for the study in hand. This posits the idea that:

> Systems of housing supply in which the state plays a very different role can produce similar housing production outcomes. This is, to a significant extent, due to the way in which the systems are structured.

The hypothesis, which is regularly re-visited as the book progresses, necessitates a choice of three countries in which the state does play a significantly 'different role'. The case study framework for the three countries is derived from two underlying factors associated with integrity of method and feasibility of approach. First, that the United Kingdom, the Netherlands and Germany are seen by other researchers (Barlow and Duncan, 1994: B.M.Bau, 1993) as being examples of very different housing systems; in the United Kingdom, the role of the state may be considered minimalist, whilst in the Netherlands, the state at the central and local level has adopted a more interventionist stance. In Germany, the role of the state appears less clearly associated with either of these extreme positions. Second, the study must be capable of being carried out; in this respect, personal contacts and language possibilities meant that this three way comparison was a feasible option.

In formulating a methodology to investigate the hypothesis, it is important to consider the many possible interpretations of the concept of 'structure' within housing systems. There are many potential combinations of state-market 'mixes' (Barlow and Duncan, 1994) and the relationship between the way in which systems function and production outcomes occur, is sometimes poorly understood. This lack of understanding results from a number of causes although insufficient attention to theoretical and methodological complexities of comparative analysis is a common fault. Whilst the social sciences provide a number of frameworks, which range from Marxist paradigms to neo-classical economic models, these are often seen as vehicles through which *all* events *can* or even *should*, be explained. This study attempts to look much closer at the question of the way in which systems function and are structured. It does not fully accept the conclusion that what matters is the 'state-market mix' (Barlow and Duncan, 1994). That conclusion is only important in so far that in some way governments and market agencies matter in determining how much housing is built and of what tenure or type. The nature of the 'mix' should be further investigated; what policy makers need to know is the way in which this 'state-market' mix functions, and hence to be able to make policy adjustments in line with demographic change or changes in the macroeconomy. Whether they can do this, depends very much on how the structure of housing systems are understood and in turn, how they are modelled.

The focus on the state and market therefore needs to be more fully explored in the context of concepts of structures and systems. This book aims in no small part to elaborate the link between theory, research paradigm and substantive knowledge of systems. The approach questions, for example, the utility of functional perspectives which are evident in authoritative pieces of recent research (B.M.Bau, 1993; Healey, 1991; Healey and Barrett, 1990). In this way it is intended to provide stronger conclusions on the relationship between the nature of systems, the way they are structured and the outcomes which ensue.

1.3 European systems of housing supply and housing production: between state and market

Because in the previous section a case has been made for comparing the United Kingdom, the Netherlands and Germany, it is appropriate in this introductory section, to highlight some of the most important aspects of housing supply and production in these countries.

The scope for government intervention in housing supply

The role for governments in influencing housing production is determined by a number of factors. These can be historical, demographic, economic, social or ideological. Together these factors serve to influence the land, planning and housing policies and processes determining housing production outcomes. In looking at the 'scope for intervention', it is important to consider the impact these factors may have.

Historical events, and most importantly in the 20th Century, the 1939-1945 War had a marked impact on the overall need for housing. In Germany, damage to the housing stock was enormous (Power, 1993). Leutner and Jensen (1988) have calculated that in 1950 there were 5.5 to 6 million too few dwellings in Germany. Housing shortages were also significant in the Netherlands in the immediate post-war period (Boelhouwer and Van der Heijden, 1992, p.57).

Housing shortages have always tended to provide a raison d' être for government intervention. High levels of house building in all three countries throughout the 1950s, 1960s and 1970s have been the response. Demographic factors have also had an important part to play. Particularly significant is the fact that in the Netherlands, there has been a very high rate of household formation. Between 1970 and 1987, the number of households increased by 50% (Boelhouwer and Van der Heijden, 1992, p.24). This may be contrasted with the United Kingdom and Germany where the rate of increase over the same period was only 23% in both countries (Boelhouwer and Van der Heijden, 1992, p.24). Shortages resulting from historical factors, combined with high rates of household formation mean that rates of house building per head are very high in the Netherlands. Figure 1.1 highlights the main historical differences in the volume of house building output.

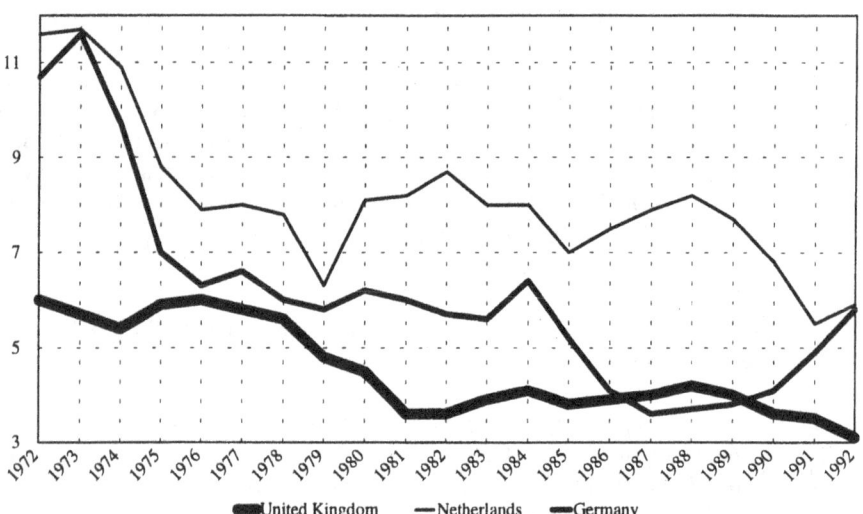

Source: United Nations Economic Commission for Europe; Annual Bulletin of Housing and Construction Statistics

Figure 1.1   Dwellings constructed per 1000 inhabitants

Figure 1.1 shows the rate of dwelling construction per head has also been high in Germany, particularly until the mid 1970s, although the population in Germany was stagnant for long periods since the 1960s. The consequence of this has been a decline in the level of housing construction per head. The trend falls below that of the United Kingdom in the late 1980s.

Differences in the extent of government intervention can be understood to be a reaction associated with particular economic, demographic and social pressures; the changing relationship between these factors will inevitably influence the need for the state to intervene in housing markets. On the basis of the data identified in Figure 1.1, a more interventionist housing policy might be predicated for the Netherlands and Germany, where levels of housing production have been significantly higher than in the United Kingdom. One objective of this investigation is to examine the nature and extent of state intervention in each of the countries.

Housing policy: tenures and sectors

Having looked briefly at the broader scope for government policy and intervention, it is also important to look at housing tenure and production by individual sectors. These aspects are significant as a reflection of housing production policy at a more detailed level.

In the United Kingdom, the main focus of housing policy since 1979 has been towards expanding the owner-occupied housing sector. This has been well documented by commentators such as Saunders (1990), who has considered in particular, the financial benefits of being a home owner in the 1980s (ibid, pp.120-202). The importance of the new housing policy of the 1980s is understood very much in terms of tenure, and furthermore in terms of private sector provision. Malpass (1986, p.11) sees housing policy during this period as being subsumed within a 'tenure policy', where broader aspects such as new building and rehabilitation lose their impetus.

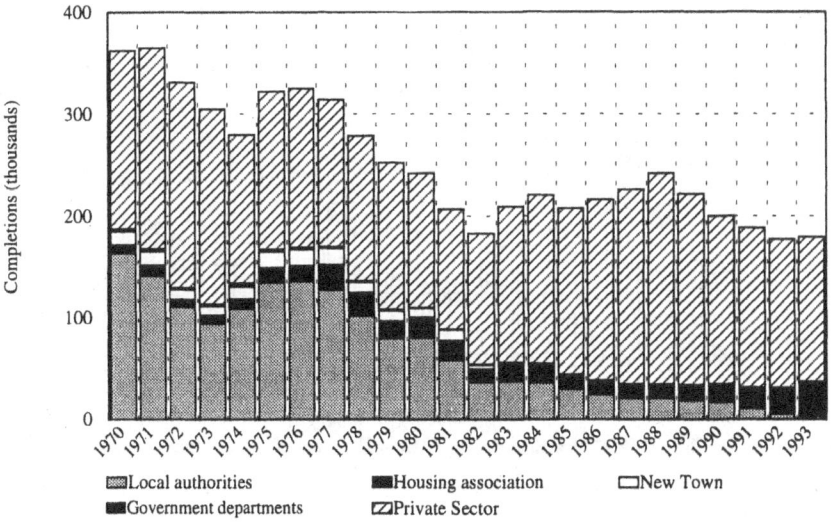

Source: Department of the Environment; Housing and Construction Statistics

Figure 1.2   Housing production in the United Kingdom

7

The policy of promoting owner-occupation in the United Kingdom has, since 1980, been (Figure 1.2) very much at the expense of other housing tenures. Production levels of social rented housing have been in decline, particularly that of local authorities, although housing associations are now taking an increasingly larger share of all completions in the 1990s (Figure 1.2). Private rented housing production has been an insignificant contributor to the new build picture. Measures to revitalise the sector have been few. The main exception of recent times is the Residential Business Expansion Scheme (BES). This scheme (formerly related to commercial businesses) was extended in 1988 to housing, although the measure has arguably come too late for a tenure that has been declining steadily since 1945.

The particular system of housing production in the United Kingdom can be usefully compared and contrasted with that in the Netherlands and Germany:

> In the Netherlands, France and Great Britain there is more emphasis upon a two way system of promotion: owner occupied and social house building. In Germany on the other hand, there has been for decades a three way division: owner occupiers, private rented housing market and the social rented housing market (B.M.Bau, 1993, p.136).

This general conclusion will be used to broaden the discussion on production policy and tenure to the other two countries. Figure 1.3 shows housing production by a number of different sectors in the Netherlands. Although a fuller explanation of the relationship between sectors and tenures is given in Section 5.3 of the book, a few introductory remarks should be made at this stage to address the comparative context.

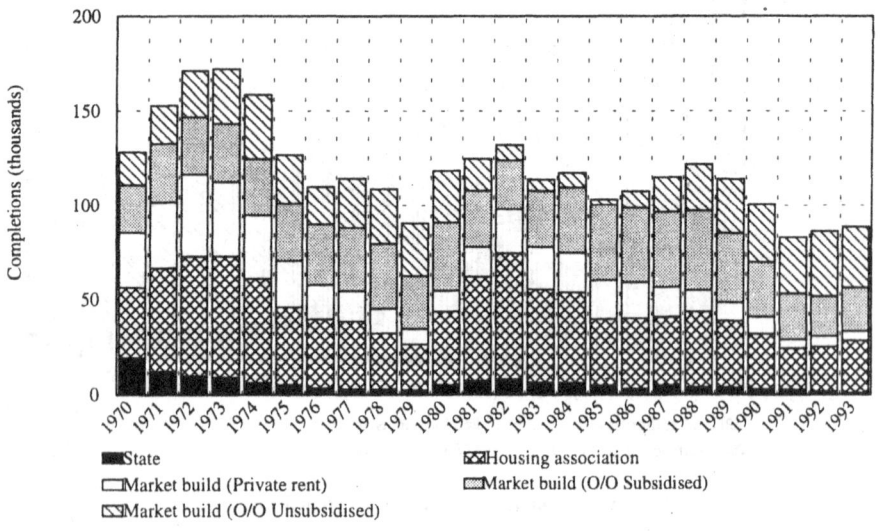

Source: Central Bureau of Statistics, Maandstatistiek Bouwnijverheid

Figure 1.3   Housing production in the Netherlands

The sectors 'Market Build (O/O Subsidised)' and 'Market Build (O/O Unsubsidised)' (Figure 1.3) are production by 'Market builders' for owner-occupier end users (Boelhouwer and van der Heijden, 1992). Production levels of private housing of this nature have fluctuated quite significantly since the 1970s, although the policy since the 1990s has been, to a significant extent, to expand the tenure: the policy document 'Housing in the Nineties' foresees an increase in the owner-occupied housing stock from 44% to 50% before the year 2000 (MVROM, 1989), from its existing level at around 46%. The other important sector in the Netherlands is production by housing associations. Figure 1.3 shows the relatively high number of housing completions by the sector. This is the case particularly in the early 1980s, a period in which the Dutch economy was stagnating (Priemus, 1991). Less significant to the picture (Figure 1.3), and decreasingly so, over time, is the private rented sector, whose completions ('Mkt Build/Priv Rent') can be seen to be falling fast, relative to total production.

The extract (B.M.Bau, 1993, p.136) suggests a promotion system in Germany based around three housing tenures: owner-occupation, social renting and private renting. It is the private rented sector which provides a third important dimension to the analysis; the housing stock in Germany is, at 43% of total German housing stock, the largest in Europe, with the exception of Switzerland (Maclennan, 1993).

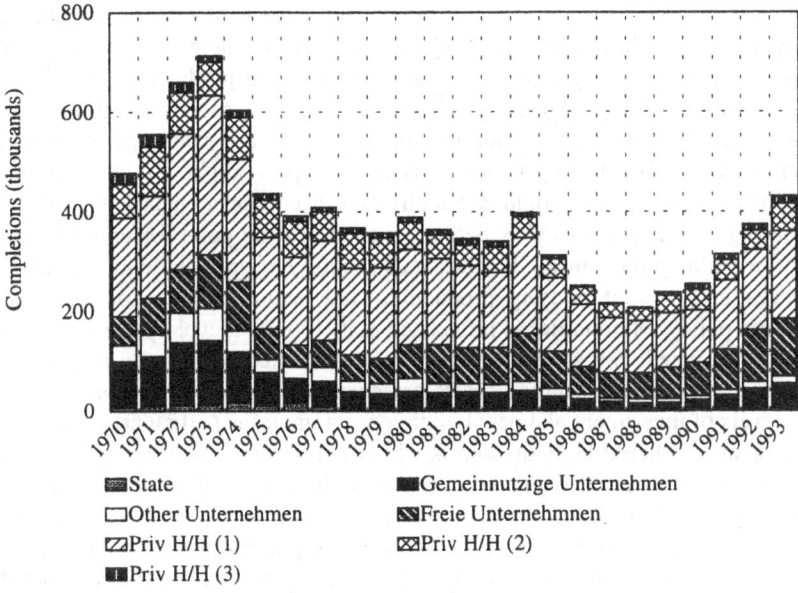

Source: Statistiches Bundesamt; B.M.Bau, Jenkis (1996)

Figure 1.4   Housing production in Germany

The relationship between housing tenure and sectors of housing production is more complex in Germany however. No official data is available which fully reconciles all housing suppliers with the tenure of housing produced (Ulbrich, 1991, p.286). This is however not the case for all sectors and tenures and it is an objective of this book to help clarify where this it is possible to overcome the problems. Figure 1.4 identifies seven different types of housing supply. These can be analysed within the context of the 'three way system' of promotion in Germany: where new build completions by private households are, to a important extent (Priv H/H (1)), completions for owner-occupation; where housing supplied by the Gemeinnützige Wohnungsunternehmen (Figure 1.4) is production largely aimed at fulfilling social needs, and where private rented housing derives from a number of suppliers, of which the Freie Unternehmen are important.

Facets of housing supply: policy and processes

The factors that bring about differences in housing outcomes are many and varied. The aforementioned demographic and macroeconomic influences are very important, although in some respects their consequences have already been widely researched (Burns and Grebler, 1977; Barlow and Duncan, 1994, Oxley and Smith, 1995). This book attempts to look more at aspects of policy and process. Together, 'policy' and 'process' can be conceptualised in a 'system of housing supply'; an idea explained more fully in Chapter 2. This 'system' can be broken down for the purposes of analysis into a number of elements: housing production policy, land policy, planning policy, the process of land supply, the process of infrastructure provision and the housing construction process. These are examined in detail in Chapter 3. Before explaining how the facets of supply might influence housing production outcomes, there should be an introductory comment on each aspect.

'Housing production policy' is perhaps a good starting point for understanding new house building outcomes. The previous section has provided data identifying differences in levels of housing production, and tenure of new housing. The 'production policy' of countries is influenced at its broadest level by the interaction of factors associated with general levels of investment and subsidy regimes. In the first section of Chapter 3, these aspects are examined. The relationship between overall levels of investment and new building programmes is particularly important; a question which should be addressed is whether differences between countries in levels of investment help to explain differences in the volume of new production. A further question which follows is about the nature of investment and in particular about the role of government subsidies. A potentially useful way of analysing and comparing production policies is provided by Oxley (1987) who sets out a subsidy framework classifying object and subject subsidies according to the extent to which the beneficiary (supplier or consumer) fulfils pre-determined income or cost criteria. In this way, the nature of production policy can be broadly gauged in terms of the way in which it encourages affordable housing across a range of tenures. The framework is exploited further in the comparative context in Chapter 3.

'Land policy' as a second facet of housing supply can be concerned with land ownership (Massey and Catalano, 1978; Adams and May, 1990; Carter et al, 1986), with betterment (Prest, 1981; Balchin and Kieve, 1988; Harvey, 1987, p.340), with land pricing (MVROM, 1991b) and indeed taxation (Dieterich et al, 1993:87; Needham et al, 1993, p.75; Williams and Wood, 1993, p.59). The issue of 'ownership' concerns questions about who should own (and hence supply) development land for housing. There are significant differences between the three countries examined in this respect. Questions about 'pricing' are concerned with the way in which land prices or values are established; in some countries land values are explained by reference to the 'market', where value is established by the 'invisible hand' principle. In other countries land prices are prescribed and detailed in a much more overt way; the Netherlands being a good example in the comparison.

The issue of 'betterment' is one about who should receive the financial uplift which accrues when land moves from one use, which is for example 'agricultural, to another which is for example a potential for housing or some other 'built' use. Questions about land policy hinge very much on the desirability of the state in trying to capture some of this, with an aim to realising externality benefits or indeed to reducing harmful side effects arising from development. Betterment is shown in this study to be caught in very different ways and by very different agencies depending on the country being examined. Finally, questions about the taxation of land can consider any significant policy instruments relating to the transfer of ownership of land, to increases in value of land, or even to issues such as inheritance or death duties on land, since these may all occur in relation to the development of land.

The way in which the land policy operates depends to a large extent on the functioning of the planning system. 'Planning' can be used initially to denote what in the United Kingdom may be understood by 'physical planning'. This is probably best reflected in the term 'Town and Country Planning'. That concept may be best equated with the Dutch term 'Ruimtelijke Ordening' and the German term 'Raumordnung'. These may both be broadly translated as 'spatial ordering', which is associated with planning at the national and Federal levels (Davies, 1989, p.345; Hooper, 1989, p.274). When comparing 'planning', however, in its broader sense, care needs to be exercised, because it is not a stand-alone facet of housing supply. It can be variously linked with what might be termed economic or social policy. One of the most important consequences of these relationships is the way in which planning can be used to prescribe particular tenures of housing. In this respect planning may take on a more comprehensive nature, and have particular consequences for social housing production.

By examining the nature of policy facets, the housing development process itself can be better understood. Indeed, the way land is supplied (by private interests or public bodies) is very much dependent on land and planning policies. The relationship between the allocation of land in development plans and its availability for house building is a key issue, and one which differs significantly between the three countries. Differing supply policies bring about different roles and responsibilities for agencies involved in the development process. One of the most important consequences in the comparative context is to give land owners a specific influence in housing markets. The extent of this 'influence' tends to drive the research agenda in different ways in particular countries; private land owners, for example are the main focus in the United Kingdom, (Massey and Catalano, 1978; Goodchild and Munton, 1985), whilst in the Netherlands the discussion is focused more on the role of municipalities (see Needham, 1992; Needham et al, 1993).

The focus on infrastructure provision as a key stage in the housing development process raises a number of important questions. 'Infrastructure' can be considered simply to be a response to a practical need to service new housing development. In achieving this, the main question is 'who provides it?'; or indeed, who or which is the most appropriate body to carry the task out? Yet the issue of infrastructure provision raises a number of economic and social issues concerned particularly with the question of 'who pays?'. Whilst this is increasingly proving to be the housing consumer, since the supplier at all stages passes costs on, the way the process is organised inevitably has implications for the timing by which housing is completed. The three countries make a useful contrast in this aspect of development, where there is no common division of labour between public and private sectors. There are also different assumptions as to what 'infrastructure' actually should comprise, in terms of primary (roads, services, green spaces, etc) and secondary infrastructure provision (schools, health care, etc).

The 'building process' might be expected to be the final main stage in a development process. The construction of a dwelling is expected to follow from the supply of land and the provision of infrastructure. The 'building process', is hence important as a facet of housing supply. The term 'building process' as with other terms used comparatively, should be scrutinised carefully. It should be clearly distinguished from the phrase 'development process', which is argued to be broader. As previously stated, the focus of research in different countries tends to lead to an emphasis on different issues. In the United Kingdom, this is, for example, on the 'private sector housing development process' (Carter et al, 1986). In the Netherlands, it is the 'building process' which is often scrutinised in more detail (Priemus, 1984).

The 'building process' raises not only definitional questions, but also questions of procedure; 'how' is house building carried out? In particular how 'speculative' is the operation? Speculative activity in the land market is one issue. The extent to which the building process is 'speculative' is another. A key relationship in this respect is that between 'client' ('Opdrachtgever' in Dutch, and 'Bauherr' in German) and source of construction. This is because the housing 'supplier', in practice, may also be, or may not be, the source of construction. The decision to build comes from a 'client' (Opdrachtgever or Bauherr). Yet this 'client' may either have to rely upon a source of construction not owned or controlled by him or herself. Alternatively, the 'order' or 'instruction' from the client 'to build', can be carried out by the same person or organisation; a sort of 'self-supply'. These relationships are all key to understanding how housing is developed in the different countries.

1.4 Structure of the book: chapter contents

There are six chapters to this book. This section essentially completes the first chapter, although an outline of what is to come in the following, should be provided at this stage. Generally, the aim is to avoid putting material into appendices, therefore graphs (figures) and tables have been inserted at the point of argument, hopefully aiding the comparative process. Section 1.5 is a crucial point of reference, since it provides a number of key definitions for the research investigation.

Comparative housing methodology

Chapter 1 has introduced the main focus of the investigation and given a context and raison d'être for the countries involved. The nexus of state and market has been given a rationale in the book. Chapter 2, which is primarily concerned with comparative method and analysis, develops some of the main themes already introduced.

In particular, the chapter will explain in some depth what it understands by the differing theoretical and methodological approaches to comparative housing questions. Having discussed some of the common comparative problems, it will explain how a variety of different methods can be employed to tackle the particular hypothesis forwarded in this research. To do this, it includes a section on the relationship between housing systems and the way in which the structure of these can be conceptualised. Above all, the aim of Chapter 2 will be to strongly link the analysis of housing systems with contemporary social scientific thinking.

European systems of housing supply

Chapter 3 mainly represents a structured description of the facets of housing supply introduced in the previous two chapters. The way of doing this, is on an 'issue-by-issue' basis, where the objective is to be able to conclude at the end of the chapter on the nature of housing supply in each country.

The chapter shows that as a result of the research process how some countries, most notably the United Kingdom and Germany, have relied on deregulated land markets to promote new housing supply, whilst in the Netherlands, municipal control of development land represents an entirely different set of options for actors in the Dutch development process. Yet the examination of the elements in the systems of housing supply reveal a number of perhaps unexpected similarities and contrasts. The role for government is by no means predictable in these European countries which makes it even more interesting to review and analyse concepts of structure; the private and public sector roles are not necessarily consistent at all stages of the development process in different countries and hence the final conclusion about the nature of systems of supply in each country must always return to the methodological framework set out in chapter 2.

Structure and agencies in the system of housing supply

Chapter 4 aims to examine further the nature of systems of housing supply and to look at different interpretations of their structure. It picks up where Chapter 3 leaves off by going further than the straightforward 'state-market; approach to looking at housing systems and their outcomes. From a number of different perspectives, the housing systems of the three countries are examined. The first approach is to look at each country in the light of the key linkages between aspects of public policy. The second approach to the idea of structure examines the main agencies involved in housing supply. By 'agencies' is meant means primarily, central government, local government, private sector housing suppliers and suppliers of social housing. The chapter attempts to show how 'private' and 'social' sector housing suppliers relate to each other within the context of state land and planning policies. In progressing the discussion, the political nature of central and local government is critical to understanding how housing, land and planning policies are formulated and implemented. A final focus of this chapter considers 'structure' by reference to the macroeconomic conditions in which housing policy has been implemented. Here there are significant different between the three countries.

Empirical investigation of the relationship between systems of housing supply and production outcomes

In Chapter 5, there is a statistical investigation reflecting aspects of the system of housing supply, and their concrete housing production outcomes. One aim is to explore how theories of housing production can be applied to data representing outcomes. Initially some detailed commentary is provided and attention devoted to the construction of a useful comparative framework. This involves looking back to the different assumptions about private and social sector housing suppliers.

The aim of the chapter is to find out how closely production trends over a twenty year period in different countries can be referenced to a number of assumptions about variables affecting housing supply. The chapter is broken down into three areas which look at: the total volume of housing production, the volume of private sector production and the volume of social housing production. The conclusions are instructive for showing how well the individual systems of housing supply (the policy and processes) can cope with demographic, macroeconomic and political change.

Conclusions

The conclusions of Chapter 6 consider both the policy implications and the utility of the research frameworks which are applied to understanding. One of the key conclusions considers the hypothesis and whether very different systems can produce similar outcomes. This involves to no mean extent, a review of the different interpretations of structure considered in Chapter 4.

Aside of this, the conclusions review the assumptions made about the objectives of systems of housing supply and look at the practical implications for policy makers in the United Kingdom and elsewhere in Europe.

1.5   Important issues of definition

Relating to the hypothesis

The hypothesis itself contains a number of potentially complex terms. The hypothesis is:

> *Systems of housing supply* in which the state plays a very different role, can produce similar housing production *outcomes*. This is, to a significant extent, due to the way in which the systems are *structured*.

The key terms are highlighted in *italics*. It is important to state at this stage how and where these terms are defined. This is now highlighted:

> '*Systems of housing supply*': these are defined in Section 2.5. This deals with what is meant by the 'system', what elements are included therein, and how the 'system' is distinguished from its broader 'environment'.

> '*Outcomes*': these are also fully explained in the methodological chapter. They relate to a set of statistical relationships which represent specific assumptions about systems of housing supply. The way outcomes are used, namely in a confirmatory manner, to provide understanding of systems and the way they are structured, is explained fully in Sections 2.6.

> '*Structure(d)*': the term 'structure' has many potential interpretations. It is therefore not explained at this stage in any detail. Chapter 4 considers primarily the way in which systems of housing supply are structured. This considers four main conceptual frameworks which relate to previous and contemporary research.

Relating generally to the research

In addition to clarifying the terms in the hypothesis, there are a number of other terms used in the research study which it may be helpful to clarify at this stage. These are:

> '*Housing supplier*': this term refers to various sectors of production which supply housing. A 'housing supplier' is, in this research,

considered to be the source of an instruction to build. In this respect he or she may be considered to be the commissioner of a building project, however large or small. The term 'supplier' is of course, an English term. The nearest equivalent in the comparative context is the Dutch word 'Opdrachtgever' ('giver of commissions') and the German word 'Bauherr' ('master of building'). It is important to note that the 'housing supplier' need not necessarily be the agency who physically builds the dwelling. Very often this will not be the case. However, in certain sectors (and this differs between countries), the housing supplier will be both the commissioner of the building project as well as the physical enabling agency; i.e. (s)he both commissions *and* builds. The differences between countries and sectors in this respect is expanded upon in Section 3.6.

'*Housing supply*': this term refers to new housing supply. *Supply* therefore means *additional* physical dwelling units. As a result of this form of supply, the dwelling stock increases, so long as such factors as the level of demolitions can be regarded 'ceteris paribus'. 'Housing supply' in this research may be distinguished from housing supply which results from changes in the 'flow' of dwelling stock. That is to say, where landlords may be able to increase or decrease the housing 'supply', by virtue of decisions about whether to let, or not to let their dwelling stock.

'*Private*' and '*social*' sector housing supplier: these terms refer to specific sectors of housing supply. The comparison is not easily made. The important point to make is that suppliers are defined from sectors of supply which are provided in national statistics on housing production. Unless otherwise stated, the following meanings should be implied:

- '*Private sector*' in the United Kingdom: this is housing supplied by the 'private sector' (also under the heading 'private enterprise'), where data for the sector is derived from the Department of the Environment's Housing and Construction Statistics.

- '*Private sector*' in the Netherlands: this is housing supplied for owner occupation by 'market builders', which is unsubsidised and where data for the sector is derived from the Dutch Central Bureau of Statistics', Maandstatistiek Bouwnijverheid.

- '*Private sector*' in Germany: this is housing supplied by 'Private households', where data for the sector is derived from the German Statistiches Bundesamt.

- *'Social sector'* in the United Kingdom: this is housing supplied by local authorities and housing associations, where data for the sectors is derived from the Department of the Environment's Housing and Construction Statistics.

- *'Social sector'* in the Netherlands: this is housing supplied by housing associations and municipalities, where data for the sectors is derived from the Dutch Central Bureau of Statistics' Maandstatistiek Bouwnijverheid.

- *'Social sector'* in Germany: this is housing supplied as a consequence of the three Förderungswege' or methods of social housing promotion, where data for the sector is derived from the German Statistiches Bundesamt. In the statistical investigation in Chapter 5, production by the sector, Gemeinnützige Unternehmen is initially considered an example of social housing output.

A final point to clarify relates to the definition of the three countries. In this respect it is important to clarify that where 'Germany' is used, the meaning is for West Germany prior to re-unification in 1990. Thereafter, the unified Germany is considered. It is also important to state that this research is concerned with the United Kingdom. Some of the sources referred to, however, use Britain or England and Wales as a basis for analysis. Where this occurs, the context is explained at appropriate points in the text.

2 Theory and method in comparative analysis

2.1 Introduction

Chapter 2 aims to explain how the particular research focus outlined in Chapter 1 is approached. This chapter is mainly concerned with showing how the hypothesis is to be investigated. The chapter aims to deal extensively with the methodological and theoretical context. This is for the social science framework (Section 2.2), the housing studies context (Section 2.3) as well as for the comparative analysis (Section 2.4). The analysis of housing systems is a relatively under researched area and hence no apology is made for the emphasis given to theory and method. This chapter may prove to be instructive to those interested not only in housing supply issues, but also to those with a broader remit to look at comparative questions and the relationship between empirical and rational approaches.

Comparative housing analysis can be viewed as a 'nesting' process, whereby housing studies forms an intermediate focus (Section 2.3) between the social science context and the special methodological aspects of comparative analysis. Inevitably perhaps, the lion's share of the commentary is given over to the hypothetical standpoint (Section 2.5), where three particular facets of the hypothesis: 'systems', 'structure' and 'outcomes' are scrutinised. Of these aspects, the most challenging to deal with is the concept of structure. This is examined in many of its potential guises. Especially important is the focus given to the concept, by researchers looking at housing and other built environment issues; the work of Healey (1992), Ball and Harloe (1992), Barlow and Duncan (1994), Simmie (1981) and Form (1954) is referred to in particular. Work by these authors has been of a pioneering nature and given comparative housing analysis new contexts for investigation.

The discussion of the hypothetical stance (Section 2.5) includes a definition of the 'system of housing supply' and outlines the facets involved. The link between systems and structure is also discussed in the same section. In this area, there are potential pitfalls, particularly since 'system' and 'structure' can be viewed as two different entities; the section sets out the research position. Further, the chapter attends to the issue of outcomes and shows how these are dealt with by comparative housing researchers.

The final section of the chapter (2.7) attempts to draw together all the methodological and theoretical aspects and show how they are incorporated in the approach to the hypothesis. Section 2.7 advocates a middle-range approach, where rational conceptual models are set within the context of an empirical research method.

2.2 The enveloping social science framework

The social sciences provide several philosophical standpoints from which research may be undertaken. Understanding of any issue or set of issues may be furthered if the researcher adopts any one of a 'positivist', 'empiricist', 'rationalist', 'realist', or 'phenomenalist' standpoint. These approaches usually provide a benchmark for more specific investigations in comparative housing analysis and therefore it is important at this contextual stage to outline some of the linkages.

Positivism, as one approach, may be regarded as an historical forerunner of 'scientific empiricism' (Kaplan, 1968, p.389). The term 'positivism' derives from an emphasis upon 'tested and systematised experience rather than on undisciplined speculation' (ibid, p.389). Positivism looks to the 'replacement of pictorial models' (ibid) and it has as its epistemology or main theme, the idea that the researcher should proceed towards understanding on the basis that there are no given a priori truths about the world (Hospers, 1970, p.183). All disputes therefore about positive statements can be solved by an appeal to the facts (Lipsey, 1973, p.4) which can be either proven or not proven in a scientific way. This is in contrast to disagreements about normative approaches or statements which cannot be resolved by an appeal to the facts (Lipsey, 1973, p.5) since they are based upon opinions about what should or ought to happen.

Associated closely with the positivist approach is the empiricist. 'Empiricism' is particularly associated with the 'British philosophical tradition' (King, 1995:10). Its proponents have been Hume (1711-1776), Locke (1632-1704) and Berkeley (1685-1783) (Facione, 1994, p.89). These philosophers gave weight to empirical statements in the development of their philosophical position. This 'position' would be arrived at only on the basis that beliefs could be shown to correspond with the facts of reality (ibid, p.90). The positivist approach was adapted by the Austrian school of philosophy and in particular through the work of Karl Popper (1911-1994) (Hughes, 1990, p.71). Popper was the proponent of the 'principle of falsification', the idea that knowledge is expanded by the process of 'Versuch und Irrtum' (Der Spiegel, 1994), or 'trial and error'. Hypotheses should be tested until proven true, and if proven untrue, should be adapted or discarded altogether.

In comparative housing research Oxley (1991), in his review of the Aims and Methods of Housing Research (ibid) adheres partly to the approach advocated by Popper, where he states in relation to the comparative method that:

Fear of error at any of these steps should not be a deterrent for even if the results or the interpretation are wrong they can be challenged and we have something more than a mere assertion or the use of terminology as a basis for an argument (Oxley, 1991, p.71).

Further, this principle should be exploited, particularly where a strong hypothesis can be identified and where the hypothesis can be quantified (Oxley, 1991, pp.71-72).

'Empiricism' in the social sciences is often discussed in the same context as 'rationalism', (King, 1995, Facione, 1988, Hospers, 1970), which is another, although very different method of developing theory. A main tenet of the rationalist approach is the belief that 'we can arrive at knowledge of the world through the application of reason without appealing directly to observation' (King, 1995, p.8). Rationalists hold that a priori truths exist even though they cannot be observed to be proven. Thus, as a rationalist, it can be stated that '2 + 2 = 4', or that 'parallel lines never meet' (Hospers, 1970, p.100), but there is no need to worry about being able to prove this through observation.

Rationalist philosophy has a different historical tradition which was developed in the 16th Century by writers in mainland Europe such Descartes (1596-1650), Spinoza (1632- 1677) and Leibnitz (1646-1716). They tried to establish what has since become known as the 'coherence of truth' (Facione, 1988, p.90). This can be done by identifying a number of beliefs which, because they are not inconsistent with each other (ibid), can be held to be rational. 'Rationalism' can be reflected in political thought and political 'projects': 'Federalism', 'Nationalism', 'Votes for women', or the 'Destruction of the Austro-Hungarian Empire' are all examples (Oakeshott, 1974, p.6). In the social sciences, a rationalist is 'anyone who holds the view that reason can be a source and justification of truth' (Facione, 1988). From this it may follow that if something can be argued in a 'reasonable' way, then it may constitute a 'rational' theory.

A counter approach might suggest, however, that rationalism does not provide the source of real theories at all, since ideas or concepts cannot be empirically deduced or tested. As such, rationalism might be seen as an example of what Popper saw as 'pseudo-science' (1963, p.33). In the theories of Adler, Marx and Freud, Popper saw ideas which could explain 'practically everything' (1963, p.35), such was their transcendental and eclectic nature. In housing research the problem of empirical versus rational approaches has been explored. There is a strong school of thought which relies to a large extent on rational theory. These approaches are identifiable in Oxley's (1991, p.69) evaluation of comparative method, and can be seen in concepts such as 'privatisation', 'social (and supplementary) policies', and 'structures of housing provision'. These concepts cannot be tested empirically and are arguably only 'terminology' posing as 'explanation' (Oxley, 1991, p.67). The 'Structures of Housing Provision' thesis, for example, which is considered in more detail later in this chapter, can be seen to be a way of 'tying things together' (Oxley, 1991, p.69).

The link between the philosophy of social science and comparative housing analysis is a complex one. Yet it is vital to identify and explore the relationships. Too often in housing research an antithetical stance is taken on a housing issue without reference to the very different methods and traditions from which conclusions are being drawn. This research draws on both empirical and rational traditions. The precise methodological approach and its link to the hypothesis is explained in Section 2.7, although two main reasons for combining such an approach can be given here.

First is the nature of the research, which attempts to compare housing systems and the way they are structured. In doing this, there is a necessity to use conceptual framework of housing systems, rather than empirically 'constructing' them in a 'bottom-up' fashion. This has much to do with the scale of the analysis. Also the interest is not simply in evaluating the outcomes, but in identifying the merits of different interpretations of housing systems alongside those outcomes.

And second is the belief that rationalism and empiricism are not always so juxtaposed as comparative housing research might anticipate. As Machlup (1978, p.196) suggests:

> although most writers use the terms 'empirical' and theoretical' as opposites, and thus contrast 'empirical correlations' with 'theoretical relationships', there are some who speak of 'empirical theories'.

Thus in comparative housing analysis we should not simply reject theories which cannot be empirically tested, but should look at the extent to which the theories themselves are empirically grounded. This is analysis on a very specific dimension.

2.3 The housing studies framework

Although this book represents a comparative analysis, whose methods are accorded a separate section (2.4), it is first perhaps worth dealing with the wider field of housing studies and some of the issues that are raised thereby. Researchers and commentators involved in housing studies come from a variety of different disciplines. They describe their backgrounds variously as economists, political scientists, sociologists, geographers, planners and so on. People are encouraged to investigate housing as a result of the multi-faceted nature of the study which continues to challenge, frustrate and reward individual researchers.

This diversity of interest can be viewed as both advantageous as well as disadvantageous, as has been highlighted by Forrest (1995, p.3):

> The general trend in the academic world has been for greater degrees of specialism. Disciplines have fragmented into subdisciplines...These developments are however, double edged. While they serve to sharpen policy debate and deepen our knowledge of particular processes at work in the production, distribution and

financing of housing, they may also contribute to a narrower perspective on housing studies. We can become over-specialised. Policy relevance can too easily degenerate into a policy-led agenda and a confined, consensual debate divorced from broader theoretical discussion and mainstream disciplines. It is instructive that the ideas with the longest shelf life often seem to have come from outside the mainstream housing research community (Forrest, 1995, p.3).

This comment suggests that whilst, on the one hand, the specialist approaches which researchers are able to provide on housing issues are helpful with the policy agendas, such narrow foci might to some extent be counter-productive in shedding light on the broader forces influencing housing outcomes. Understanding of housing outcomes may therefore be better provided by a combination of differing academic disciplines looking at specific housing problems. As Priemus (1991, p.1) has suggested 'housing may be regarded as being symptom-oriented' and that the 'processes with which we are confronted in the field of housing often find their roots outside the specific field of housing'.

In practice however, the idea that research should proceed from a multi-disciplinary standpoint, is not one which is easily realised. The search for a consensus on the methods and limits of housing studies and housing policy is never too far away and the desire to simplify things can be viewed as a reaction to the complexities created by many different disciplinary approaches. In trying to establish agreement, there are many difficulties; what constitutes a 'robust' or 'useful' framework is a common point of dispute. Economists may tend towards econometric modelling, based upon quantitative analysis and regression techniques, whilst sociologists may lean towards qualitative analysis. The end result of the former will be expressed in a numerical 'model' whilst the conclusions of the latter may be expressed in terms of some behavioural 'concept' or 'paradigm'. It may be argued that because the former can be 'tested' it is by necessity a more 'useful' approach than the latter. This is not necessarily the case and it is even possible that researchers from different academic backgrounds can be analysing the same issue and coming to the same conclusions, but not recognising the fact, since they are using two different methodologies and two different ways of expressing conclusions.

In so far that housing studies is a problem area (and there is little evidence to the contrary), this investigation recognises the contribution that can be made by researchers of differing academic disciplines. This almost has to be the case where housing systems are looked at; they cannot be 'proxied' and 'tested' as though they were a singular variable or factor. Hence there is a strong case for looking at the political background to housing in each of the different countries as well as for examining the role of agencies in the development process. At the same time however, it is difficult to gauge the consequences of different systems without basic quantitative techniques. Thus a mix of approaches is necessary.

2.4 The comparative framework

Anyone who has ever carried out research into other countries will be able to sympathise with the fictional character Gulliver, in Jonathan Swift's novel Gullivers Travels. It was Gulliver's aim on returning from his travels to convince those at home that things abroad were exactly as he described: primarily that in some countries he was relatively 'big' but that in other lands he was relatively 'small'. Although this situation may not arise to any significant extent between housing researchers from different European countries, there are nevertheless issues to do with policy and practice which present problems in the comparative context.

These practical problems are openly recognised in research. A very good example is given in the German ministry of housing report (B.M.Bau, 1993) which examined the functioning of urban land and property markets in Europe. This apportions a number of 'stars' against particular facets of these markets. For example, development plans in Britain are given one 'star', whilst in the Netherlands and Germany they are given three 'stars' in recognition of their relatively greater significance (ibid, p.98). Likewise with other aspects of supply (ibid, p.83; p.109). The report attempts to evaluate therefore the significance or importance of particular facets of policy in the particular context of individual countries; where a given policy or procedure, whilst being outwardly comparable, has a very effect in particular (country) contexts.

To enhance our understanding of comparative housing analysis and methodology we need to look again at the broader framework. In doing so, we ought probably to examine more closely the problem of translation and its related discourse. What the aforementioned report (ibid) is concerned to highlight, is the problem of explaining dynamic (in)equivalence. This is to do with 'equivalence (or inequivalence) of effect' (Hatim, B and Mason, I, 1990, p.240). An associated and more straightforward problem is that of 'formal equivalence' which is about whether 'things are the same'; in very simple terms, whether, 'one man's coq-au-vin' *is* another man's chicken-in-a-basket' (Cole, 1994); hence, whether, for example, 'land use planning' in one country is the same as 'land use planning' in another. Formal equivalence would then be disputed on the basis of whether the 'coq-au-vin' and the 'chicken-in-basket', were related to a homogenous object. A dispute about dynamic equivalence, on the other hand, might assume they are the same object, but that the 'coq-au-vin', for example, would have a greater significance in France, than the chicken-in-a-basket might, in England.

In so far that there is a valid distinction between the two concepts, both formal and dynamic equivalence are a potential problem for comparative housing researchers. First, there is a need to establish whether the same thing is being discussed and second, in drawing conclusions, there is a need to know whether that object has the same effect on the issues or outcome under investigation. The problem, however, in the analytical process is that the consequences of one cannot be distinguished from the consequences of the other. In analysis, is it thought that outcomes are different because there is a failure to establish how similar an agency or process *is*? This is a failure to establish formal equivalence at the outset. Or, is it concluded that outcomes are different because it is believed that an agency or process, which is formally equivalent, has a different effect in different circumstances? This is a failure to establish dynamic equivalence.

The challenge of comparative analysis is immense and a task which is made increasingly difficult by the nature of housing studies itself. There is scepticism expressed by some housing researchers about doing comparisons. Matznetter, for example (1995, p.5) states that:

> Comparative housing studies are a cinderella amongst comparative social sciences, in a similar way as housing is itself disliked by all kinds of social scientists: it is neither exclusively a technical problem, nor is it market-supplied, nor is it provided only by the welfare state.

Ball and Harloe (1992, p.6), have suggested that 'housing parables from other countries tend not to travel well'. Hence whether the concern is with the means or the ends, the message is a guarded one. Despite these reservations however, comparisons are nevertheless carried out. If there is a lesson from previous research, it is that the field of study should not be too narrowly defined. This is particularly if problems of equivalence are not to overshadow all the analysis. In summary, if an holistic approach is adopted, which takes housing systems (and housing supply systems in this particular study) as a basis for looking at outcomes, then the fact that individual facets are not directly comparable, becomes less significant an issue in the methodology.

The way in which this 'housing supply system' can be defined and managed in the methodology will be explained in the following section.

2.5 The hypothetical framework

In approaching a methodology for comparative housing analysis a process has been recommended (Sections 2.1 to 2.4) whereby the broader social scientific issues are looked at before the specific research question. Before making a final methodological statement, particular aspects of the hypothesis should be more closely examined. In this section, two concepts and their inter-relations are explained and scrutinised. These are the concepts of 'system' and 'structure' which are italicised in the research hypothesis below:

> *Systems* of housing supply in which the state plays a very different role can produce similar housing production outcomes. This is, to a significant extent, due to the way in which the systems are *structured*.

The concept of systems

It is argued that the way a 'system' is defined, is determined both by the subject or topic selected for analysis, as well as by the method of its investigation; that is to say, what is understood by 'systems analysis'. Both the particular research question, as well as broader perceptions of what a 'system' might be, play a part. Given these parameters, there is a need to discuss both issues of 'choice', and broader questions of how systems are analysed.

We begin with the latter; the 'analysis of systems', and as previously, look outside the field of housing for a starting point. In doing so, it can be helpful to consider the nature of a 'political system'. In the form of a simple model, a 'political system', (Easton, 1965) can appear thus:

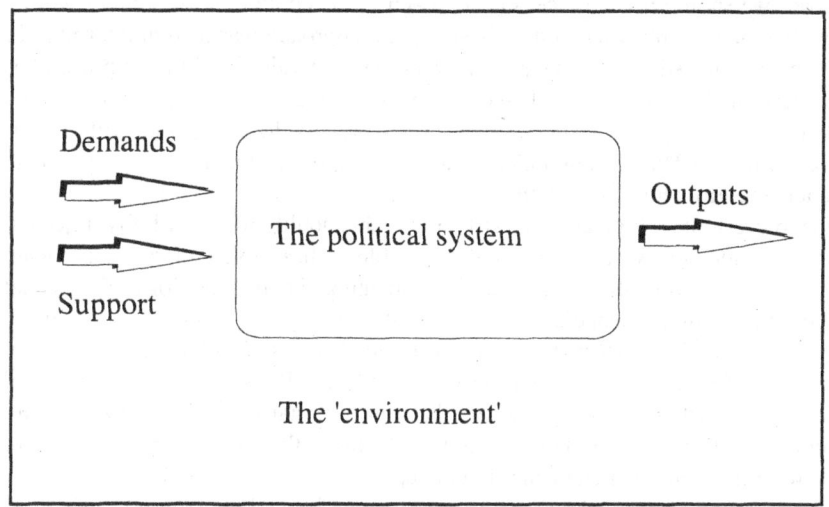

Source: Easton (1965)

Figure 2.1   The political system

Figure 2.1 shows two 'input' factors, namely 'demands' and 'support'. These derive from the many democratic, economic or other influences on the political system. The system itself has a particular nature which brings about specific 'outcomes' as shown in the diagram. Easton's model is not complex. It is perhaps most interesting however, since it attempts to draw a conceptual distinction between a 'system' and its 'environment', an approach not unique to Easton.

Ross (1952), writing even earlier than Easton, sets out five steps for analysing systems. These are:

1) The system to be investigated is explicitly distinguished from its environment.
2) The internal elements of the system are explicitly stated.
3) There are relationships between the elements of the system and its environment.

4) Where these relationships involve deductions, the canons of logical or of mathematical reasoning are employed.
5) Assertions concerning the relationships between the system and the real world are confirmed according to the canons of scientific method (Ross, 1952).

This (ibid) is a prescriptive approach which attempts to provide a methodology for systems analysis. In this it is useful, especially in circumstances where it is actually possible to specify the limits or boundaries of systems and their environments. However, we should perhaps see this approach in the context of the time of writing (early 1950s), arguably when a positivist, logical approach was a common route for social science investigations. Over time, however, the validity of this approach has been questioned. Barlow and Duncan, (1994, p.39), for example suggest quite correctly, that in field of the social sciences, researchers do not operate within 'test-tube' conditions. This situation can be argued to apply to the analysis of political, social and therefore housing systems.

The prescriptive, logical positivist approach should not be wholly rejected. Whilst the approach is now rather unfashionable, it has nevertheless a significant role to play. Its potential is greatest in managing the methodology of a social science investigation. Hence as social scientists we may not accept the proposition that 'systems' and ' environment' can be divided, as is possible in the physical sciences. However, we might be attracted to Ross's second and third methodological 'steps' which prescribe that the 'internal elements of systems are explicitly stated' along with their 'relations'. If this is the case, the next stage is to decide what these internal elements should be.

Thinking first about a 'housing system', it may be difficult to know where to start in identifying the elements, particularly where the investigation is comparative because of the problems relating to equivalence. Using however, the concept of a 'political' system as a foundation, we may begin to see more clearly what broader elements could be included. Here the study area is concerned with two main elements: 'policy' and 'process'. Hogwood and Gunn (1984) make a broad distinction between the substantive issue of 'policy' (knowledge *of* the nature of policy) and knowledge *in* the policy process, which is analysis of the policy process itself. These two major elements of the political system are important. 'Policy' because this may reflect the 'objectives' of a 'system', and the 'process' since this determines how, and whether 'policy' can be implemented in practice. The implementation aspects are stressed heavily in associated texts which deal with the analysis of systems (Ham and Hill 1984; Dunsire 1978); an original focus on policy process and implementation was given by Weber (1947) however, who looked in particular at the bureaucratic nature of decision making in organisations. This focus helps sometimes to bridge the gap between the policy rhetoric and the outcomes of the systems under consideration. As Ham and Hill (1984, p.102) point out, 'policy' can be purely symbolic, being sometimes in the form of government statements or at other times in the form of the 'Queen's speech'.

The system of housing supply and choice of elements

The purpose of this section is to show how the framework for the analysis of systems helps to define the idea of a 'system of housing supply'. In doing this the 'policy' and 'process' framework introduced in the previous section can be utilised. However, as suggested earlier, there is inevitably an element of choice involved in defining how that 'system' is arrived at. In doing so, previous research has an important role in indicating the elements or facets to be included. Comparative research at the present time generally casts a net quite widely (Boelhouwer and van der Heijden, 1992; B.M.Bau, 1993; Barlow and Duncan, 1994; Ambrose, 1992) in so far as the study of housing systems is concerned. These studies provide the framework for an holistic approach; the idea that where many individual facets are considered, outcomes reflect not simply the sum of facets, but the sum of the interaction of the individual facets.

The main focus being comparative housing *supply* however, does make it arguably easier to manage the methodological process, especially when the 'policy-process' framework is re-considered. In this research there are three 'policy' facets considered:

1) Housing production policy
2) Land policy
3) Planning policy

and three 'process' facets. These are specific to the development process and include:

4) Land supply
5) Infrastructure provision
6) The house building or construction process

In addition, and inextricably linked with housing, land and planning policy and the development process are the agencies involved in policy making and in the development process itself. Although there are many including the providers of finance, exchange professionals, etc, we are concerned mainly with:

7) Central government
8) Local authorities
9) Housing suppliers (private and social)

The relations between the elements of the system and the aspects of policy and process which form the basis for this study are shown in Figure 2.2:

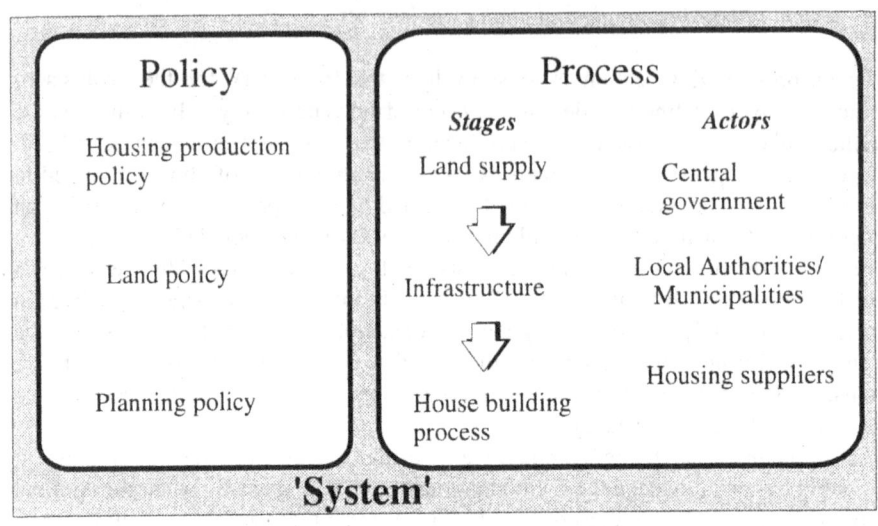

Figure 2.2   Elements of the system of housing supply

The 'policy' facets to be investigated relate to 'housing production', 'land' and 'planning'. The 'process' aspects to be investigated are sub-divided between 'stages' and 'actors', or 'agencies'.

These nine elements form the basis of the investigation into the structuring of housing supply systems and the consequences for housing production outcomes. They are examined mainly in Chapters 3 and 4, where the focus is on the role of state and market (Chapter 3) and on the role of agencies and the structuring of supply (Chapter 4).

Structures of housing supply and production: rationalism re-visited

In Section 2.2 'Enveloping social science framework' it was held that two methodological approaches have predominated in the social sciences and that to some extent these are diametrically opposed. It was also explained that it would be difficult to empirically construct *systems*, housing or otherwise. In this section, rational explanations of housing systems are examined by considering a number of differing interpretations of the term 'structure'. 'Structure', which is compared with the 'system' in a later section, can be useful to analysts of housing in the same way that the concept has proved useful to other researchers of the built environment.

Structure as a functional concept: linkages and event-sequences

If the housing system has a structure, then it may be considered to be a functioning structure; one where the system of housing supply is seen as a series of linkages or events which are connected in variety of ways. Previous research provides the possibility, where structure is considered as a rational model, to look at what is termed (Healey, 1992, p.223) the 'event-sequence' model. This is applied in the context of the development process where the focus is on a number of stages: 'evaluation', 'preparation', 'implementation' and 'disposal' procedures (Cadman and Austin Crowe, 1978). Healey (1992) and Goodchild and Munton (1985, p.65) see the process as being to do with the 'maturing of circumstances', 'purchase of land' 'preparation of land', 'construction of development scheme' and 'occupation by...developer, a new owner or a tenant'. Development is hence seen to be about the circumstances of a process; in particular the way in which the process or sequence of events may be held up, interrupted or constrained in some way.

The idea of constraints, interruptions or obstacles within a process is a theme of the report by the German Housing Ministry (B.M.Bau 1993). This arrives at the conclusion that 'simple property-market systems function better than complicated ones' (B.M.Bau 1993, p. xxxii) and as was shown in Section 1.2 these findings are specifically directed at the juxtaposition between countries which adopt differing degrees of state intervention. The conclusion is accounted for by a number of factors of which are related to 'clear distribution of the tasks involved among a small number of players', 'one channel of supply for building land', and 'clarity and transparency' which reduces 'uncertainty' (ibid). The research findings therefore suggest that a knowledge of the linkages, distribution of tasks and sequences of events is imperative in understanding housing outcomes.

The case for looking at the system of supply in terms of 'events' and the way in which they link or do not link together is strengthened on the evidence of other research. For example, by considering Ball's (1988) investigation of the British construction industry. Ball (1988, p.19), in refuting the utility of neo-classical economics in explaining outcomes, also rejects 'conjunctural' explanations. Whilst this is in effect a case against a narrow focus on linkages in the production process, it is nevertheless a recognition that protagonists (Healey, 1992; B.M.Bau, 1993) following Ball (1988), have a distinct approach which will no doubt be used again in the future. Ball's approach is arguably an appeal for an agency focus, one which is looked at in the following section. The focus adopted by Healey and others concerned with the development process (Cadman and Austin-Crowe, 1978) however, is nevertheless significant as it can be closely linked with the work of earlier analysts of systems such as Durkheim. Durkheim saw systems in terms of their 'functional dependence' or 'organic solidarity', terms which, if anything, determine the need to focus closely on the functional aspects of systems.

The 'event-sequence model' of the development process can be seen to be the built environment's version of a much broader analytical tool used in the social sciences to analyse systems. When using the concepts of 'events', 'sequence' and 'linkages' therefore, it is perhaps helpful to relate it to something broader. At best this is argued to be the wider system, where the links between policy making and the process or processes of development are investigated. From this starting point a number of questions can be posed which are intended to address and define the epistemological framework of the event-sequence paradigm. This approach follows the logic that the 'meaning of a proposition lies in the method of its verification'

(Wittgenstein, 1951) and that it is not only necessary to understand more about the individual nature of systems of housing of housing supply, but also to confirm or refute our understand of models, propositions or concepts. Questions which might assist this process are, for example:

1) How integrated is the system?
2) How simple or complex is the system?
3) What links exist for determining housing outcomes?

Structure as a concept of power relations: agency perspectives

Agency perspectives incorporate a number of themes. Perhaps the most important is that an agency approach focuses on individuals, organisations, institutions or interest groups (Simmie, 1981; Massey and Catalano, 1981; Healey, 1992). Rational models assume that individual agencies might have some bearing on a particular outcome or set of outcomes. This can be a result of particular motivations, or because an agency enjoys a position of dominance or power, or because an agency is in some way a catalyst to, or indeed an obstacle in, a process. In these respects, the agency paradigm is a closely linked to the previous focus which looked at systems and processes from an event-sequence perspective. However, whereas the first analysis tends to consider agencies as subordinate to the process, and where problems arise only due to lack of organisation, the agency perspective requires us to examine the ways individual agencies or actors exercise power in their responsibilities. Within this approach, problems can occur in the production process notwithstanding the fact that it is technically well organised. Conceptually, this is the difference between a two dimensional and a three dimensional model. The event sequence idea provides a structure or chain of events. The agency paradigm works within this structure, yet may aid or exploit it in its own particular way.

As with the event-sequence model, there is a history to agency models. These have their roots in sociological explanations in that there is a focus upon behavioural aspects of individual actors or institutions. In the more recent past, however, agency has been promoted as a medium for understanding issues relating to land and the built environment. Form, (1954) was probably the first to promote agency and institutional frameworks when he introduced the idea of 'organisational congeries' in the land market. Aggregations of 'real estate, 'big business', 'residents' and 'government' all having differing interests and motivations compete to influence outcomes within the built environment. This focus has been extended quite widely in the context of the development process, by Healey (1992), and by Goodchild and Munton (1985), the latter who looked in particular at the role of landowners in the development process. The importance of power relations between important players in the land market has been a focus adopted by Simmie (1981), who examined various agencies in business, local authority and education and their influence on the design of development plans. The importance of particular agencies, 'urban gatekeepers', in the process of gaining access to housing is the focus of a study by Pahl (Pahl, 1977). The agency paradigm is used in a broader context by Giddens as a foundation for the theory of structuration, which is seen to be a 'correlation of agency and structure' (Dallmayr, 1982, p.21).

If the agency model has a specific thesis, it will be difficult to define, however. The focus on agency comes from several angles. The one focus is upon the motivation of agencies in the system of housing supply. Yet there can be profit maximising motivations as well as altruistic motivations. Another focus can be on way in which the agencies themselves are constituted; their nature, either as individuals or organisations may be significant for understanding outcomes. Yet another focus can reflect the balance of power between agencies and the nature of conflict between them. These themes can be identified in many of the studies cited in the previous section.

The lesson of these studies is however that it is very difficult to quantify the significance of 'motivation', or indeed, the extent of 'conflict'. The best that can perhaps be done, as suggested by Hooper (1992, p.46) is to reflect such concepts in the neo-classical theories of perfect competition and monopoly. The idea that some agencies operate from a position of monopoly power, whilst others function in perfectly competitive markets, is one which can be helpful in explaining particular outcomes. The theories, however, are based upon rational assumptions about market behaviour which do not necessarily apply in practice. That is to say, do agencies in a monopolistic situation necessarily restrict output in order to maximise profits (as economic theory often suggests), or is 'profit' not a motivation? Or, do agencies in perfectly competitive markets necessarily maximise production in response to the need to maximise revenue? These are questions which need to be considered alongside the classical economic assumptions. Hence, although theories of 'monopoly' and 'perfect competition' can be applied, they need to be applied judiciously.

Despite the problems with the agency model, we need to keep the underlying tenets of the framework fully in mind when examining the details of European systems of housing supply. For as will be shown, in Chapter 4, the motivations of agencies, in particular state governed agencies, are not consistent between countries, in the same way that housing suppliers are not in equivalent positions of power relative to central and local government. These differences should challenge the researcher to strengthen the epistemological framework rather than discard it.

Other models of structure: structuration, welfare state regimes, structures of provision and equilibrium models

In using the rational concept of 'structure' in the hypothesis of the research, many interpretations can follow. The idea of structure as a functional or a series of power relations between actors has already been introduced. 'Structure' however is potentially more than these things, and any analysis of housing should keep an open mind to alternative frameworks. These are introduced in this section as a means by which differences in European systems of housing supply may be explained, although it should be emphasised that there may be only some overlap between the systems of supply as described in Chapters 3 and 4 and the way structure is conceptualised. This is largely uncharted water in so far as housing research has been concerned and the specific claims made for particular models have not been investigated to any great extent elsewhere.

One way of trying to make sense of housing systems might be to use the 'structuration' thesis. For many, this thesis is associated with the work of Giddens (1979,1982,1984). In the context of theoretical approaches, the place of 'structuration' lies between 'system' and 'structure' (Giddens, 1982, p.35; Giddens, 1979, p.66). Within this framework Giddens defines 'structure' as 'recursively organised rules and resources', and the 'system' as 'reproduced relations between actors or collectivities'; 'structuration' is the 'conditions governing the continuity or transformation of structures, and therefore the reproduction of systems' (Giddens, 1982, p.35).

How 'structuration' is further interpreted or applied to the analysis of housing, however, is a matter for much debate. Dallmayr (1982, p.21) has suggested that the chief contribution of Giddens in this respect is to draw a correlation between 'agency' and 'structure' foci. This may be something akin to a bringing together of the agency and linkages (event-sequence) models. If this is the case then it is useful at least as a guiding concept. However, as with all concepts of this nature, its origins are difficult to trace. How far the 'structure' facet of structuration is derived from deterministic Marxist ideals of structure, is not fully clear. Dallmayr (ibid) sees the framework of structuration as one in which functionalist perspectives develop: a sort of 'structuring of structure' interpretation (ibid, p.21).

'Structuration' is viewed in this research focus as a middle ground. It is useful in that it appears to go beyond simple functionalist approaches. However, it is a problem, in that is difficult to operationalise or empirically question. The idea, however, that an intermediate stage of analysis can be introduced, which fixes agencies and events (the 'system') within a broader context is an attractive one, particularly where this 'broader context' is not seen in a fundamental (Marxist) way, and when the context can be meaningfully expressed or measured. In research relating to the built environment, Healey and Barrett's approach to 'structure' and 'agency' is probably the nearest we can get to Giddens' assumptions of structuration. Their methodology prescribes that:

> The analytical task is to link the institutional analysis of the development process with the dynamics of the economy as reflected in resource flows, and with political organisation and cultural values as reflected in rules and ideas (Healey and Barrett, 1990, p.93).

This heady methodological challenge incorporates many different aspects of sociological and economic thought. The combination of structure and agency, from which 'structuration' is derived, is an important ingredient here and possibly underpins the thinking on the 'institutional' analysis ('agency' and 'events') on the one hand, and the '(structural) dynamics of the economy' on the other. As an empirical challenge, this approach presents many problems, largely because of the expansive framework. Holistic approaches, however, can have merit, and sometimes their advantages are revealed more evidently in the comparative method. An example of this can be see in Crouch, (1993, p.93) who when examining business institutions in Europe states that:

> There is a paradox about the German (also the Austrian, Dutch and Swiss) economies: they combine exceptionally strong forms of corporatist co-ordination and co-operation among firms with a virtually neo-classical rigidity of central banking institutions.

This particular paradox would present problems for those using the narrower institutional or agency approach. According to Crouch, countries like Germany, Austria, the Netherlands and Switzerland all have institutional structures which can be considered 'corporatist'. Yet the consequence of this is to have an economy which is run along 'neo-classical' lines. To understand more about this paradox, data should to be used to illuminate the relationships better. Indeed, this is an issue which is looked at further in Chapter 5, once more information has been presented about the systems of housing supply.

An important 'benchmark' to keep in mind in the discussion of structure is the work of Barlow and Duncan (1994). Something of their thesis on the welfare state regimes and the consequences for European housing outcomes has been introduced in Chapter 1. Yet their approach has not yet been given a context here. Indeed, the 'welfare state regimes' can be regarded as a model of structure. This is in the sense that Barlow and Duncan look to use Epsing-Andersen's social policy and labour market framework as a determinant of policy on housing provision (ibid, pp.28-29). This is not a structural approach which is wholly deterministic. This would not be possible. They indicate this by stating that there are no 'pure' cases (ibid, p.28) of welfare states. Thus differences in housing systems and their outcomes are only broadly determined by differences in social policy. However, the approach is rational in the sense that it attempts to link outcomes to what it sees as generally fixed and structured entities. On this basis the approach can be operationalised to some extent, where concrete housing outcomes can be measured against a broader framework.

It is however difficult to apply the same tests to the analysis of systems and the way they are structured. One such approach is the 'Structures of Housing Provision' (SHP) thesis. The 'SHP' approach is a focus which has evolved in housing research and which is attributable mainly to the work of Ball and Harloe (1988, 1992), but arguably also to the work of Ambrose (1986, 1992, p.173), who promoted the idea of 'chains of housing provision'. The main focus of these approaches is on the modes of 'production' 'consumption', and 'finance' through which housing is provided and the emphasis is upon the social relations between agencies in the housing system. Although the SHP is in name a 'structure' approach, the method by which it intends to throw light on housing systems, owes more to a neo classical equilibrium framework, than a deterministic 'structural' approach. A concern of Ball and Harloe (1992) is that the framework should not attempt to explain how things happen, but simply that they do, in the same way that the 'invisible hand' (ibid, p.4) works within free markets.

Another model which can be associated with this sort of approach is known as the 'Equilibrium' model. This is also founded in neo-classical economics. Healey (1992) has analysed how supply, demand and the market influence the development process. In this scenario, land and property markets are portrayed as a sort of self-reconciling process where there are a number of assumed goals: housing, 'in the right place' 'at the right time' and at the 'right price' (Healey, 1992, p.222). These 'golden rules' are implicit objectives of the system, which takes full account of all agencies and all structural relations. The system works in such a way as to achieve the goals, but does not explicate how it is done.

Although SHP and Equilibrium concepts are broad they serve a function in that they provide a safety net, or 'long stop' against which questions about structure can ultimately be posed. In this research, the broader perspectives are also useful. This is because simpler models of structure do not provide the whole answer. They cannot get beyond the functional level of analysis which may not account for the values and objectives implicit in systems. Ambrose (1992, p.171) has alerted researchers in the comparative context to the possibility that implicitly, housing systems may have differing aims and objectives. If this is the case, then no amount of analysing the functional and political relationships between agencies will reveal wholly why housing outcomes occur as they do. Housing is built not only as a function of the organisation of the development process and its social relations, but also as a result of markets and the justification for state intervention.

Structure and political perspectives: towards an analysis of systems and structure

A potential difficulty with 'structure' is that the concept implies many different interpretations of a system's make up or constitution. A further potential complication is introduced by the political dimension attributed to structural approaches. These two aspects are debated across and within different academic disciplines and it is important to highlight some of the problems before suggesting an approach to systems of housing supply and their analysis.

Where 'structure' is discussed, it is often linked with theories about society. Marx's emphasis was upon the relations of capital, production and class. At the time Marx was writing, households from different social classes could be empirically defined: 'working class' people, for example, were given cheaper admission fees to some public places. 'Gentlemen' had to pay more. Societal divisions came about for Marx, since 'economic and political power were closely linked' (Giddens, 1984, p.39), and where labourer existed only by leave of his ability to sell his labour. The analysis of these divisions could be referenced to either political or economic factors, and the class system explained accordingly. The underlying structure determined the overlying structure or system. Capitalism was linked to the organising of society and to the distribution of power. A logical progression was made from shared values and consensus to economic event although these were conceptualised as being two things: the nature of the 'Überbau' or 'superstructure' of society and class systems being determined by the underlying capitalist ethic (ibid). Deeper structure, or 'Unterbau', the root of such an ethic, implicitly influenced, and was inseparable from, the superficial or superstructural level. The expectation is therefore that systems (of whatever kind) derive their raison d'être from the underlying rules, which are both omnipotent and omnipresent.

The politicisation of 'structure' creates further anarchy for comparative housing analysis. The Marxist thesis of structure, which makes the conceptual division between upper and lower stratas, has been allowed to infiltrate discussion of built environment issues for some time. It is linked quite strongly with approaches discussed in recent sections. The SHP thesis, for example, (Ball and Harloe, 1992) is linked with the Marxist fundamental position in more than one instance (Kemeny, 1987; Healey 1991), although this connection is challenged by Ball and Harloe (1992, p.9). They refute the link, mainly it seems, on the basis that the Kemeny confuses questions of provision, with issues of production (ibid). In this area the conceptual difficulties are significant. One reason for linking structures of housing provision with Marxist approaches may be founded on the very broadness of the thesis. This may in some way be considered to be trying to bridge the conceptual divide between surface and substructure; a confusion between a sort of 'horizontal' and 'vertical' concept of structure.

Barlow and Duncan's methodology (1994) can be similarly approached from a fundamental angle. This framework originates from the premise that 'liberal', 'corporatist' and 'social-democratic' states each have their own essential rules and values which impact upon policy making at the surface. Such things as the 'work ethic', the 'catholic church' or 'one-nation' states (ibid, pp.29-29) all play a part in shaping policy, which is part of the system. These perceptions are 'bottom-up'; whatever the subject of interest to research, this will be influenced by the underlying organic forces,. The discussion of a 'system' therefore, whether this be a political, social or housing 'system', derives its character from the underlying forces. Policy and process (the 'system') will always be a function or reflection of these forces.

Healey and Barrett (1990), and Healey's (1992) research has attracted criticism for its reluctance to address the political aspects of the analysis of structure. The focus in the former article is upon Giddens' concept of 'structuration', whilst the latter is upon the 'development process'. There are many difficulties with these subjects. Healey's discussion of the models of the 'development process' has been criticised by Hooper (1992, pp.47), not least because of the way in which Healey presents 'structure' models as a 'superior explanation'. This (ibid) presents an 'artificial separation between the sphere of the economy and the non-economic conditions of its existence'. Healey therefore creates a conceptual separation between surface structure, which may function in accordance with economic rules or values, and, on the other hand, substructure, whose raison d'être is not necessarily 'economic'. This approach (Healey, 1992) is very much a functionalist one. It focuses more upon the observable manifestations of processes and systems, than upon the underlying values, in an attempt to provide a more empirical approach. This is in a sense an anti-Marxist position since from the Marxist standpoint, surface structure, (what is arguably more 'observable'), exists only from the fundamental and is hence not to be given priority or weight. Healey's focus is on 'sequences' of 'events', 'agencies' or 'institutional' perspectives. These tell us about the mechanics of systems, but from a Marxist standpoint they have no utility, since structure is more fundamental, and cannot be questioned by looking at the way in which systems function.

It is clear therefore that researchers, philosophers or others draw boundaries around concepts of 'structure' in different ways and hence the term creates methodological problems. The use of the concept of 'structure', as it relates to 'system' (Section 2.5) in the hypothesis therefore, needs careful definition. Indeed, the terms 'structure' and 'system' are sometimes regarded in social theory as being interchangeable. This is particularly the case with functionalist approaches. Dallmayr (1982), for example, chooses to dispense with the term 'system' altogether. Within this adopted framework, the 'Unterbau' can be interchanged with the 'Überbau' and it does not matter whether we call the whole or part of the thing a 'system', or 'structure'. This circumvents the definitional problems, but does not overcome the possibility that explanations of outcomes can be better understood using a conceptual division between 'systems' and 'structure'. In this research hypothesis the focus is upon this precise juxtaposition; systems producing unexpected outcomes, a consequence of the way in which they are structured. A choice is made to perceive systems differently from the way they are 'structured':

'Structure + Function = System' (Giddens, 1982, p.34).

Within this conceptual framework it is possible to isolate the two terms 'structure' and 'system' from one another; the analogy of a human body can be applied, whereby the structure of the body could exist independently of its functioning. An extreme and inverted example of this might be where the body is dead and therefore has ceased to function, despite the fact that its 'structure' can still be described or analysed.

Structure, systems and hypothesis: towards a methodology

Inevitably in carrying out an empirical analysis of housing systems, there will be a need to rely on models, concepts and theses of the nature of systems. These models are to some extent empirically grounded although they rely also on rational conception for the way in which they are seen to function. In examining systems, this balance is very important in prescribing a methodological approach. Whilst therefore Healey and Barrett's (1990, p.93) 'analytical task' 'link(ing) the institutional analysis of the development process with the dynamics of the economy as reflected in resource flows, and with political organisation and cultural values as reflected in rules and ideas', cannot in its holistic form be operationalised in any empirical way, it nevertheless can be broken down into a series of more discrete investigations; the results of which, can be compared and eventually linked together to evaluate systems of housing supply.

From this prescribed standpoint however, very eclectic approaches, should be left until last. The challenge of the 'analytical task' should be taken up in stages. Models of structure should be approached first within their own particular context. This can be through functional or 'event-sequence' models. In other cases it is a matter of looking at agencies in the system of housing supply. Initially models are isolated from one another. These are, however, re-considered as the level of analysis becomes more complex and models of the macroeconomy are brought to bear. Finally the very eclectic 'equilibrium' and 'structures of housing provision' paradigms might be considered as all encapsulating analytical frameworks.

Figure 2.3 shows how structure and system are conceptualised in this research in the context of previous attempts to explain housing and other outcomes in social science:

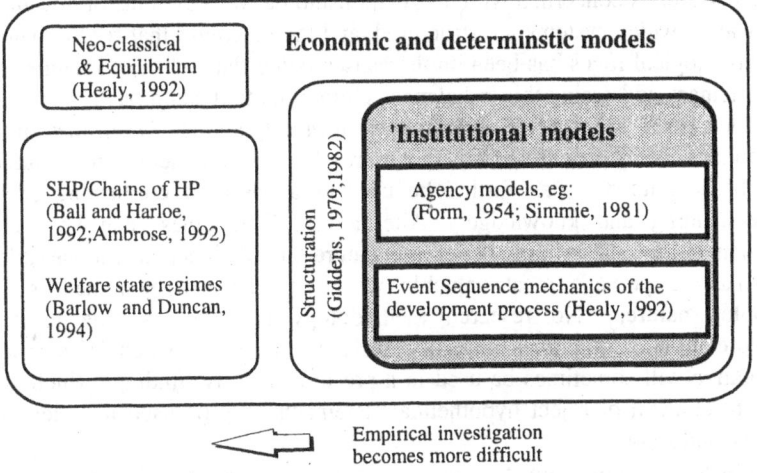

Figure 2.3 Structure and systems: conceptual framework

Figure 2.3 provides a conceptual distinction between models which are 'institutional' in nature and those which are 'economic and deterministic'. This is a not wholly valid distinction since the institutional framework is not in reality distinct from the economic context. The case for the distinction is based more on the extent to which empirical investigation is made possible via the particular perspectives engendered in the models. As has been argued in previous sections, empirical investigation is very difficult with models such as the SHP or the equilibrium. These are arguably, more, descriptive, than operational or empirical frameworks. A different methodology proceeds from the assumption (Figure 2.3) that 'institutional' models which focus on specific aspects of the development process and the policy making agencies, lie within the economic framework and are encompassed by the ethics or ideals underlying the political system.

The link between the two aspects is seen to be captured by, for example, theories of structuration (Figure 2.3) which see outcomes as being driven both from within institutional arrangements as well as by political and economic change. The relationship between 'structure' and 'system' can also be explained via this linkage, where initially the 'system' is defined as being a functional entity and where 'structure' is depoliticised. However, a broader approach to housing outcomes is also useful; one which considers the historical background to systems of housing supply, the ethos for economic policy as well as the institutional context. This is a broader measure of the 'housing system' and one which is considers 'structure' to be a much more encompassing or holistic entity.

2.6   Housing systems and their outcomes

This research is concerned with the relationship between systems of housing supply, the way in which systems are structured, and the *outcomes* that result. Thus far the methodological focus has been on the causes rather than on the consequences and a commentary addressing this imbalance is important to the approach.

'Outcomes' are used in several ways in investigations. Often they are seen as dependent events providing only a measure of a particular set of circumstances. On this basis, outcomes can further be used as a basis for confirming or rejecting understanding and knowledge. Alternatively, 'outcomes' can be seen as an evaluative tool, describing better the nature of the independent variable. This approach is perhaps most valuable where systems are examined, given their complex nature. No research methodology however, is able to make the interpretation of outcomes mutually exclusive: research which is intended to be evaluative will sometimes be used in a prescriptive way; findings which are meant only to confirm or reject hypothetical statements may be used in order to predict events, and so on.

'Outcomes' are seen to have two main functions. To provide concrete conclusions to specific hypotheses or to help describe better the nature of the system or entity from which they originate. In the second scenario they can be considered as 'measures' of housing systems. With either function, however, the way outcomes are expressed is critical to the conclusions: when investigating the consequences of housing systems, for example, inappropriately specified variables will neither inform about differences between countries, nor improve understanding about individual countries. A short overview of contemporary research reveals a number of problems relating to questions of evaluation and specification. Ambrose (1992), for example, has highlighted the difficulty of evaluating the 'performance' of systems:

> Was the GDR system a success because it renewed over a third of the stock between 1970 and 1990 and kept rents to a very low proportion of income? Is the Italian system a success because it consumes very few state resources as subsidy? Is the Swedish system a failure for the

opposite reason? Has Britain scored a success in the 1980s by offloading over 1 million units of public stock?...the evaluation will depend largely on the observer's politics (Ambrose, 1992, p.163).

Above all, the problem of evaluation lies in not knowing what the 'system' itself is trying to achieve (ibid). In this respect, Barlow and Duncan's (1994) choice of variables might be criticised where an evaluative approach is implied in 'Success and Failure in Housing Provision' (1994). To evaluate housing systems, they choose outcomes which represent assumed ideal goals or objectives of systems. To do this, they use measures of 'production efficiency', 'allocative efficiency' and 'dynamic efficiency' (ibid, pp.53-84) to form the basis of judgements about 'success' or 'failure'. These terms are rather problematic however, mainly because they require further definition to a number of more concrete housing outcomes; 'allocative efficiency', for example is seen as being two sided (ibid, p.75) and is measured in terms of 'product diversity' and 'consumption patterns' (Barlow and Duncan, 1994, p.54). But 'product diversity' is ultimately reflected by:

> the physical form and characteristics of the dwellings (which relies on 'cultural expectations')...housing entry costs, expenditures, access forms, security of tenure, property control and ownership (Barlow and Duncan, 1994, p.75).

and is hence more to do with mainstream issues of housing type, tenure and cost. The most difficult measure, however, is 'dynamic efficiency' which is 'the development of economic efficiency over the long term'. This is 'harder to operationalise empirically' (Barlow and Duncan, 1994, p.54) and in the event (ibid, pp.114-143) is dealt with under headings of 'house builders strategies', 'promotion forms', and 'developers risk and survivability'.

Apart from such operational problems, measuring success and failure, as Barlow and Duncan set out to do, is an ambitious objective, and one which has to make normative assumptions about the goals of housing systems. Whilst such an approach is sometimes necessary in comparative studies to create a framework, the emphasis is on looking at outcomes to evaluate systems, rather than on selecting measures to describe better how systems function. The attempt to be prescriptive relies upon a link between systems and outcomes which in comparative housing research has yet to be properly established. This research study therefore, begins from the present and arguably unsatisfactory position. The emphasis in using outcomes is not to say whether systems are 'good' or 'bad', but to use outcomes as a basis for understanding differences in systems of housing supply. In this sense, it is intended that 'outcomes' are seen as a mode of confirming or rejecting certain assumptions about systems and structure, rather than the latter being considered as a predictive tool for outcomes.

What are the outcomes to be investigated?

In this research methodology, there is an attempt to provide measurable outcomes, as well as a reason for measuring them. In looking at outcomes, three relationships are considered:

1) The relationship between total housing production and total housing need.
2) The relationship between production in the private sector and profit in house building in that sector.
3) The relationship between production in the social sector and the performance of the macroeconomy (mainly reflected in the variables of economic growth and levels of unemployment).

The reasons for using these variables are provided in Chapter 5. Here it is more important to say something about the broader research context. In doing this, it would be misleading to suggest that the results of the investigations carried out in Chapter 5 do not to some extent 'evaluate' the systems: inevitably, some countries will 'measure up' better against these criteria than others. It is important to know how the system of housing supply reacts to demographic change and to changes in the size of the housing stock; this could be considered a broad measure of 'production efficiency' in the same vein as Barlow and Duncan (1994). In the same way, a hypothesis of Ambrose and Barlow (1987, p.111) is used to examine the relationship between private sector production and profit for private housing suppliers. This could be considered a measure of market or 'allocative efficiency' in that private housing supply increases or decreases according to profitable housing market conditions reflected in variables such as house prices, land prices or building costs. However, the aim in using these quantifiable outcomes is also to consider the extent to which the implicit goals of systems of housing supply can be understood. Hence, the focus on the relationship between social housing production and changes in the performance of the macroeconomy. Here the interest lies in questions of whether social housing production increases or decreases in response to changes in growth and levels of economic activity as reflected in employment data. Given these outcomes, what can then be said about the implicit goals of housing systems in different countries? In turn, the results help to challenge other hypotheses about the underlying aims of housing systems. A good reference point is Jaffe (1989) who makes a distinction between housing systems which he classifies as 'private', 'social entitlement' and 'distributive justice'. Another good reference point is Schmidt (1989) whose investigation questioned the extent to which housing systems exhibited individual characteristics.

The measurement of outcomes

The use of outcomes to confirm understanding about systems and structure, conditions the way in which outcomes are measured. That is to say, definitive answers are neither a necessity nor a reality. The objective is not to use the results to predict or forecast housing production in the future. The outcomes need only indicate whether or not certain models of systems of housing supply are apposite or not. The method of investigation in Chapter 5 looks only for the broad relationships between variables using correlation coefficients as a measure. There is however no attempt to synthesise the results in a bolder (econometric) model of housing production. The method of analysing the relationships, or 'outcomes', should then remain fully accessible. Figure 2.4 shows the approach:

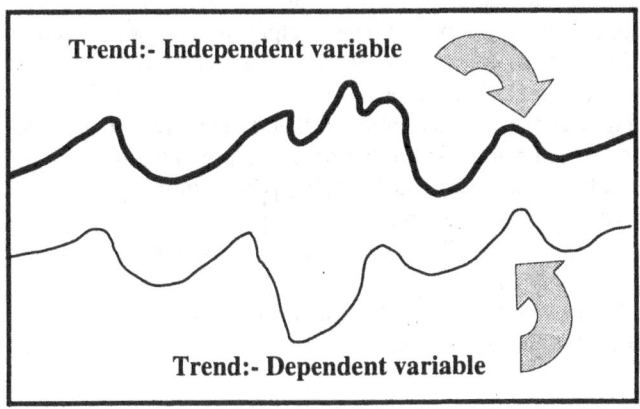

Figure 2.4   The measurement of housing outcomes

Figure 2.4 shows two trends: a trend for a 'dependent' variable and a trend for an 'independent' variable. This will apply for each of the three investigations introduced in the previous section and will apply to all three countries. This will be the case since total housing production, private housing production and social housing production will be examined with their independent variables for each of the three countries.

Measuring outcomes is a result of correlating together dependent and independent variables. 'Similarity' of outcome, a focus of the main research hypothesis, occurs where the variance between the dependent and independent variables is more or less the same. This is reflected in the correlation coefficients, which will be high when the association between the variables is high, and vice-versa. It is important to emphasise in comparative analysis that the results are a function in differences in the 'gaps' and not in differences the 'height' of the trends. Hence there could be a large absolute difference in values between two variables in one country and only a small difference in another, yet the correlation coefficients could be the same for the two countries.

2.7 Synthesis of methodology: between empirical and rational approaches and towards middle-range methods

Previous sections have considered two main methodological standpoints: empiricism and rationalism. Examples of these approaches are championed by particular schools of thought and they are applied to various research problems with varying degrees of success. With the analysis of systems, however, there is a need, it is argued, for a dual offensive, using both empirical method and rational concept. This is due to the shortcomings of the empirical method which is to some extent 'bottom-up piecemeal', atheoretical or even anti-theoretical (King, 1995, p.12), as well as to the shortcomings of the rational approach; whose method is in its least scientific form, purely à priori. It hence helpful to have somewhere to begin, yet at the same time, not to forget what these conceptual models represent. The route incorporating empirical and rational approaches is one which may be described as 'middle range theory'. This form of theory identifies a need to define some methodology which can deal with the problems presented in trying to reconcile the 'concrete' with the 'abstract' (Sayer, 1995, p.24). In this area there may be a link identified with the realist approach which questions the validity of any form of modelling, whether rational or empirical as a means of explaining real world happenings (ibid, pp.24-26).

Figure 2.5 provides a view of the relationship between the research question and the broader philosophical standpoints.

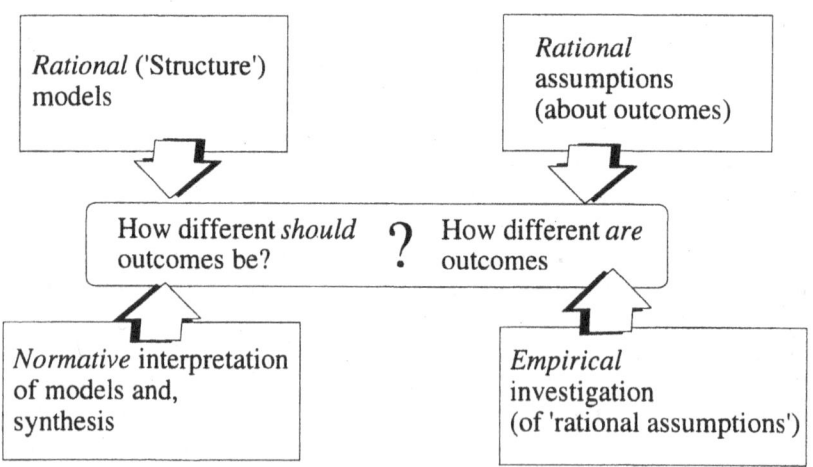

Figure 2.5   A philosophy of method

Figure 2.5 attempts to draw together the approaches introduced in this chapter. The main focus is on the relationship between expected outcomes ('how different *should* outcomes be'?) and the actuality (how different *are* outcomes?), once the results are known. To reach this stage, we need to examine the different 'rational' models of housing systems. This is done mainly in Chapter 4. Given this information, similarities and differences can be identified between pairs of countries in respect of their housing systems. This will be a 'normative' interpretation. From this stage, some 'rational' assumptions can be made about what the outcomes will be: for example, country x will produce similar outcomes to country y, but not to country z. The empirical stage of the investigation is a check to see whether the rational expectations are borne out in the empirical research.

3 Systems of housing supply: between policy and process

3.1 Introduction

Systems of housing supply are made up of several facets. The previous chapter has introduced these in terms of housing production, land and planning policies, as well as aspects of the development process: land supply, infrastructure provision and the building process. A main aim of the research, incorporated within the hypothesis is to investigate the nature of the different systems and the way they are structured. Chapter 3 begins this process, by comparing the different elements of supply in six sections (3.2-3.7). The outcome of this process is given in Section 3.8, which attempts to summarise the extent to which there is state and market sector involvement in the systems of supply.

The chapter is mainly descriptive, although because it compares countries on an 'issue-by-issue' basis, it is inevitable that cross-border analyses are used. This approach has considerable advantages over some of the traditional 'country-by-country' texts. The approach used here serves much better the objective of immediate comparison. This is particularly possible where facets of supply can be described by data on land and housing markets. However, where facets of supply are more difficult to quantify, problems of inequivalence may occur. In these cases, definitions need to be carefully set out; for example, with the comparison of planning in the three countries, a number of key definitions and policy landmarks allow the discussion to be taken forward.

Chapter 3 shows how housing supply is promoted very differently in the three countries. However, differences in the extent to which policy and process are polarised between countries, depends on the particular facet of housing supply chosen for examination. Across the spectrum, systems of housing supply will be shown to vary most between the United Kingdom and the Netherlands. However, Germany's relative position is by no means consistent with the other two countries, across different facets of housing supply. The approach also considers a broad time scale, which sometimes makes it difficult to be very concrete about conclusions.

Mainly the summary tables at the end of each section relate to the period of the late 1980s to early 1990s. However, where significant policy changes were implemented during the 1970s, this is also taken account of in the conclusions.

3.2   Housing production policy

This section on 'housing production policy' represents an examination of the first 'policy' facet of the system of housing supply introduced in the previous two chapters. The aim of Section 3.2 is to analyse the primary differences in production policies of the three countries with a view to understanding two main aspects of the research: first, differences in the levels of overall output, as well as differences in the volume of completions in specific tenures; and second, to provide a basis for understanding how production policy might link in with other facets of supply such as land and planning policy.

Production is one of the most important aspects of housing policy. Historically, production has been one way in which governments have shown success or failure in the broader housing policy field. 'Success' or otherwise has been measured in terms of the total number of houses built or in terms of their tenure, type or source of production. It was shown in Figure 1.1 (Chapter 1) that European governments have been under varying degrees of pressure to intervene with housing policies to ensure that production levels keep pace with demographic and economic change. To do this they have used public and private sector means to boost production of particular tenures in response to housing consumer needs. The main differences in sector output were outlined in Chapter 1.

Since the beginning of the 1970s, housing production has been demoted within the broader public policy agenda of many European countries. General levels of housing need have fallen and other priorities have overtaken housing. Figure 1.1, for example, shows a generally declining trend in output from a peak in the early 1970s, to a trough in the mid to late 1980s. However, this is a general conclusion only, and particular countries do not fit the trend for all the period of time. Whereas production levels in the United Kingdom (per 1000 head of population) have shown only a fairly low variation, as they have declined, the trends in the Netherlands and Germany are (Figure 1.1), much more volatile. These variations, as was also suggested in Chapter 1, may explain differences in the individual policy stances to housing production in the three countries.

Against this backdrop, the main issue to address is how a 'housing production policy' can be understood, and if possible, be compared? Whilst outcomes themselves (total production levels and tenure of new housing) are a reflection of policy in the broader sense, what is needed is a measure of government responses to housing production problems.

If we are interested for example, in the role of governments in influencing the volume of output and the tenure of new housing, we should not ignore levels of housing investment. Levels of investment, whilst they account also for private sector activity, are historically highly dependent on government policy. Whilst the private new build housing sector as well as the repair and maintenance sector contribute to total housing investment, state investment in housing is usually a significant part of this; hence a focus on investment may be helpful in explaining differences in production policy stances.

Important in determining the nature of housing production policy in the three countries, are the production programmes themselves. The extent to which housing production falls within specific 'programmes' is significant in helping us to understand the nature of intervention or regulation. There are meaningful differences in these respects, particularly in the extent to which central governments have defined housing production programmes at the national level. Whereas both Germany and the Netherlands have subsidy channels defining quite clearly production programmes at the national level, the United Kingdom has tended to rely more on the central-local government negotiating process. This the framework for investigation in Section 3.2.

Investment in housing

Levels of investment in housing can be measured in a number of ways, although comparative data sources are limited. Perhaps the best available is that provided by the United Nations, which is the Annual Bulletin of Housing and Construction Statistics. This provides data on: first, the total levels of Gross Fixed Capital Formation (GFCF), i.e investment in the economy as a component of total Gross Domestic Product (GDP) which is made up of the elements of consumption, investment and government spending (Begg, 1989, p.429); second, the GFCF in residential buildings as a percentage of GDP and third, GFCF in residential buildings as a percentage of total levels of GFCF. The latter two data sets are useful in the analysis of production policy. GFCF in residential buildings is defined as the:

> value of work put in place on the construction of residential buildings, including major alterations in and additions to such buildings, but excluding the value of the land before improvement. Expenditures in respect of new permanent fixtures are included (United Nations, 1993, p.190).

Included in data on GFCF in residential buildings is the value of new housing construction. This includes both private and public sector investment, although excludes (Oxley and Smith, 1996, p.3) the land value of plots connected to those dwellings. The measure also includes an estimate of expenditures on improvements and major renovations to existing dwellings.

Figure 3.1 shows two measures of investment in housing for the United Kingdom, the Netherlands and Germany. They attempt to relate investment in housing to the broader economic context at two levels. The graph shows the GFCF in residential buildings as a percentage of GDP ('Hsg %GDP') and GFCF in residential buildings as a percentage of total GFCF ('Hsg %GFCF'). Investment in housing constitutes a significantly higher proportion of total investment, than it does of GDP. This is the case for all three countries (Figure 3.1) and is explained largely by the fact that total GFCF is only one element of GDP. The data is taken over the period 1972 to 1993, where an average for each of the variables is given. For Germany, the relevant period is 1972 to 1991, which relates primarily to West Germany.

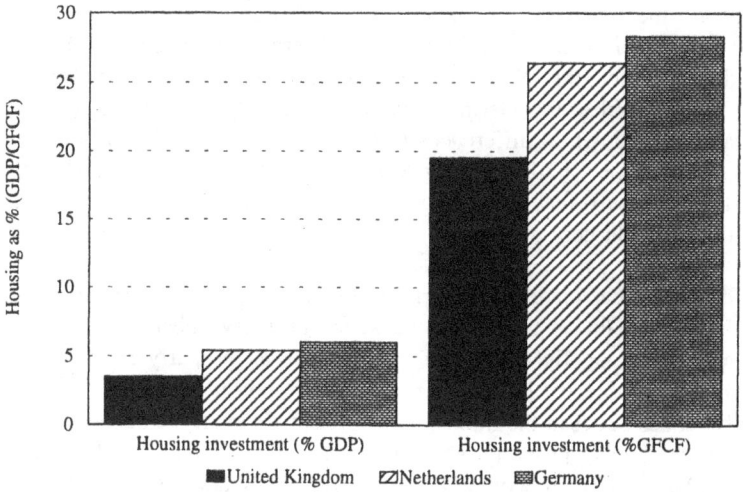

Source: United Nations Bulletin of Housing and Construction Statistics

Figure 3.1 Housing investment as a percentage of GDP and GFCF

Figure 3.1 shows significantly lower levels of investment in housing in the United Kingdom, than in the Netherlands and Germany. This is the case both where investment in housing is related to GDP and where investment in housing is related to total investment in the economy. These are perhaps not surprising findings, when it is considered (Figure 1.1) that the overall level of house building in the United Kingdom has been much lower per head of population than in the Netherlands and Germany. However, the relationship between housing investment (as a % GDP/% GFCF) and the level of production output per head is by no easily predicted. This can be seen in comparing the Netherlands with Germany, where in the former, output per head has been higher (Figure 1.1) than in the latter; although where in Germany, 'the latter', levels of investment in housing have been higher than in the Netherlands (Figure 3.1). The conclusions about these relationships are therefore determined by additional factors and depend on the assumptions made at the outset: where a percentage or proportion of GDP or total GFCF is used as a benchmark for example, is it the case that housing investment is expected to follow changes in GDP and total GFCF, or are levels of GDP and total GFCF regarded as being independent of housing?

One of the most critical elements of GFCF in housing is that of investment in levels of new building. The relationship between new build and total GFCF in housing has not been extensively investigated. Oxley and Smith (1995), however, have researched the relationship in more detail. In particular, they found (ibid, p.191) a weak relationship for the United Kingdom, between the two variables, whereas in both the Netherlands and Germany, a much stronger association could be established over time, between the number of dwellings constructed per 1000 inhabitants and the level of housing investment as a percentage of GDP. This was particularly the case for the Netherlands, although the statistical relationship between the two variables for Germany is not insignificant. The differences highlighted can be put down to differences in government policy. In particular, to the emphasis on either new build, or improvement and modernisation. Oxley and Smith suggest (ibid, p.190) that the difference between housing investment in total and housebuilding is 'largely a function of the volume of resources going into improvement work'.

Papa (1992, p.172) has made a comparison of direct government expenditure in European countries. This is a division between 'property subsidies', 'housing allowances' and 'foregone fiscal income'. In so far as property subsidies are concerned, which are 'object' (ibid, p.8) or 'bricks and mortar' subsidies, there are significant differences between the three countries. Papa's evidence suggests (ibid) that for the Netherlands, property subsidies make up a significantly greater proportion of GDP than in the other two countries ('England' is used for one comparison). Taking the greater part of the 1980s decade (1980-1988) it is shown that on average, Dutch property subsidies account for around an additional 1% of GDP over and above the other two countries.

Taking these findings together with the earlier data from the United Nations leads to the conclusion that the focus on the relationship between direct government spending and overall levels of investment in housing, needs to be sharpened. Some conclusions based on all the issues considered however, can be suggested about the role of governments in stimulating new housing production and these should be set out with a view to drawing together the relationship between state and market at the end of the chapter:

> In the Netherlands, there have been high levels of housing production (Figure 1.1). These are accompanied over the period by high levels of housing investment relative to both GDP and GFCF (United Nations). An empirical study (Oxley and Smith, 1995) shows a high statistical association between levels of new production per head of population, and levels of housing investment as a proportion of GDP. Further research over the shorter period of time (Papa, 1992) shows that in the context of the other two countries, governments in the Netherlands have made large expenditures in the form of object property subsidies.

In the United Kingdom, there have been low levels of housing production (Figure 1.1). These are accompanied over the period by low levels of housing investment relative to both GDP and GFCF (United Nations). There is however, only a weak relationship between new production and investment. This may suggest, amongst other things, that government has attempted to divert investment into the improvement or rehabilitation of the existing housing stock. The level of property subsidies spent in England (Papa, 1992) has been low in the European context for the 1980s.

In Germany, there have been high levels of housing production (Figure 1.1), although not as high as in the Netherlands. High levels of new build in Germany have been accompanied by very high levels of housing investment relative to both GDP and GFCF (United Nations). The empirical study (Oxley and Smith, 1995) shows a high statistical association between levels of new production per head of population, and levels of housing investment as a proportion of GDP. As with England, the level of property subsidies (Papa, 1992) has been low in the European context.

Housing production and subsidy programmes

An examination of levels of investment in housing may provide an indication of why there are different *overall* levels of housing production between countries. In attempting to understand more about the specific outcomes relating to housing tenure and the role played by private and social sector suppliers, it is necessary to look at the particular production programmes implemented by governments to support new housing production. The nature and extent of these programmes can give an indication of the way in which governments aim to make new housing both accessible and affordable to households.

Where production programmes are considered however, there is a question of what constitutes a 'programme'? In the pre-1970 period, most governments in western Europe, particularly those with a war-damaged housing stock had what they would call 'production programmes' with definite housing targets. In the United Kingdom, during the 1950s and 1960s the production programme was mainly targeted towards a number of dwelling completions, predicated on the rise in the number of households and the level of slum clearance. The 'building programme' during this time was identifiable because both major political parties had an idea about how much new housing could be achieved. This was a 'numbers game' (Malpass and Murie, 1994, p.65) in which political capital could be made if the targets were reached. One example of this was the Conservative government's drive in 1950 towards 300,000 dwelling units per year (Holmans, 1987, p.119).

In the other European countries, a number of initiatives were taken during the period 1945 to 1970 in order to stimulate housing production programmes. In Germany, two laws were passed in 1950 and 1956: the Erste and Zweite

Wohnungsbaugesetz (first and second housing law(s)). These two laws introduced the Erste and Zweite Förderungwege (Leutner, 1990, pp.iv-v), which are literally, 'ways of promotion' (of new housing). The Erste and Zweite Förderungwege represent a defined channel of potential subsidy for a number of private and social sector housing suppliers. As such they are a good example of 'production programmes'. The Förderungwege have been arguably successful throughout the post-war period and their role since 1970 has continued and is considered below in more detail.

In the Netherlands, it also became important in 1945 to lay the foundations for new production programmes. In 1948, the Bijdrageregeling Woningwetbouw was introduced. This was a grant scheme for Housing Act dwellings (Boelhouwer and Van der Heijden, 1992, p.58); that is to say, production primarily in the social sector. This initiative was updated two years later to take more account of the better targeting of subsidies between rent levels and size of dwelling. Over the immediate post-war period, a number of other subsidy programmes were also introduced across the rented and ownership sectors. These were broad ranging (Van der Schar,1987, p.58) and generous; Boelhouwer and Van der Heijden suggest (1992, p.58) that as much as 95% of all new housing construction was subsidised. However, it is also shown that over the longer run (ibid, pp.59-71) it has been continually difficult to strike a balance between government support for production programmes, the demands of public expenditure reduction and the very high levels of Dutch household formation.

Since 1970, the concept of a state 'building programme' has become less meaningful as levels of production have fallen off. This is in part explained by the very acute levels of demand of the 1950s and 1960s being reduced by the beginning of the 1970s. The way in which housing production has been achieved in the three countries cannot be consistently associated with building programmes sponsored by the state. This situation varies, however, and the following commentary is aimed to provide an overview of the specific differences.

Housing production during the 1970s in the United Kingdom was dominated mainly by two sectors of supply: the private sector and local authorities, although housing associations also enjoyed an increase in activity between 1974 and 1979 (Malpass and Murie, 1994, p.73). Production by the private sector was largely unsubsidised and so its building programme became dependent on fluctuations in the housing market. These changes were very significant, particularly in the first half of the decade. Local authority housing production during the 1970s was also hit by economic downturn; but perhaps more important, by a number of differing financial provisions, which together, ensured that an ongoing 'production programme' did not become a reality. The 1972 Housing Finance Act, for example, was based around the idea that local authorities would be able to provide more housing if subsidies were increased, but only up to a level where 'fair' rents would cover the building costs. During the initial period of implementation, the system began to work as expected (D.o.E, 1977). However, it soon became clear that, due to the stagflationary economic conditions of rising inflation and unemployment, the twin goals of low loan repayment costs and rents above a 'fair' level, were mutually exclusive. In 1975, the system was abandoned by the incoming Labour government.

The most significant housing policy document of the latter part of the 1970s was the Green Paper (D.o.E, 1977). This was wide ranging, but lacked incisiveness. Harloe (1978) has described the policy as 'insipid' and Short (1982, p.62) has described it as disappointing. Mainly the critique of the Green Paper is that it lacked an innovative edge, reiterating old themes, and that it failed to address the 'thoroughgoing reform of housing finance' (Malpass and Murie, 1994, p.72) that was needed.

One legacy of the Labour government and the Green Paper of 1977, which might have put a production programme back on the rails, was the Housing Investment Programme (HIP). This was built on the existing policy relating to improvements of the housing stock (Malpass and Murie, 1994, p.88). That policy stated that local authorities could bid for funding, and central government would allocate according to what they felt was needed. Housing Investment Programmes were to provide flexibility and allow local authorities to balance their efforts between new build and modernisation programmes. With the election in 1979 of a Conservative government, the HIPs were retained. However, there was to be no resurrected production programme. Rather the Conservative government exploited the HIP system so that local authorities were forced to reduce their new building programmes: because the HIP allocation was made up of two elements, the 'net' allocation' (grant from central government) and capital receipts (in the 1980s mainly from 'Right-to-Buy'), it became possible for central government to reduce its ('net') contribution at the expense of the receipts which local authorities obtained from the sale of council house stock. For a while, local authorities simply spent capital receipts anticipating 'top-ups' from government. However, central government not only began to ring-fence the spending of receipts, but also cut the overall level of funding. Gibb and Munro (1991, p.72) sum up the period in the following way:

> The 1980s have been characterised by the identification and exploitation of loopholes in the regulations, which are subsequently closed by the government.

In the 1990s, the Housing Investment Programmes have been more closely integrated with the Approved Development Programme for housing associations, leading to a greater role for the latter, although production still emanates mainly from the private sector (Figure 1.2).

In Germany and the Netherlands, government housing production programmes have proved more durable than those in the United Kingdom. This is for a number of reasons; one explanation might be less adversarial nature of central government politics, an aspect covered in more detail in Chapter 4. Another explanation might lie in the fact that the subsidy channels in those countries have been open to a broader range of housing suppliers. This is particularly the case in Germany, where subsidies for the construction of social housing have not been limited to non-profit making organisations, but also to private investors. By looking in more detail at the German Förderungwege or 'promotion ways', it is possible to see how production programmes have been maintained. Figure 3.2 shows production output achieved in Germany via the First and Second Förderungwege over the period 1975-1988:

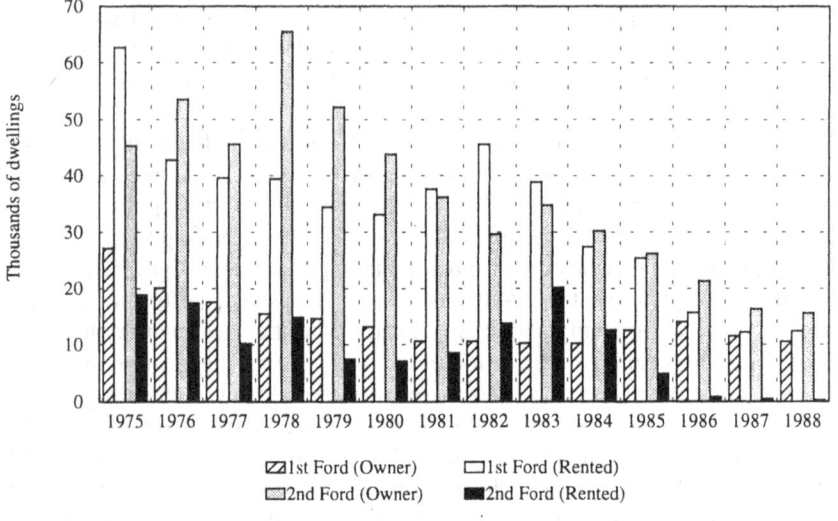

Source: Papa (1992)

Figure 3.2 Housing production in Germany: first and second Förderungswege

Figure 3.2 shows that the two Förderungswege have encouraged housing supply for both ownership and rent. Mainly rented housing has been produced under the Erster (First) Förderungsweg, whilst the Zweite (Second) Förderungsweg has enabled more dwellings for ownership. To attract subsidy under the Erster Förderungsweg, the dwellings must be built for households with 'an income under a given maximum' (Papa, 1992, p.57). To attract subsidy under the Zweiter Förderungsweg, the dwellings must be built for households with income 'no greater than 40% above those households in Erster Förderungsweg type dwellings' (ibid). In 1975, around 170,000 dwellings were produced as a result of the First and Second Förderungsweg. This constituted 37% of total German housing production. In 1988, production from these two sources had fallen however to 39,000 dwellings, and to 19% of total production.

Production of the nature described above, has helped Germany to maintain a housing policy which can be identified by a consistent supply of new dwellings. The cornerstone of production policy lies in the many possible sources of supply which the Förderungswege have helped to create as social housing providers: these are non-profit making organisations as well as private individuals. Provided that central government has had ultimate control over the allocation of tenancies, the rate of interest and some minimum housing quality standards (Boelhouwer and Van der Heijden, 1992, p.120), then it has not attempted to distinguish between housing suppliers.

In so far as other housing sectors are concerned in Germany, central government has intervened more sporadically to stimulate production programmes. By far the largest supplier of new housing is the 'private household' sector. This sector (Figure 1.4) sources and provides housing for several ends. Not only for social tenants, but also for its own (owner-occupation) use. Mainly this sector has relied on the system of Bauspar capital, but with some grant assistance given by central governments, particularly during the 1980s during the period of the CDU-CSU-FDP right wing-liberal coalition.

Dutch housing production during the 1970s was motivated primarily by a policy document published in 1974 (MVROM, 1974): the Nota Huur en Subsidiebeleid (White Paper on Rent and Subsidy policy). This had a distinct aim of stimulating housing production; but particularly to 'ensure that new non-profit rented housing remained within the reach of those on average incomes' (Boelhouwer and Van der Heijden, 1992, p.63). The system was complicated and led to VVD Liberal-PvdA Labour coalition into financial problems towards the end of the decade. Essentially, government undertook to guarantee the level of rent increases for a 50 year period (Priemus, 1991) for all new production in the non-profit and private rented sector. This it did on the basis that although a low initial rent would be contracted between tenant and supplier, eventually, the contract rent would catch up with the guaranteed cost rent, hence absolving government from future commitments. Until that happened, property subsidies would be paid to the supplier on an annual basis to bridge the shortfall.

The scheme, however, was based on the assumption that inflation would continue and therefore the contracted rents could rise fast and hence reduce the protracted subsidy period. In the event, a period of economic stagnation set in (ibid); unemployment rose, making it difficult to increase the contract rent, and hence the subsidy increased. Furthermore, investors in the private rented sector rejected government intervention in rent setting and production began to fall (Figure 1.3).

During the 1980s, two main production programmes are identifiable in the Netherlands. These are known as 'Sector A' and 'Sector B' programmes, which relate to the construction of owner-occupied homes. Under these programmes, (Figure 3.3) annual subsidies were available for the construction of dwellings for households with a specific income limit (Sector A), or where the dwelling construction costs were under a stipulated limit (Sector B) (Papa 1992). These programmes worked to the advantage of both supplier and occupier. The housing supplier, often a housing association, received a loan at reduced rate, backed by the local municipality, and households received an annual subsidy (B.M.Bau, 1993, p.134) to help with the purchase, provided that their income did not exceed a stipulated limit (Papa 1992, p.17). Sector B grants were discontinued, however, in 1988.

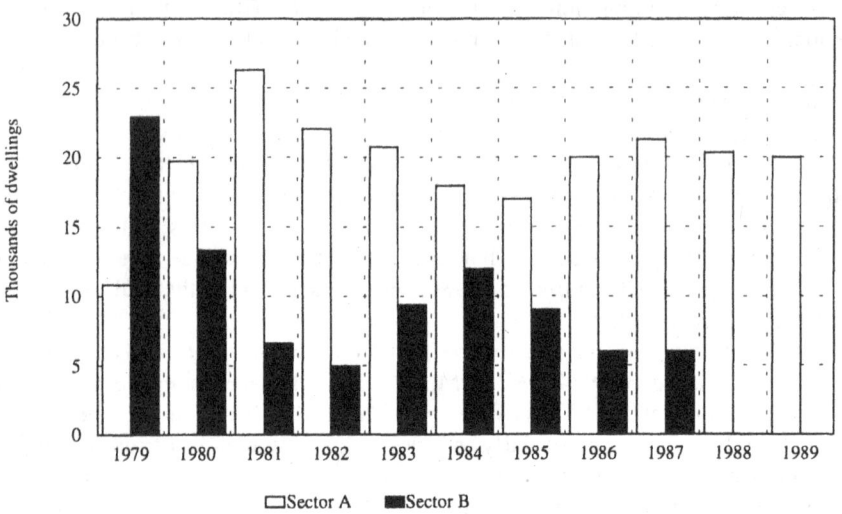

Source: Boelhouwer and Van der Heijden, MVROM

Figure 3.3   Housing production in the Netherlands: Sector A and B housing

Figure 3.3 shows production under Sector A and B production programmes. Sector A and Sector B dwellings accounted for around 33,000 units in 1980 and around 27,000 in 1987. In 1980, this was around 27% of all Dutch housing production. In 1987, it was around 25%. The total volume of Sector A and B production is similar to the total volume of 'subsidised ownership' housing, supplied through the market builder sector. This may give an indication of the origins of the 'subsidised ownership' production in Figure 1.3.

The policy towards owner-occupation in the Netherlands gained impetus towards the end of the 1980s and this has continued for much of the 1990s. The policy document 'Housing in the Nineties' (MVROM, 1989) foresaw an increase in the owner-occupied housing stock from 44% to 50% before the year 2000 (MVROM, 1989). This is to be achieved through an increasing proportion of new unsubsidised production and by leaving housing supply increasingly to market forces.

Evaluation: a note on affordability and equity

In concluding this section on production and central government programmes, it is evident that governments deal with housing need in very different ways. Sometimes this involves providing subsidy to a very broad number of suppliers, as in Germany;

in other cases, as in the United Kingdom, government is concerned more with creating distinct channels between particular housing suppliers and the source of subsidy. There are other effects to consider, however. These concern both the control of supply, as well as the housing consumer. In both Germany and the Netherlands, housing production programmes are based quite specifically around a targeted household end user. These are systems where the subsidy is made dependent on income or some other specified criteria. Oxley (1987, p.166) classifies this type of subsidy as a 'conditional object' (subsidy), since it is given conditionally, and is a property (object) subsidy. In the United Kingdom, subsidies are generally of a different nature. These are characterised by Oxley (ibid) as 'pure object subsidies'. These occur where governments provide subsidy for the construction or provision of a dwelling, but do not make this subsidy conditional upon specific criteria relating to the intended occupants of the dwelling.

On the basis of these criteria, it might be argued that housing production is targeted more directly to affordable ends in the cases of the Netherlands and Germany: government production programmes tying in housing suppliers to low cost dwellings or low rents. In the United Kingdom, 'affordability' is implicit of the process of housing association and local authority production, where it is assumed that central government, albeit indirectly enables affordable housing to be produced. The different systems, however, have their critics. In particular, Germany is singled out (Jaedecke and Wollman, 1990, p.143) for its overemphasis on supply policies, which has led to the concentration of housing capital in a few hands only (Boelhouwer and Van der Heijden, 1992, p.120). One explanation for this is that rents are controlled at the social level for a limited period only; after this time, social housing suppliers can increase rents to the market level, taking advantage at least in part, of state subsidy. Such possibilities may lead to speculative behaviour on the part of investors.

Table 3.1 summarises the main issues relating to housing investment and production programmes:

Table 3.1
Synthesis of production policy issues (1970-mid 1990s)

	Investment in Housing	Production programmes
UK	• Low levels of housing production. • Low levels of housing investment. • Low correlation between new production and investment (Oxley and Smith, 1995). • Low levels of property subsidies (Papa, 1992).	• 1970s local authority programmes, but declining into the 1980s. • HIPs (1978) as an opportunity for revival of production programme, but used as measure to reduce public expenditure in 1980s. • Market driven, private sector production 1980s-90s.
NL	• High levels of housing production. • High levels of housing investment. • High correlation between new production and investment (Oxley and Smith, 1995). • High levels of property subsidies (Papa, 1992).	• Nota Huur en Subsidiebeleid (1975): a production policy for the rented sector, but unsustained. • 1980s: Sector A and B programmes for the owner-occupied sector. • 1990: Housing in the 1990s Policy document: increased emphasis on unsubsidised private sector housing.
G	• High levels of housing production. • Very high levels of housing investment. • High correlation between new production and investment (Oxley and Smith, 1995). • Low levels of property subsidies (Papa, 1992).	• First and Second Förderungswege: historic from the 1950s and 1960s. Significant for social housing (rented and ownership) production in 1970s and 1980s. Non-supplier specific. • Increased subsidies for private households in 1980s with CDU-FDP coalition.

3.3 Land policy

Section 1.3 considered initially the facets of land policy which are to be described for each country. These facets encompass issues associated with land ownership, land values and pricing mechanisms, betterment and taxation of development land. By examining the sources of land supply, the way in which land values are derived as well as the manner by which betterment is treated, we can make informed judgements about the stance the state adopts on land policy. These aspects are considered in turn.

Land ownership

The focus on 'land ownership' means examining the main differences in land ownership patterns for the three countries. In a comparative study such as this, the discussion has to be fairly embracing, and hence the concern is largely with the extent to which development land is owned 'publicly' or 'privately'. Public ownership of development land is ownership by the state in its broadest form; therefore, either by central government, by regional authority or municipal land owner. Private ownership here means private individuals, private households, or ownership by large private housing developers or intermediary land speculators. Significant differences are apparent in respect of the three countries. In particular, between the United Kingdom and Germany on the one hand, and the Netherlands on the other. Figure 3.4 highlights these differences:

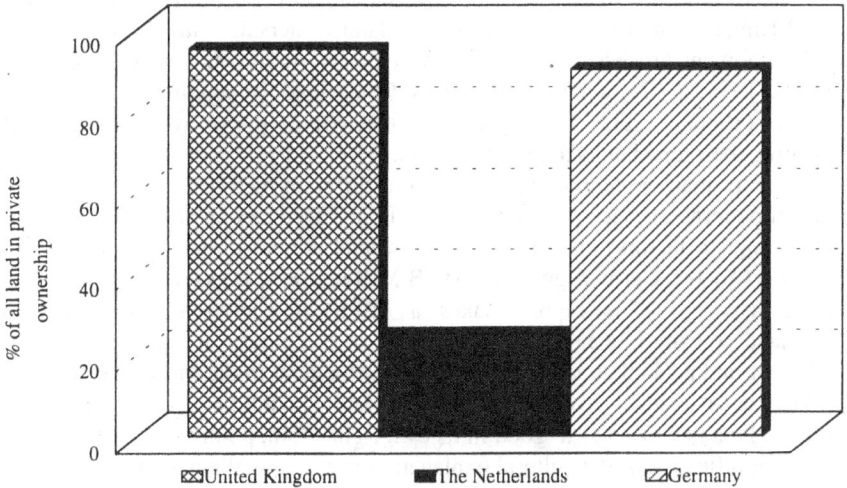

Sources: Allgemeine Vermessungsnachrichten (1987); Needham (1992); Barlow and Duncan (1994)

Figure 3.4   Supply and ownership of land for housing development

Figure 3.4 is compiled by using a number of different sources emanating from studies of the individual countries. The main conclusion is that development land is supplied mainly by private interests in the United Kingdom and Germany, whereas development in the Dutch case depends to a much greater extent on ownership of land by the state. However, care should be exercised in considering this general conclusion not least because 'ownership of development land' needs to be related to a particular and consistent stage in the development process, in order for the comparison to be meaningful. Perhaps the most appropriate stage to consider from the comparative standpoint, is where land is in a state ready for building. At this stage, planning permission for housing will have been given. In Germany, land in this state is known as Baureifes Land (Dieterich et al, 1993, p.119). This is land that already has the main infrastructure provided. In the Netherlands, the equivalent of 'building ready' land is that sold by municipalities to various building sectors. This is 'building ready' in the sense that the main infrastructure is in place. In the United Kingdom, the data relates to land supplied through the open market.

It should be stated that for Germany and the Netherlands, the data sources are more comprehensive and detailed than for the United Kingdom. The overview in Figure 3.4 shown for Germany is derived from Scholland (1987) and reported in Dieterich et al, (1993, p.109). Scholland's study breaks down land supply by ownership and by planning and land development stages. The study reveals that only 12% of all Baureifes land is owned by the state; this is primarily by municipalities and with a small percentage being owned by the church. For the Netherlands, Needham (1992, p.670) provides evidence that 77% of serviced building land is supplied by municipalities. This figure is based on detailed data from the Central Statistical Bureau's Maandstatistiek Bouwnijverheid. For the United Kingdom, it is more difficult to link land ownership with specific stages in the development process. One of the most recent studies, however, (Barlow and Duncan, 1994, p.42), suggests around 90% of land is supplied through 'open markets' (1980s). This is in part explained (ibid, p.48) by local authorities offloading their land banks to private buyers.

There are many potential explanations for different methods of land supply and different patterns of land ownership. Some importance can be attributed to cultural and ideological factors; the esteem in which land is held in each of the countries. The report of the German government (B.M.Bau 1993, p.xxxiv) picks up on the cultural aspects. The report makes a distinction between Britain and the Netherlands on the one hand, and Germany on the other. It suggests (B.M.Bau 1993, p.51 and p.71) that actors in housing development in the former two countries see land as a product from which 'groundrent' should be derived, whereas in Germany land is viewed as a 'good in its own right' (ibid, p.xxix).

The significance of the cultural explanation is easily challenged, however, in the face of the facts. The distribution of land ownership at the development stage, for example, shows, in particular, great differences between the United Kingdom, with its system of private land supply, and the Netherlands, where municipal land supply predominates (Figure 3.4). The differences are explained more easily, it might be argued, from a practical analysis of the individual process of housing development. In the Dutch case, for example, Faludi (1989, p.5) and Davies (1989, p.340) attribute the extent of the role of municipalities in the ownership of development land to the problem of land preparation and service provision. These operations might otherwise be too expensive for private sector interests. In the United Kingdom, equivalent problems do not really occur, perhaps explaining why (Section 3.6) the private sector plays a more significant role in infrastructure provision.

Land values and land pricing systems

When land is supplied for house building, it is sold at a price which reflects many factors including the strength of the existing housing market and prevailing levels of building costs. The state has a key influence on these relationships and land markets are a function not only of housing markets, but also government activity. In the comparative field, Barlow and Duncan (1993, p.1130) have shown how different forms of regulation affect land markets in different ways.

Methods of regulation are both overt and covert. Sometimes land values are determined by market agencies negotiating in a covert way; alternatively, land values are determined more overtly by the state stipulating the price at which land is sold for housing. This is an entirely different model, although the extent to which the process is 'overt' is ultimately influenced by the availability of data.

In the United Kingdom, the land market has largely been regulated in a covert manner by government over the last twenty five years; although government 'inaction' undoubtedly influences the price of land, the basis of determining land prices has remained 'market value'. This has been a rule of thumb for housing and land policy with the notable exception of the period following the introduction of the Community Land Act in 1975. This deliberately set out, as did its predecessor, the Uthwatt Report in the 1940s, to use the market mechanism to re-distribute land values in favour of particular housing and other needs. In practice, the policy was a failure for a number of reasons which are well explicated by, amongst others, Prest (1981). As a model for land market intervention, the Community Land Act created similar possibilities as are engendered within the Dutch development process in that the state can intervene to achieve social housing objectives. The principle of the market prevailed throughout the 1980s in the United Kingdom, and the policy has been re-inforced during the 1990s (D.o.E, 1994). This (ibid) policy states that local authorities must provide good reason for selling land at less than market value to the social sector.

By contrast with the United Kingdom, land prices in the Netherlands were for many years prescribed quite overtly by central government. Although the situation is changing now to a more flexible system, land prices up until the mid 1980s, were fixed for most housing sectors (MVROM, 1991b, p.3). In other words, a private house builder would know what price had to be paid for land if housing were to be built in a specific location. This price would be even more rigidly fixed for the social sector and hence housing associations, the main suppliers, could calculate quite accurately the amount of subsidy required to build the house itself. The system also has another advantageous side effect, although in another quarter: the process of land pricing has produced, perhaps not surprisingly, very comprehensive data sets, a source of great utility to the researcher in this field. Two of the most important categories are land prices in the 'market' and 'social' sectors. Land prices are also classified according to housing which is 'subsidised' and 'unsubsidised'.

The very prescriptive role played by successive Dutch governments in land pricing is perhaps only equalled elsewhere in Sweden, where municipal land supply is also the norm (Barlow and Duncan, 1994). To understand more about the price mechanism and the land market under conditions of public sector land supply, the reader is referred to Needham (1992, pp.681-5), who suggests an 'institutional' approach to be apposite, when understanding the determination of Dutch land prices.

Further understanding of the relationship between land ownership, land prices and land policy can be gained by looking at the situation in Germany. This is particularly the case in comparison with the United Kingdom. In both countries, development land is predominantly in private hands, and neither country has a tradition of land prices which are prescribed by government. The principle of determining land price according to the market value is one which has also been used in Germany since the 1960s and negotiated solutions are the norm. The only exception to this situation is where large scale city re-development schemes are carried out: the so called 'Städtebauliches Entwicklungs Maßnahmen', or 'City Planning Development Measures'. Under these circumstances, land can be purchased by municipalities 'for a price that does not include hope value' (Dieterich et al, 1993, p.73). In such a case, the way in which land prices are arrived at may be regarded as similar to that in the Netherlands. That is to say, the municipality may be considered as the only or main purchaser of potential development land; a situation of 'monopsony' (Needham, 1988, p.69), and hence any 'hope value' is driven from the equation.

Betterment

Land is a commodity which usually increases in value over time. This can happen slowly: where physical planning systems do not permit alternative uses; or it can occur overnight, where say agricultural land is given planning consent for housing. This increase in land value is known as 'betterment' and different countries adopt different ways of dealing with it. Mainly governments in the United Kingdom have taken a 'hands-off' approach and allowed developers to take the profits accruing from speculative land acquisitions. However, this was not always the case, particularly during the 1970s, where the issue of betterment was highlighted in a government paper (D.o.E, 1974):

> The growth in value, more especially of urban sites, is due to no expenditure or thought on the part of the ground owner, but entirely owing to the energy and enterprise of the community...it is undoubtedly one of the worst evils of land tenure that instead of reaping the benefit of the common endeavour of our citizens, a community has always to pay a heavy penalty to its ground landlords for putting up the value of their land (D.o.E, 1974).

This philosophy provided the grounds for the enactment of the Community Land Act 1975. This Act, however, did not realise its objectives. There were problems with land holding as well as the administering of the Act due to poor legislative drafting (Prest, 1981, p.99). The Act was repealed in 1979, although Development Land Tax, introduced as a partner mechanism to the Community Land Act, remained until 1986. The role of the state in proactively attempting to introduce formal measures to recoup betterment is seen to be a short lived one in the United Kingdom.

State ownership of development rights in Germany is not identified as a major issue in this study: there are no state betterment levies in principle and attempts to introduce them in the past have failed (Dieterich at al, 1993, p.72). In Germany, betterment value is often shared between housing supplier and municipality, via the role of the latter in the process of Erschließung or infrastructure provision (Section 3.6). This is also often the case in the Netherlands, although there, the municipality has in theory the upper hand, because the opportunity for speculation for private land owners has not arisen.

The way in which betterment is shared between the different actors is one of the most interesting comparative issues. Whichever side it is approached from (public or private), betterment cannot be ignored as it raises fundamental questions about equity within the development process. In the United Kingdom, betterment is apportioned between developers and the objectives of planning authorities via the particular circumstances of each development. Planning agreements have been the norm for some while, although developer's planning 'obligations' have been possible during the 1990s. Within this processes, many detailed aspects of costs and benefits are hidden, or difficult to uncover. In the Netherlands the primary objective when selling land to private sector builders or housing associations is to cover the costs of land acquisition and the costs of preparation and servicing (Van der Schans, 1995). Details of schemes are sometimes available in the form of land exploitation statements (see also Section 4.2.2). There is evidence to suggest that municipalities do take advantage of their advantageous situation on occasions. In Germany, as elsewhere, the apportionment of development gains is a hotly debated topic; in particular, the amount which private households have to contribute for infrastructure costs in larger development schemes is increasing and can become a significant deterrent to new housing supply. The actual extent to which municipalities in Germany gain from the increase in land values created by the planning system is very much dependent on the way in which they are able to re-structure private land plots within the street plan.

Land taxation

In the United Kingdom, perhaps the most important tax on land has been the Development Land Tax. This operated from 1976 until 1986 when it was abolished by the second Thatcher government. It applied on a percentage of the increase in the value of land between acquisition and disposal. The applicable rate fell with time. When the tax was introduced around 80% of the increase (after allowing for given exemptions) was taxable, whilst in 1986, when the tax was abolished, the rate was 40%.

In the Netherlands no such tax exists (Needham et al, 1993, p.191). A tax can be levied, known as a 'bouwgrondbelasting' ('building land levy') where, due to municipal improvements to land, (for example, drainage), land becomes easier for private operators to build on (Needham et al, 1993, p.69). Its main purpose, is however, not punitive, but to encourage landowners to contribute to the necessary public works (ibid). If they do this, landowners then become exempt from the tax.

In Germany a 'speculation tax' exists for land which is acquired and sold within two years (Dieterich et al, 1993, p.89). This is linked to incomes and can also apply where the land concerned relates to inheritance. In practice, however, this form of tax does little to hinder speculation since 'two years is too short a period' (ibid, p.92).

Table 3.2 provides an overview of the issues discussed in Section 3.3:

Table 3.2
Synthesis of land policy issues (Time frame: 1980s to early 1990s)

	Land ownership	Land pricing	Betterment	Land taxation
UK	• Supplied mainly through open market. • Private individuals, development companies.	• No overt state pricing policy. • Land values, strongly market driven.	• Apportionment of betterment via planning agreements and obligations (negotiated solutions).	• Development Land Tax (1976-1986): tax on disposal land acquisition costs.
NL	• Development land owned mainly by municipalities. • Sources suggest c.75%.	• Overt pricing policies for land by central government. • Especially for social housing production.	• No formal mechanisms to apportion betterment. • (However) development gain accrues to municipalities.	• Taxation ('Bouwgrondbelasting') used for recalcitrant landowners.
G	• Supplied mainly through the private sector. • Private individuals, development companies: (c.90% of all land supply).	• No overt state pricing policy. • Land values, strongly market driven. • Exceptional intervention: 'Städtebauliche Entwicklungsmaßnahmen'.	• Betterment shared between public and private parties through process of Erschließung (infrastructure provision).	• 'Speculation' tax on land acquisitions & disposals < 2 years. Easily overcome however.

3.4 Planning policy

In examining planning as a facet of housing supply, the objective is mainly to understand its implications for housing production. To do this, an overview should be provided of the most important development control mechanisms. This focus should show how the planning system works at the ground level. At the same time however, a more strategic review of planning policy is needed so that different interpretations are discussed. This point is particularly important in the comparison since without such a strategic overview, the limits of planning policy in each country are not easily gauged.

Section 3.4 thus looks at two particular aspects: The nature and limits of planning policy, and in particular the extent to which it is a 'comprehensive' socio-economic policy; and second, the investigation will make a comparison of development plans in the three countries. This second aspect is particularly important for understanding the relationship between spatial development plans and their effect on land values and the development process.

The limits of planning: a 'comprehensive' planning policy?

Initially it should be stated that a 'comprehensive' planning policy is hard to define. It can be a number of things, although the concept is introduced here in terms of a policy which appears to integrate in a proactive way, spatial, demographic, economic and social demands. In housing terms, this means a policy which sets out to provide a framework for a changing economy; one in which planners can anticipate not only where the housing market will provide, but also where it will fail. Whether this framework is operational, can only be judged by looking at what happens in practice. Nevertheless, for the sake of analysis, it is important to be able to link these outcomes with the policy rhetoric or policy stance. This begins with the various definitions of spatial planning in the three countries.

In the United Kingdom, spatial or physical planning is commonly understood in the term 'Town and Country planning'. This has been defined (Keeble, 1969, p.1) as:

> The art and science of ordering the use of land and the character and siting of buildings and communication routes so as to secure the maximum practicable degree of economy, convenience and beauty.

This can be compared with definitions of spatial planning in the Netherlands and Germany. In the Netherlands, Brussaard (1986, p.1) describes Dutch physical planning as:

> The search for the establishment of the best possible mutual adaptation of space and society for the benefit of society.

In Germany, the concept of physical planning is incorporated in the term 'Raumplanung' which means the planning or ordering of space (Kimminich, 1986):

> The comprehensive, superior planning and ordering of space, superior in the sense that it is above the local level combining and harmonising the various special planning activities.

Although there are undoubtedly other definitions of spatial and physical planning, it is useful to compare the above three, which are native definitions. Given that the question is about 'comprehensive' planning, one might first pick out the German definition as being the most 'comprehensive'; at least in its aims. This statement is quite ambitious and one which attempts to define the lines of responsibility between national and local levels. It assumes also a degree of integration in the planning process: the 'harmonising (of the) various special planning activities'. Yet despite these aspects, it is not the most inclusive. For this attribute, one should select the Dutch definition, whose objectives are more overtly directed to serving the needs of society. One consequence of this standpoint might be to interpret the limits of planning policy as being beyond spatial planning; up to a point where the latter must explicitly and consistently adapt to demographic and social forces of change.

The definition of Town and Country planning in the United Kingdom given by Keeble is arguably a much narrower one. It is also more technically orientated ('art and science') and is more specifically related to ('the siting of') buildings and land. This perception of physical planning is undoubtedly influenced by the significance of case law, where the state has traditionally found it difficult to use the planning system to achieve social or economic objectives. Although the picture is changing now, the difficulties for local authorities in imposing planning conditions has a long history. Some of the most important cases are set out in Morgan and Nott (1988, pp.275-287).

A changing planning policy: how comprehensive?

Where planning policy is analysed, it should be related to a time frame. The aim will be to look at policy over time and question the role which planning has played in influencing land and housing markets.

In the history of Dutch planning policy, there are a number of landmarks which provide distinct themes for analysts of planning and land systems. These 'landmarks' are reflected in a series of four National Planning Reports, which have been produced since the 1960s. These have been very significant in determining the nature and location of new housing development. Mainly we are concerned with the third and fourth reports, although the second should be mentioned in passing; this was the planning document setting out the pattern of 'deconcentrated concentration'; a period of new town planning.

The Third Dutch planning report of 1973, was focused on keeping development within the bounds of the Randstad, the main cities of Amsterdam, Rotterdam, Den Haag and Utrecht; this was a policy of 'clustering' development within the boundaries of the existing new towns at the outskirts (Zonneveld, 1989, p.44). The most recent Physical planning report, the Fourth (1988) and the VINEX (Fourth Report Extra 1992), (Alders, 1991) are interpreted as being a further move to consolidate housing and industrial development. The main spatial theme is that cities should become more 'compact' and that green space should remain undeveloped. The other important focus is on strengthening the existing strong economic areas in the large cities (Buijs, 1993, p.138). Whereas in previous planning eras, the policy was to diversify and re-distribute, the concept of planning as a re-distributive tool has become less significant over time (ibid, p.140).

Since the 1970s there have been many changes to planning in the United Kingdom, although no very distinct framework within which analysts of policy can work. The defining point in the whole period is probably the beginning of the 1980s. This is regarded as a watershed between a period of 'blueprint planning' in the 1970s (Balchin and Kieve, 1985, p.118) and a much more flexible market dominated planning era (Brindley et al, 1989; Thornley, 1991; Healey, 1992). The beginning of the 1980s heralded a stream of policy directives aimed at facilitating development control procedures and speeding up the planning process. Two of the most important pieces of government policy guidance during the period were first, Circular 22/80, 'Development Control Policy and Practice' (D.o.E, 1980), which encouraged local planning authorities to adopt more efficient practices and speedier development control procedures; and second, Circular 14/85 'Development and Employment', (D.o.E, 1985), which urged planners to make a 'presumption to allow development' unless there were 'material' reasons why this should not do so. The policy was engendered within the catchphrase 'Rolling back the frontiers of the state' and this theme accompanied not only planning but other aspects of public policy. The planning system was to become above all, more 'market-aware' (Healey, 1992, p.13).

For housing this had advantageous implications for the private sector. Consistently throughout the 1980s, planners experienced difficulties in increasing the level of social housing through the planning system (Joseph Rowntree Foundation, 1994, p.34; Stevens, 1994, p.56; Barlow, 1994, p.2). Developers demanded that owner occupied housing should come first. This situation has changed a little since the 1990s as a result of Circular 7/91 'Planning for Affordable Housing' (D.o.E, 1991), which now allows local authorities to plan for a mix of housing development. However, this 'mix' is related more to the combination of affordable and private housing, rather than a combination of social and other housing tenures:

> policies should give clear guidance on what the authority would regard as affordable housing...policies should not, however, be expressed in favour of any particular tenure (Department of the Environment, 1992, Planning Policy Guidance Note 3).

Planning policy in the United Kingdom since the early 1980s can be argued to have had a strong bias towards the market. Although strategic planning documents validating this theme are not in evidence there are a number of other 'landmarks' in the form of urban development corporations, enterprise and simplified planning zones. These bind together planning initiatives within a market framework.

In Germany, as in the United Kingdom, planning policy has changed: 'Raumplanung' has appeared in many forms since the 1970s. In the late 1960s there was a 'comprehensive' approach (Kunzmann, 1984, p.23), where the idea that 'integrated urban planning' was possible. This was in conjunction with stronger government steering of the land market. Fürst, and Ritter (1993, p.15) suggest that the 1960s were a time of 'Planungseuphorie' in which there was a consistent attempt to bring together politicians and planners.

Since the middle of the 1970s, however Raumplanung has to some extent lost its identity and influence (Fürst and Ritter, 1993, p.16). This is the result of external factors to do with the changing of municipal boundaries and to do with the oil crisis of the mid 1970s. The stagnating population level of the 1970s also relieved some of the pressure on planners and questioned the need for 'euphoric planning' and a 'Gesamtstrategie' ('Totalstrategy') (Ernst, 1991, p.42).

In place of the strategic approach has come, throughout the 1970s and 1980s, a planning system of a different nature. Whilst the prescriptive development plan system has remained, there has been a greater role for the individual Länder, and the interest has shifted from the plans themselves to the process of planning (Fürst and Ritter, 1993, p.16). In these respects, plans have been steered increasingly from 'endogenous' factors to take on a more reactive role. Particularly important at the national level have become environmental concerns and a greater role for public participation in the planning process at the local level. The 1970s are seen as a period in which themes of 'entrepreneurship', 'nostalgia', 'conservation', the 'village ideal' were to the fore (Adrian, 1976, p.16). Planning came within the 'market mechanism' to a greater extent and there was a greater role for participation in planning. 'Raumplanung' in the 1980s at the national policy level became concerned with particular regional problems to do with 'energy' and 'local traffic problems' (Ernst 1991, p.43). This was a period in which planning was in a state of 'stagnation' (Fürst and Ritter, 1993, p.16) and in which attempts to co-ordinate at a more strategic level were largely not carried through.

The objectives of planning in Germany in the 1990s have been directed towards the demands of the re-unified economy. This has put pressures on planning for a closer relationship with housing policy (Lauschmann 1991, p.289) and in particular the need to provide 1 million dwellings in the early part of the 1990s. From within this broad target, 100,000 social dwellings should result (ibid, p.289). To achieve this goal, a break with tradition has been needed. The enabling of social housing through the German planning system has always been written into law (Dieterich, 1994), although in practice there must be 'very special reasons' for doing so (ibid). It is however possible to see how in Germany, planning and housing policy are being brought closer together because of the particular social housing needs. This is to some extent, similar to the planning policy changes in the United Kingdom during the 1990s.

Development plans: a comparative summary

Key studies of planning control (D.o.E 1989; B.M.Bau 1993) indicate an historical distinction between the United Kingdom and mainland Europe in respect of the significance of the development plan within the development control process. The plan at the local level, the Dutch bestemmingsplan and the German Bebauungsplan are in practice legally binding documents prescribing the location and nature of land use development. These documents virtually accord planning permission for uses shown in the plan. In the United Kingdom, a very different situation has been the case. This is best exemplified in Circular 14/85 (D.o.E, 1985) which states that 'local planning authorities should not refuse permission just because the development is contrary to the development plan'.

The situation has changed somewhat however since the introduction of the Planning and Compensation Act 1991. Now, development plans in the U.K. should be considered alongside 'other material considerations' as the basis of planning decisions. The 1991 Act represents a 'change from a market or appeal-led approach to development control to a plan-led approach' (Purdue, 1994, p.399), although there still remains doubt about the specific status of the development plan in the context of development control decisions (Purdue, 1994, p.399; Hands and Yendole, 1992, p.112).

The status of the development plan and its relations with other planning considerations is an important one for housing. A key issue in practice is the amount of certainty (D.o.E, 1989, p.440) which the plan provides for actors in the development process. In the United Kingdom, the system of development plans in combination with 'other material considerations' has tended to lead to a planning situation in which there is a good deal of uncertainty. This is of course an advantage as well as a disadvantage, in that it builds flexibility into the system. The development control system in the United Kingdom is typically contrasted with systems in mainland Europe in which plans are legally binding and hence provide greater certainty. Attempts to evaluate the advantages of one particular type of system over another will however, always be difficult. The conclusion of the Department of the Environment's report on 'Planning Control in Western Europe' (D.o.E, 1989) is that these two situations do not provide any particular advantages over each other:

> On permits, overall there is probably not much difference between England and overseas, the shorter time for proposals in conformity with legally binding plans being offset by the longer time likely to be needed for a permit based upon the preparation of, or amendment to, a plan, and the combination of building and planning control (Department of the Environment, 1989, p.439).

In many ways, the traditional method of making distinctions between development control systems, is not helpful. Very often, and as in the previous quotation, the discussion is about the trade off between time taken in plan preparation as against the time taken in making development control decisions. Also, even if planning systems can be polarised between the 'certain and inflexible' and the 'uncertain and discretionary', then these differences can only go a limited way towards a framework which explains differences in housing production outcomes. Two legally binding plan systems will not lead to the same outcomes, unless all other policy variables are the same. Figure 3.5 can be used to emphasise the importance of looking at the individual country context, and in particular, to consider planning and land policy stances together.

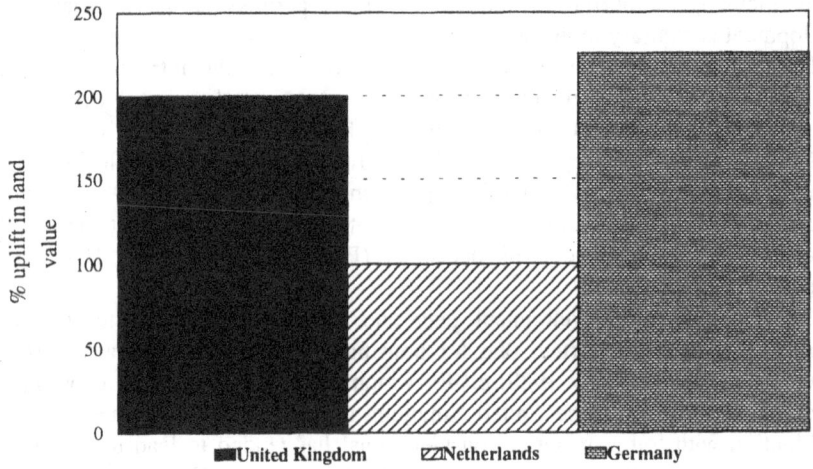

Source: B.M.Bau (1993)

Figure 3.5 Development plans and land values (% uplift in value due to development land status in development plans)

Figure 3.5 shows the general uplift in land value attributable to development plans. By this is meant the effect on land values, from land being allocated for specific uses in development plans. It does however, in every case, indicate uplift from the grant of planning permission. The plans concerned are the local plan in the United Kingdom, the bestemmingsplan in the Netherlands and the Bebauungsplan in Germany. For the United Kingdom, the uplift between agricultural values and land allocated in development plans is in the region of 200%. The uplift in the case of Germany is higher at around 225%. In the Netherlands the uplift in value is only around 100%. The figure relates to land markets in the mid to late 1980s (B.M.Bau, 1993).

There are several factors at work influencing the uplift in land values in each of the countries. Two of the most important are: first, the significance of the development plan in relation to the granting of planning permission; and second, the economic and political relationship between the agency granting planning permission and the land supplier.

If we looked only at one aspect, namely the relationship between development plans and their significance for the grant of planning permission, then it might be expected that in the Netherlands and Germany, the uplift in land values would be similar. Both countries have legally binding plans in which land use allocation is virtually tantamount to granting planning permission. However, Figure 3.5 shows that the uplift in land value is very different in the two countries. Furthermore, it can be seen that the uplift in land values in more similar in the United Kingdom and Germany.

A shorthand explanation for these differences is that private land supply systems (the U.K and Germany) bring about different outcomes to public systems of land supply (Netherlands). However, the uplift in the case of Germany and the U.K is not quite the same and hence we might not attempt to explain all the difference in terms of ownership. Some of the difference in the uplift between the U.K and Germany is accounted for by the significance of development plans in the process of development control. Possibly, the lower uplift in the case of the U.K is explained by the fact that in Germany, planning permission is effectively a function of land use being allocated in development plans, whereas in the U.K, the applicant is not the whole way there on the basis that his or her land plot is allocated for a particular use in the plan. The grant of planning permission in the U.K, is dependent on the plan allocation being robust to the consideration of other material issues.

The relatively lower percentage uplift in land value in the Netherlands (Figure 3.5) can be explained in terms of two factors relating to physical land conditions and the market for housing land. These factors are related. In the first instance, the market for development land, particularly without infrastructure provision is relatively narrow. The municipality is in practice, the main purchaser of agricultural land and the market for housing land will be created not so much through the grant of planning permission (or housing land allocation in the plan) as by the subsequent operations of the municipality carried out at the site level.

Table 3.3
Synthesis of planning policy issues (Time frame: 1970s to early 1990s)

	Strategic planning framework	Planning & social Housing links	Development plans (DPs)	DPs, land values and gains
UK	• 1980s: Circulars 22/80, 14/85, providing for greater private sector participation. • Strategic national planning framework not highly defined.	• Historically, social housing and planning link weak, consequent of case law. • Circular 7/91 now allows LAs to plan for 'affordable' dwellings.	• Discretionary nature, flexible yet some uncertainty resulting. • Planning control based on DPs and 'other material consideration'. • 1991 Act: primacy for DPs.	• Allocation in DP creates increase of circa 200% from agricultural values.
NL	• Defined national strategic planning framework since 1960s. • Evidenced in four national planning reports. • Eg, Fourth Report and VINEX (1988-92).	• Social housing proactively promoted through planning, housing and land policy instruments.	• Planning control based on legally binding DPs (Bestemmings-plan (BP)). • Plans provide certainty, but process is arguably inflexible.	• Zoning in BP creates lower uplift; circa 100% from agricultural values.
G	• Up to mid 1970s, national 'Gesamt' (total) strategy. • 1980s: 'Total strategy' questioned: greater role for interest groups in planning & environment.	• Social housing under special circumstances. • Stronger planning & housing relationship since unification.	• Certainty, but with element of inflexibility. • Planning control based on legally binding DPs. • Bebaungsplan (BP) at the local level.	• Zoning of land use can create significant increase in land value; circa 225% from agricultural value.

3.5 Land supply; land allocation and land availability relationships

The previous three sections have set out the main policy aspects of housing supply: housing production policy, land policy and spatial planning policy. Ideas were given about how each of these policy fields might affect the supply of new housing at the ground level. The objective of this section and the following two sections (3.6 and 3.7) is to examine the development process in more detail. A critical relationship in this respect is that between the *allocation* of land: through the development plan process; and the *availability* of land which depends on factors associated with land ownership, housing market conditions and the physical state of land. To begin this analysis, a theoretical framework is provided, within which, at a later stage, each of the individual countries are considered. This framework considers (Figure 3.6) three possible relationships between land allocation and land availability.

At possibility 'A' in Figure 3.6, there is a 45° uniform relationship between land allocation and land availability. This means that for every additional acre or hectare of land that is allocated in development plans, an additional acre or hectare of land becomes available for housing construction. In this way, planning objectives are made possible by the interaction of factors associated with land availability.

At possibility 'B' in Figure 3.6, there is a situation envisaged in which land is available in the absence of any allocative mechanism. Land appears to be becoming more available in the absence of planners changing development plans. It follows that in this extreme situation there are no planning regulations, or if there are, planning has little or no bearing on housing and land markets.

At possibility 'C' in Figure 3.6, which is another extreme and opposite example to 'B', land is being allocated in the planning process, but no land becomes available. Planners further allocate increasingly greater amounts of land, but without this having any appreciable effect on land becoming available. This could occur for a variety of reasons to do with supply and demand. There could be no demand for housing and hence however much land was allocated, it would still not be built on. Alternatively, the policy of allocating more land might have the effect of reducing land prices to such an extent, that land owners would simply hold on to land until they thought planning policy would become more restrictive. Or, it might be that the problem of supply is a physical one: where land is allocated, but for a number of reasons (topographical, contamination, etc), the land would never be developed.

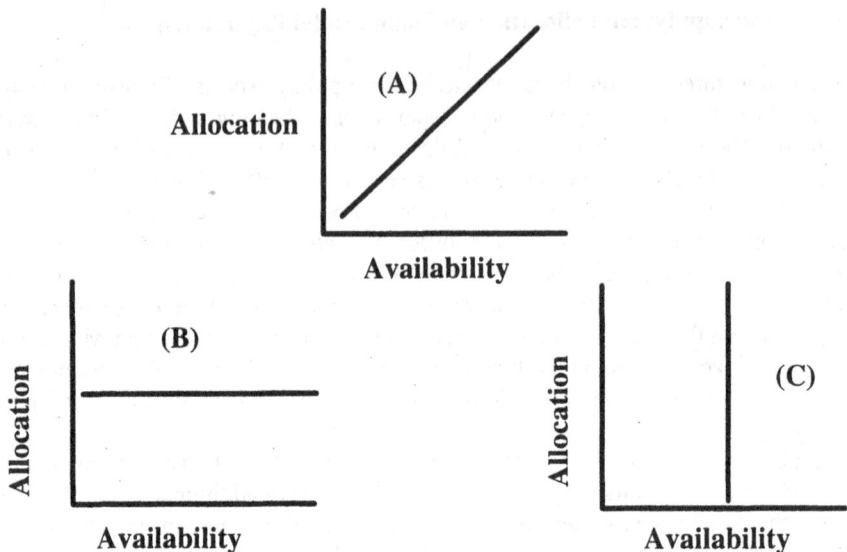

Figure 3.6 Land allocation and land availability

In practice, however neither possibilities 'B' nor 'C' will occur to any great extent, for a number of reasons. First, in most countries, planning does exist. Therefore in some form, the amount of land allocated in development plans will effect land values and hence the price of housing: planners realise this and do not allocate land willy-nilly because they realise the planning system is an important lever with which to manipulate land values. And second, the models fail to distinguish between the short and the long run. In the short run the possibilities 'B' and 'C' are a reality, because of the imperfections in housing and land markets. A main 'imperfection' comes in the form of time lags between land allocation and housing construction and subsequent sale or letting. During this time lag, the knowledge of planners, developers, owner-occupiers and/or tenants is not always perfectly shared and the forward planning of individual actors is often not possible to predict. There are also times when the housing market is moving more rapidly than the planning process. As a consequence, planning policy fails to gauge correctly the market trends and hence in the short to medium term, either 'B' or 'C' can result. Whilst it might be hoped that 'A' is constantly being achieved, the reality in the short or even medium term, is that the relationship lies either between 'A' and 'B', or between 'A' and 'C'. These would be lines (Figure 3.6) which slope upwards at around 20° or 60°.

To those without a vested interest in manipulating the development process to their own ends, situation 'A' is the most ideal. There are no obstacles in the land supply process, and planning inefficiencies are minimised. But what conditions are needed to achieve this position?

The first condition (call it say, 'condition 1') would be if planning and land supply functions were undertaken by the same agency in the development process.

If this were politically acceptable (and there are countries where this might not be the case), there would be an agency or organisation which was not only able to grant itself planning and building permission, but also to release land in accordance with its development programme. As such, the organisation might further be able to determine the amount, type and tenure of housing to be built. Such a comprehensive approach would minimise costs as well as to solve the problem of reconciling land and planning objectives.

A second condition ('condition 2') to achieving 'possibility A' would stipulate that in order to reconcile the process of land allocation with land availability, the opportunity cost of land holding would have to be increased. Land owners would have to be encouraged to offload development land in favour of investing money elsewhere. This might be brought about as a result of exogenous factors to do with housing market. However, it could be brought about by deliberate state intervention. If government, for example, was to threaten a policy of state ownership of land at some point in the future, this may cause land owners to sell up. Alternatively, changes in the housing and land market could cause owners to divest their land assets in favour of other opportunities, although this possibility might be considered beyond the control of policy makers.

Another way ('condition 3') of bringing about possibility 'A', envisages further intervention in the land supply process in order to ensure land is released in accordance with the development plan. This could be done using either taxation or compulsory purchase procedures or a combination of both. By taxing in particular, long term land holding, owners might be encouraged to release land at an earlier stage than might otherwise be the case. By using compulsory purchase measures more frequently, the state might make land owners more uncertain, as and when, housing markets reach the troughs and peaks of their cycles. By the use of either measure, the effect might be to release more land on to the market.

To understand more about the relationship between land allocation and land availability in the three countries, these 'conditions' may be helpful to the discussion.

Land supply: between theory and practice

In the United Kingdom, there is a fairly clear division of responsibilities between the public sector, which acts formally as the planning authority and private interests who as a 'group' are the main suppliers of land for housing development. This means that 'condition 1' (an organisation with both planning and land supply functions), is not fulfilled. Neither is 'condition 2' likely to be fulfilled; the market for development land in the United Kingdom is broad. It involves many types of buyers, and state ownership of development land is not the norm. Land owners in the United Kingdom, have realised, as a result of historical movements in the housing market, that it often pays to think long term in order to realise maximum profits. The speculative attitude of land owners is not one which is conducive to forward planning; haphazard patterns of land release do not help the planning process.

Under these circumstances the private landowner is an important player. In the United Kingdom, the 'land owner' is represented in a plethora of interests, ranging from large financial institutions through private development companies to individual land owners (Massey and Catalano, 1978), most of whom who are concerned with maximising the value of their land. Generally, the pattern in property cycles over the past twenty years has enhanced their ability to do this, and speculative activity has arguably been encouraged by a government reluctance to become pro-actively involved in land banking. Brown et al (1984) have identified both 'market conditions' and 'landowner behaviour' as important constraints to land availability.

Closing the gap between allocation and availability via the 'condition 3' (taxation measures), is no longer possible in the United Kingdom since the abolition of Development Land Tax in 1986. One objective of introducing the tax in 1975 was to bring development land on to the market. This did not happen however. A possible cause was that landowners were waiting for a change of government and a re-think on land policy. The use of compulsory purchase measures to make land available is still at the disposal of local authorities, although the extent of implementations have declined with a falling off in the levels of slum clearance.

There are stark differences between the United Kingdom and the Netherlands, where in the Dutch case, both planning and land supply functions are mainly municipal responsibilities ('condition 1'). Probably as a result of this, Needham is accurate in suggesting that development land in the Netherlands can be regarded as being 'on tap' (Needham, 1992, p.684). In terms of Figure 3.6, this may mean that the Dutch system gets as near as is ever possible to situation the 'A', where land can be released commensurably with development plan policies.

The Dutch land supply process should also be seen in the context of other land policy instruments. It is here that the second condition ('increasing the opportunity cost of land holding'), should be considered. In the Netherlands, the market for development land is in practice a narrow one, since municipalities are the main, and in some cases the only possible, buyer. The net result is that original landowners only have a limited market into which their land can be sold and thus the opportunity cost is relatively low in the first instance. This is the case with, or without, planning permission. The limited market for land owners may also help to explain why 'condition 3' ('coercion through compulsory purchase and taxation') is not so important. The use of 'Onteigning', compulsory acquisition, is largely insignificant. Statistics suggest that only 0.06% of all land acquired by Dutch municipalities for development between 1979 and 1982, required the use of compulsory purchase powers (Needham et al, 1993 ,p.76).

The supply of land in Germany is affected by many similar factors to that in the United Kingdom. This is hardly surprising given the similar land policy stances (Section 3.2). There is, as in the United Kingdom a division of labour between public sector planning and private sector land ownership. This makes 'condition 1' unachievable.

As in the United Kingdom, there are a proliferation of different interests in the land market in Germany. Speculation in land is significant (Dieterich et al, 1993, p.128), particularly amongst intermediate land owners, making it difficult for the state to force land owners to consider other opportunities ('condition 2'). Companies have been formed with a specific interest in investing in farmland with hope value (Dieterich et al 1993, p.110). Owners of development land in Germany are divided into three groups (Dieterich et al 1993, p.110): 'market' orientated housing companies (Freie Wohnungsbauunternehmen), 'non-profit' owners (e.g. housing associations or the Landesentwicklungsgesellschaften, which are the development companies of various Länder), and private owners. These are classified as 'intermediate' land owners. These intermediate owners, who are owners of land zoned in the Flächenutzungsplan, or regional plan, can gain from the uplift in value created when the Bebauungsplan is finally made. This is a value which can be quite considerable (B.M.Bau 1993, p.159).

A note on compulsory purchase, compensation and land values

Compulsory purchase can be used as a mechanism for making land available in all three countries (B.M.Bau 1993, p.153). The ability to use compulsory purchase is dependent upon the very particular needs of localities and there must be some common need identified (ibid). There is only limited data on the use of compulsory purchase in the comparative context. As was suggested in the previous section, there is little need for the Dutch municipalities to use Onteigning. This is because of their position in the development process as both land use planners and land developers. Rather Onteigning can be used as a method of last resort (B.M.Bau 1993, p.139). Compulsory purchase measures are not used so often for housing schemes in the United Kingdom, particularly since 1979 and their use is limited in Germany, except for comprehensive development, exemplified in the Städtebauliches Entwicklungsmaßnahmen (B.M.Bau, 1993, p.152).

The basis of compensation to be paid is also an important issue. In the Netherlands, compensation is paid on the basis of the 'actual worth' of the land, which in practice is around double the existing (agricultural) use value (B.M.Bau 1993, p.152). The price paid by Dutch municipalities to land owners is not the equivalent of what might be paid under similar circumstances in the other two countries. It is what is termed an 'institutional' value (Needham, 1992, p.672), which reflects the monopolistic position of the municipality in the land market. In the United Kingdom, the basis of compensation is the 'market value', which, in accordance with Section 16 of the Land Compensation Act 1961 should reflect both existing use value and 'hope' value where it is appropriate. In Germany, the basis of compensation is the value to the municipality of the land for 'Verkehrswert' (B.M.Bau, 1993, p.152). This is anticipated to relate to the benefits of having land for roads and other infrastructure.

Table 3.4
Synthesis of land supply issues (Time frame: 1980s to early 1990s)

	Land allocation and land availability.	Theory and practice.	Compulsory purchase and land values.
UK	• Public sector planning and private sector land supply. • Land supply influenced by market trends, & speculative activity.	• Institutional and private interest in land markets; significant for allocation-availability relationship.	• CPOs used less extensively for housing schemes since the 1960s. • Basis of compensation, 'market value', which can include 'hope value' for planning consent.
NL	• Planning and land supply through municipality. • Influences land acquisition prices in line with monopsonistic behaviour (Needham, 1992).	• Municipal role creates single market for development land. • This may make possibility 'A' (Figure 3.6) easier to achieve.	• Relatively insignificant: not used often, as municipal role as land supplier suffices. • Compensation up to double 'existing use' (B.M.Bau, 1993).
G	• Public sector planning and private sector land supply. • Land supply influenced by market trends, & speculative activity.	• Some institutional interest in land market. • Makes possibility 'A' (Figure 3.6) more difficult to achieve.	• Enteigning not often used. • Compensation basis, 'market value'.

3.6 Infrastructure provision

An understanding of the term, 'infrastructure provision' should not initially be assumed. In one form it can mean the construction of a national motorway, whilst in another, it can be a network service; for example, water or gas pipelines, electricity cabling or telephone connection to a single dwelling. The potentially diverse range of interpretations means that for comparison a common source of information should be relied on. The best available source identified for this purpose is a report of the German government (B.M.Bau, 1993).

The report (ibid) uses the term 'Erschließung', which is translated elsewhere as 'infrastructure development' (Dieterich et al, 1993, p.72). This term needs to be seen in a German context; of statutory instruments which can be used to bring about infrastructure provision. These instruments are 'Umlegung' and 'Grenzregelung', which can be used to change the shape of land plots where it is required to provide infrastructure. The term 'Erschließung' implies a comprehensive 'closed' approach to infrastructure provision, which is very different to that in the United Kingdom. In Germany, it is a landmark in the development process involving to a significant extent, public legal provisions.

'Erschließung', which will henceforth be termed 'infrastructure provision', is divided into two categories (B.M.Bau, 1993, p.153); 'primary infrastructure provision', and 'secondary'. The primary infrastructure includes 'streets, parking areas, public utility cables and green spaces'. 'Secondary Erschließung' relates to 'social infrastructure'. In so far as costs are concerned, the division between the two classifications in Germany is not relevant for housing development (B.M.Bau, 1993, p.154); costs of both types of infrastructure are borne between municipality and private party, (developer or private household). In the Netherlands however, there is a more distinct division which comes about through specific funding channels for 'secondary infrastructure', especially in relation to the construction of social housing.

The classification of infrastructure into primary and secondary forms of provision, is a necessary step in progressing the discussion. There is a need to ask what is 'infrastructure', and what is not 'infrastructure'? In the Dutch case, for example, there is a need to be alert to the fact that there is a potentially grey area between what is in practice 'land preparation' and what is 'infrastructure provision'. The 'preparation of land' may be considered as being linked to 'infrastructure', yet in the Netherlands the former is an entirely different and additional stage of the development process. This is not so much an issue in the United Kingdom or Germany. The need, very often, to raise the level of land, or to drain it in order to make it suitable for building, is an additional cost in the Netherlands over and above the usual 'infrastructure' considerations. The result of this commitment to development has been substantial and has resulted over the years in many hectares of reclaimed land. The comparative significance of this particular policy in the Netherlands is provided quite succinctly in the statement that 'God made the world, but the Dutch made Holland' (Anderweg and Irwin, 1993, p.6).

Economic theory and infrastructure

In economic theory, 'infrastructure' can be considered to be about the provision of 'public' goods, 'merit' goods and 'externalities' (Loughlin, 1985). 'Public' goods are those goods, which 'even if consumed by one person, can still be consumed by other people' (Begg et al, 1989, p.340). Examples of this might be roads or water pipelines. 'Merit' goods are 'goods that society thinks everyone ought to have regardless of whether they are wanted by each individual' (ibid). Some examples of this are health, education and leisure. 'Externalities' arise 'whenever an individual's production or consumption decision directly affects the production or consumption of others, other than through market prices' (ibid, p.322).

The question of infrastructure provision meets these issues directly. For housing development there must be roads, sewers, electricity cables and so on. These may be considered 'public goods'. The grant of planning permission, moreover, will have the effect of creating some adverse and some beneficial consequences. The planning process can be argued to be a 'non-market decision' and hence decisions on planning matters are decisions which can lead to both harmful and beneficial externalities. The 'merit good' issue enters the sphere of housing development in connection with the externality issue since it is often argued that the benefit created for those developing land or housing should be returned in some form to the wider community.

These issues are helpful in understanding why governments adopt a certain stance on infrastructure. The extent to which countries find it necessary to mitigate the adverse effects of planning decisions by making developers provide 'social' or some other beneficial 'infrastructure' is important; as is indeed in the wider context, the extent to which the state wishes to trade off planning permission for infrastructure gains. This can be argued to be the essence of the process in the United Kingdom, particularly since the introduction of planning obligations. In other countries, this trade off will be less overt, where the state takes decisions on all forms of infrastructure and passes on the costs to house builders. This is more the case in the Netherlands. Under either circumstance, however, the welfare arguments may play an important role.

Responsibility for infrastructure provision

In Germany it is the legal responsibility of the municipalities (Dieterich et al, 1993, p.70) to ensure that infrastructure is provided, in accordance with § 123-135 BauG. It is hence laid down in a (building law) statute. However, this does not mean that municipalities provide all infrastructure. It comes from a mix of public and private sector sources, although by whatever means, it is ultimately a municipal responsibility. The opposite of this situation occurs in the Netherlands. In the Dutch development process, virtually all infrastructure provision is provided by municipalities, yet they are under no legal duty to provide it (B.M.Bau, 1993, p.138). In the United Kingdom, a legal duty falls neither specifically on public or private sector.

Who actually provides infrastructure?

The question of who physically installs infrastructure is beyond the remit of this research; mainly divisions between public and private sectors, as commissioners of infrastructure works are the main focus of 'who provides infrastructure'. Figures

3.7, 3.8 and 3.9 show the sources of infrastructure provision (i.e the commissioners of works) in the United Kingdom, the Netherlands and Germany respectively. The information is taken from the German government report (B.M.Bau, 1993), and relates to the period of the late 1980s. Figure 3.7 outlines the way in which infrastructure works are divided in the United Kingdom. Figure 3.7, as well as Figures 3.8 and 3.9 show the divisions according to percentages for all development land.

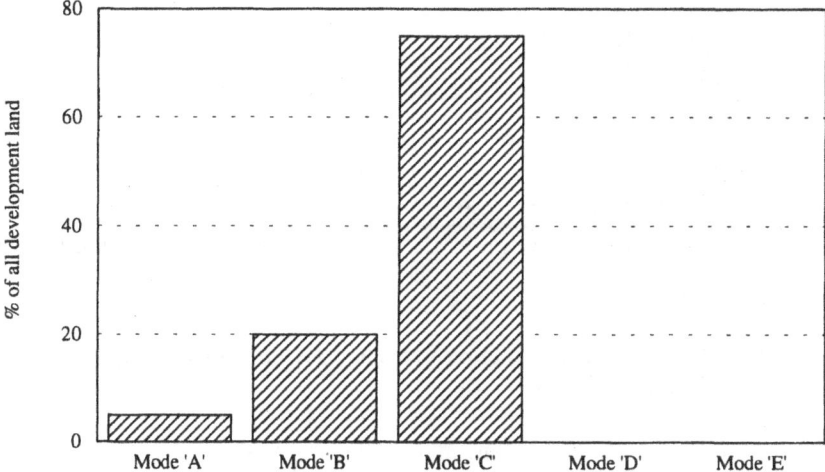

Source: B.M.Bau (1993)

Figure 3.7   Modes of infrastructure provision for housing development: the United Kingdom

Infrastructure is provided in the Netherlands in the following way:

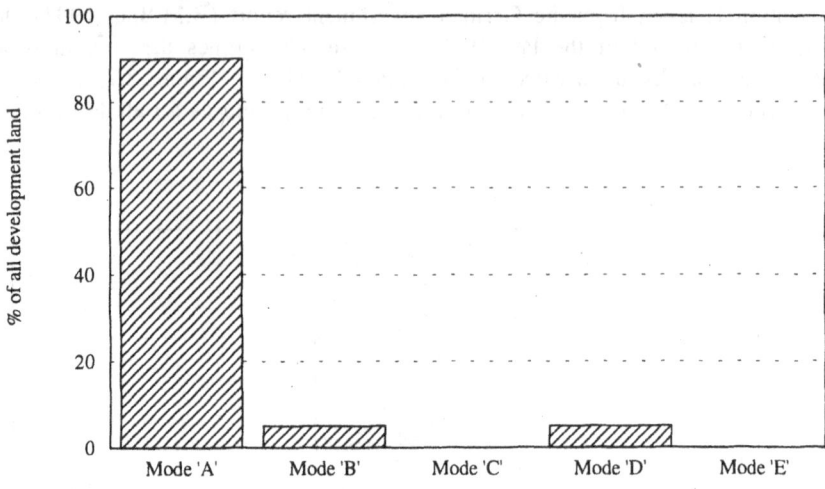

Source: B.M.Bau (1993)

Figure 3.8   Modes of infrastructure provision for housing development: the Netherlands

Infrastructure is provided in Germany in the following way:

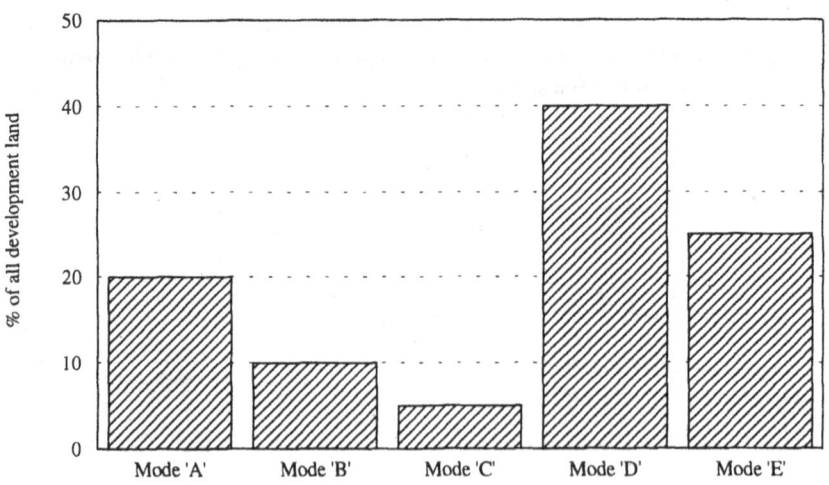

Source: B.M.Bau (1993)

Figure 3.9   Modes of infrastructure provision for housing development: Germany

Figures 3.7, 3.8 and 3.9 show five modes of infrastructure provision:

Mode 'A': Where development land is provided with infrastructure by local authorities or other municipal bodies.

Mode 'B': Where development land is provided with infrastructure by public or quasi-public bodies. Some examples of these are: in the United Kingdom, Urban Development Corporations and in Germany, the Landesentwicklunggesellschaften (regional land development companies). In the Netherlands this mode of infrastructure provision (Figure 3.8) is not so common.

Mode 'C': Where development land is provided with infrastructure by private developers.

Mode 'D': Where development land is provided with infrastructure by landowners (either original or intermediate) *without* the use of public sector legal procedures.

Mode 'E': Where development land is provided with infrastructure by landowners (either original or intermediate) *with* the use of public sector legal procedures.

Figures 3.7, 3.8 and 3.9 provide an interesting contrast. In both the Netherlands and the United Kingdom, the channels for the supply of serviced land are fairly distinct. In the former, serviced building land is provided by the state municipalities, whilst in the latter it is largely a function of private developers. Figure 3.8 shows that in the Netherlands, around 90% of land is serviced by municipalities (Mode 'A'). In the United Kingdom, almost 80% of development land is serviced by private developers (Mode 'C'). In the Netherlands, the serviced building land is sold on to a variety of house builders in both the private and public sector. In the United Kingdom, the most significant mode of infrastructure provision is by private developers who can be servicing development land for their own use, often the construction of owner-occupied houses.

In Germany, infrastructure tasks are distributed more broadly; across all five modes (Figure 3.9). There is infrastructure provision from municipalities and by the Landesentwicklunggesellschaften, who are the land development companies of the Länder. This totals around 30%. The greater volume of infrastructure provision, however, comes from Modes 'D' and 'E', which emanate from original and intermediate owners who provide infrastructure both with and without legal procedures. This amounts to around 60% of all infrastructure works.

This high level of provision (Modes 'D' and 'E') in Germany is particularly interesting when compared with the United Kingdom and the Netherlands, where there is (Figures 3.7 and 3.8) virtually no equivalent. However some care needs to be exercised in the comparison since 'intermediate' and 'original' owners in the United Kingdom and the Netherlands can also be 'private developers' or 'municipalities'. Hence, some further investigation is required. A way ahead would be to link more closely the land supply and building process to the stage of infrastructure. A possible explanation for the particular modes of infrastructure provision in Germany, may lie in the prevalence of private households as suppliers of new housing (Figure 1.4).

Infrastructure costs and modes of payment

Generally speaking in all three countries, the costs of infrastructure are borne ultimately by the housing consumer. The extent of costs borne are potentially 100% in all three countries. Traditionally in Germany, however, the municipality has contributed a minimum of 10% of total infrastructure costs (B.M.Bau, 1993, p.154) leaving the consumer or investor with a maximum of 90% to pay. However, the trend is now towards shifting an even greater percentage of costs to private parties (Dieterich, 1994).

Infrastructure costs are in practice influenced by the nature and extent of provision and the ownership of land. In the Netherlands, municipalities are the main landowners and their decisions about the level of infrastructure provision are critical to the overall cost borne by the housing consumer. In this scenario, it might be anticipated that sometimes a merit good argument is applied; high standards of infrastructure are deemed necessary, but without the agreement of individual households who could end up paying for 'meritous' levels of provision. Where 'infrastructure provision' is on an additional plane, such as with the provision of social housing, schools or green space, then the issue is much more to do with distributive decisions.

In the United Kingdom, the different patterns of land ownership at the housing development stage create different assumptions about standards of provision and hence cost. Where the boot is on the other foot, housing developers may take a minimal stance to infrastructure provision: if the scheme is for owner-occupied housing, this 'stance' may be simply 'enough to get the houses sold' Furthermore, developers frequently imply social housing is not only a cost of the planning gain to be borne at the time of new development, but is also a potential cost to the marketability of private housing.

In Germany, some of the arguments relating to the United Kingdom also apply. Because land is normally in private hands, the level of infrastructure provision is more a function of a negotiated process. Without some concessions on infrastructure cost sharing, land will not be brought on to the market. This may explain the willingness of municipalities to make some (10%) contribution. However, private households and investors also recognise the municipal power to be able to change private land boundaries (Grenzregelung and Umlegung) and therefore ultimately the latter significant leverage over the development process. Table 3.5 summarises the issues relating to infrastructure provision:

Table 3.5
Synthesis of issues relating to infrastructure provision (Time frame: late 1980s)

	Responsibility for infrastructure	Main source(s) of infrastructure provision.	Parties bearing infrastructure costs
UK	• No state legal responsibility.	• Private housing developers (80% of all development land). • Mode C (Fig 3.7).	• Up to 100% paid by housing consumer.
NL	• No state legal responsibility.	• Municipalities (90% of all development land). • Mode A (Fig 3.8).	• Up to 100% paid by housing consumer.
G	• Legal responsibility for municipalities under § 123-135 Bau.G.	• Original or intermediate owners (can be 'housing developers'). • Modes D and E (Figure 3.9).	• Minimum of 10% of costs paid by municipality. • Remainder paid by housing consumer.

3.7 The building process

Section 3.7 examines the final stage in the housing development process; land supply and infrastructure provision having been the first two main phases. The 'building process' is a comparison of a number of aspects to do with housing construction, the extent of risk and speculation and the nature of housing suppliers. But first, a much broader question should be asked about the term 'building process' to find out how applicable this is across the three countries:

A 'building' or 'development' process?

Which term is more appropriate to a particular sector of housing supply in the comparative context?: 'building', or 'development' process? The answer to this question depends essentially on two things. First, what is meant by the terms 'building' and 'development' process, and second, what housing suppliers actually *do*.

One way of making a distinction might be to suggest that whilst it is possible to describe the process of the construction of a dwelling as 'development', it is less correct to describe the cumulative process of acquisition of land, provision of infrastructure and the construction of a dwelling as 'building'. If this reflects in any way common understanding of the terminology, then the debate can be expanded, given what is known about housing production in the three countries. This begins with the United Kingdom.

Housing production in the United Kingdom comes from three main housing suppliers: the private sector, housing associations and local authorities (Figure 1.2). This is generally the case for the period since the 1960s. This means that there are three main production channels and three potential 'development processes'. Of the three sectors, the most significant contributor to the total volume of housing production is the 'private sector'. This sector have produced around 80% (D.o.E Housing and Construction Statistics), of all new dwellings since the mid 1980s (Figure 1.2). The sector is regarded as a very speculative one by comparison with other European countries (Barlow and Duncan, 1994, p.36), although it is difficult to be precise about 'how speculative' since output from this sub-sector is not disaggregated from national construction levels (Ball, 1983, p.45). Barlow and Duncan (1994, p.42) have calculated in more recent research, however, that 'speculative' production accounts for around 70% of all production in the 1980s, implying that much of production by the private sector is speculative. To determine, however, whether a house building is 'speculative' or otherwise, requires some more definition. Barlow and Duncan (ibid, p.33) relate speculative housing promotion to the total management of the development process including the acquisition of land, building and sale of completed dwelling, which is 'not for a specific client on a bespoke basis'. Ball (1983, p.50) has suggested that this category is concerned with 'development profit', which is achieved by the 'judicious purchase of land and conceiving of the appropriate residential scheme' (ibid).

The private sector in the United Kingdom is thus involved in *both* the land market and in the construction of dwellings to a significant extent. This is with an aim to a 'distinct type of capital accumulation' (ibid, p.51). There is a concern with profit taking from both land and house building, a point picked up by Barlow and Duncan (1994, p.89):

> Despite appearances, housebuilding is only partially the business of putting up houses. The houses are the socially acceptable side of making profits out of land appreciation (Cited from: Investors Chronicle 8/1/74).

Private sector production in the United Kingdom is also dominated by large firms. Figure 3.10 shows production by this sector. For the years 1985 to 1988 approximately 25% of total production derived from up to 13 firms only (Gillen, 1994). Some of these were Barrett, Beazer, Bovis, Bryant, Costain, Ideal, Laing, Lovell, McCarthy and Stone, Tarmac, Westbury, Wilcon and Wimpey (ibid). These companies, along with smaller firms in the private sector are producing housing mainly for owner occupation.

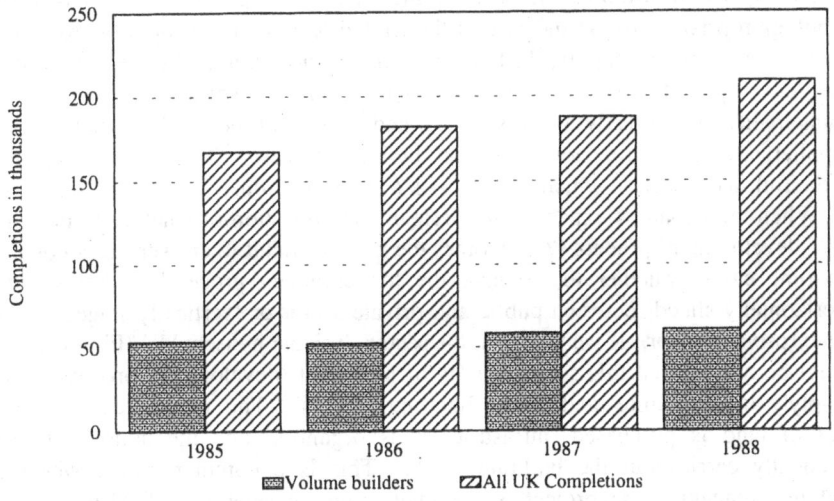

Source: Gillen, 1994; Department of the Environment

Figure 3.10 Housing supply by volume house builders in the United Kingdom

The extent to which these large firms exert an influence over the housing market is considered in Chapter 4.

The development processes of the other two sectors, 'housing association' and 'local authority' (Figure 1.2), are less well researched, perhaps because from a volume production aspect, these sectors are less important. Housing associations in the United Kingdom, now the main suppliers of social housing, rely upon a mix of sources for land supply; from both local authority land banks as well as private sector sources. Local authority housing production in the past relied very much on land banks built up over long periods of time. In the city of Leicester, for example, the land bank of the city council dates back to the last century, although production on this land is now mainly private sector and housing association.

When considering the same question, of 'building' or 'development process', in the Netherlands, a quite different situation arises to that in the United Kingdom. This is between municipal land supply and infrastructure provision on the one hand, and the building process which is carried out mainly by market builders and housing associations (Figure 1.3), on the other. In the United Kingdom, the process is 'vertical' in the sense that each sector has many responsibilities within its own development process. In the Netherlands, the development process of most housing suppliers is sliced 'horizontally' in the sense that a division of labour is reached between public and private sector (market builders and housing associations in the broadest meaning of the term 'private').

An expansion of the debate on 'building' and 'development' in the Netherlands is not appropriate here. In the case of the United Kingdom, it is possible to explain the link between land supply, the building process and 'volume' builders in terms of the 'development process'. In the Netherlands, however, the role of the municipality has already been stressed and it should be evident that housing suppliers are mostly concerned with the 'building process'. This stage is examined in the following section which looks at risk and speculation.

When the debate is expanded to Germany, the question of whether a 'building' or a 'development' process (?), becomes the more difficult to answer. It is not clear in some cases, whether to perceive the 'development process' as being either 'horizontally sliced' between public and private sector or 'vertically staged' by the same (private) actor. If we take first the sector, 'private households' (Figure 1.4), it could be argued that this sector has its own distinct 'development process': 'land supply', 'infrastructure' and 'house building process'. This may be case, where a plot of land is purchased, infrastructure is organised and the household itself physically carries out the building work. This is a common route, where an architect managing the project is the main point of reference (B.M.Bau, 1993, p.170). However, the need for municipal involvement in infrastructure provision is also often necessary and hence the 'private' process becomes momentarily 'sliced' by public sector involvement before the building process can begin. This can also be the case for production by housing investors, or social housing providers.

The building process, risk and speculation

The previous section looked at the terms 'building' and 'development process' and suggested how they may apply across different sectors within different countries. One important consequence of the housing supplier's involvement is that firms, households or individuals may speculate in land markets for financial gain. Generally a distinction can be made here between the United Kingdom and Germany, where this is possible, and the Netherlands, where it occurs infrequently. However, there are a number of other aspects to do with the relations between the housing supplier, the building process and the housing market which are significant for understanding the extent of risk involved in the supply process. These are complex issues, particularly in comparisons, and hence a framework should be established. This can be built essentially on the relationship between a 'client' and the 'source of construction'.

The 'client' in this comparative framework is the 'supplier' of housing. The volume of production emanating from 'clients' ('opdrachtgevers' in the Netherlands and 'Bauherren' in Germany), is that recorded as 'production by sector' in national housing production statistics. However, the 'client' or 'orderer' of production is not always the same entity as the source of construction. In the United Kingdom, it has been suggested that housing is 'speculatively' built by 'private house builders' (Barlow and Duncan, 1994, p.36). The extent to which this is a 'speculative' operation will depend mainly upon two factors: the size of the house building firm, and market conditions; for example, building housing when housing demand is weak, with a large labour force retained by a company, may be seen to be 'highly risky' or 'speculative'. Building in a strong housing market, under the same conditions may be less 'risky' or less 'speculative'. Either way, the cyclical nature of the housing market may lead to a notion that the private sector operate in a 'speculative manner'. The degree of speculation should also be referenced to the question of land supply. The involvement of the volume builders in the land market may compound the speculative nature of housing supply in the United Kingdom.

In other sectors in the United Kingdom, and perhaps housing associations are the most relevant today, the relationship between 'client', and source of construction is normally a separate one; a 'contract' arrangement. If there is risk or speculation in the building or development process then it may be measured in terms of the sum of money not guaranteed by government Housing Association Grant, or the risk that rents will not cover the building costs.

A starting point for understanding the building process in the Netherlands is the 'opdrachtgever'. The 'opdrachtgever' is the 'client'. or 'giver of commissions' (Renier, 1992, p.215). In the 'market sector' (Figure 3.11), there are five main 'opdrachtgever' (Priemus, 1984, p.55). The 'beleggers', the 'makelaars', the 'particulaire personen', the 'bouwbedrijven' and the 'projectontwickkelaars'. Figure 3.11 provides an interpretation of the building process in the market sector.

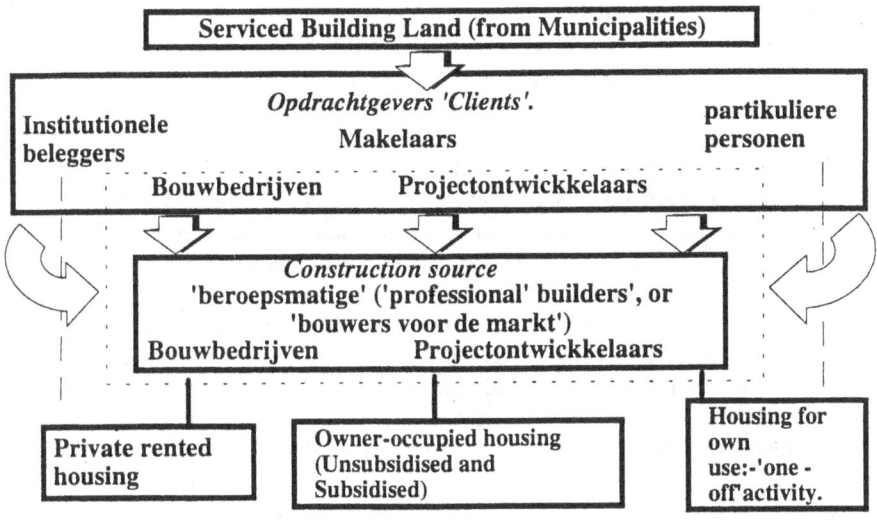

Figure 3.11   The building process in the Dutch market sector

Production for 'beleggers', 'makelaars' and 'particulaire personen' is production for specific clients. In this sense it is not a speculative exercise for house builders themselves. The risk is taken by institutional investors ('beleggers') who require production for private rent, by real estate agents ('makelaars'), who require production for a variety of sources, both rented and ownership housing, and by private individuals ('particulaire personen') who require production for their own use. The beleggers produce for a very specific end use, private rented housing (Figure 3.11), which can be both subsidised or unsubsidised (Boelhouwer & Van der Heijden, 1989, p.30). Private individuals 'particulaire personen' requiring production comprise a significant amount of the market sector. This type of production will be a 'one-off' (ibid, p.31) and will be produced by market builders who rely on this particular small scale commission. The housing for these three 'client types' is produced by the 'market builders'; the 'bouwers voor de markt'. Whilst they provide a 'professional' ('beroepmatige') service in that they fulfil contracts as a source of construction, they also function as a 'client' for production and therefore come therefore under the heading 'opdrachtgever'. The dotted line in Figure 3.11, conceptualises the dual function, where:

> the client is not simply a *demander* of building capacity, but also has the potential to fulfil certain needs within the process. When the opdrachtgever plays an active role, he breaks away from the one sided demand - supply equation which characterise other production sectors (Priemus, 1984, p.55).

What this implies is that the 'market sector' as a whole operates in what might be termed a 'partially speculative' manner. Much of the time it 'demands capacity' from 'opdrachtgevers', but it can also 'create work for itself', so to speak, by anticipating trends in the housing market.

Market builders have a particular function in the Dutch building process:

> The market builders differentiate themselves from other clients, in that they specifically direct themselves towards a (calculated) need in the market, while other clients look to their own user interests in housing production (Boelhouwer and Van der Heijden, 1989, p.29).

These 'other clients' are housing associations and municipalities. They provide a demand or need for production capacity for social rented housing. This 'need' is met to a significant extent by building companies which are associated with municipalities (B.M.Bau, 1993, p.174); 'gemeindeeigene - Wohnungsbaugesellschaften', who may be considered the 'source of construction'. In 1988, there were 250 of these companies (B.M.Bau, 1993, p.174).

It is clear that the building process of market builders is affected by a number of factors. The sector needs to be carefully analysed since market builders can operate in both a speculative manner, as well as building on a bespoke basis.

The extent to which the building process is 'speculative', is argued to depend upon the relationship between the 'client' and the 'source of construction'. In Germany, a translation of 'client' is 'Auftraggeber'. However the term 'Bauherr' is suggested to be more apposite in the comparative context. This is because types of

'Bauherren' define the way in which German housing production is categorized. A 'Bauherr' is defined:

> Any person, who technically prepares and realises *in his own name* (*for himself or for a third party*), a building project, or prepares and allows (the project) to be realised (on his behalf) (Frank, 1978, p.27).

The definition of the Bauherr is significant to understanding the building and development process of private households in particular. It is made explicit in the definition, that two possibilities exist from a single decision: either the 'Bauherr' realises the building him or herself, or leaves it to be contracted out. 'Realises', is taken to mean 'physically' carries out, whilst 'contracting out' implies what might be understood as a 'design and build' process. The market for new owner-occupied housing is further supplied by contractors involved in the 'building and sale' of dwellings (B.M.Bau 1993, 170):

> In the building phase there are two common routes (for the supply of owner-occupied dwellings); the construction by the individual party who will eventually be the occupier, or a 'build and sale' route through building contractors (B.M.Bau, 1993, p.170).

The degree to which the building process is 'speculative' will depend upon which of the three possible routes are chosen. In two of the routes; 'own construction' and 'design and build', it will essentially be a question of who ties up capital in the building process; the household or the building contractor Under the third route, the 'Build and Sale' (B.M.Bau, 1993, p.170), there may be a greater element of speculation in terms of the funding of land costs, or need to find a purchaser for the dwelling.

The term 'Bauherr' relates also to other sectors; the Gemeinnützige Unternehmen, whose interest as a housing supplier is directed towards social needs (Ulbrich, 1991, p.278), the Freie Unternehmen and other Unternehmen. These 'Bauherren' provide a demand for housing of various tenures. These are mainly across the rented sector; either 'private' or 'social' rented.

It is difficult to analyse the extent to which these are 'speculative' processes. Information on the relationship between these Bauherren and sources of construction was not identified in this research. Furthermore, the Freie Unternehmen produce both housing for rent and for sale (Jenkis, 1993, p.286). This may involve a long term investment commitment or a short term financial gain. A final difficulty may be presented by the diverse nature of the German construction industry, which is stated to be an industry of 'small enterprises' (Boelhouwer and Van der Heijden, 1992, p.118).

Table 3.6
Synthesis of the building process (Time frame: late 1980s to early 1990s; private sector)

	'Building' or 'development' process?	'Client', 'source of construction' and 'speculation'.
UK (Private sector)	• Housing development process; 'volume builders active in land and house building. • 'Vertical' process utilising resources & skills of development firms.	• 'Client' and source of construction'; same in case of 'volume' house builders: c 40% of all production (Gillen, 1994). • Viewed as a mainly speculative sector.
NL (Market builders)	• 'Building process' for all housing suppliers or 'opdrachtgevers': market builders and housing associations. • Land supply through municipalities to all these sectors.	• 'Market builders' function as a source of construction. • But also as 'client', or 'Opdrachtgever, where they act speculatively. • May be viewed as a partially speculative sector.
G (Private households)	• Public-private sector development process. • Private households and municipalities shared responsibility.	• 'Clients' are 'Bauherren'. • Private households are main Bauherren. • Speculation is reduced via 'self-promotion', or 'design and build' processes.

3.8 Between state and market: a summary of systems of housing supply

This final section of Chapter 3 aims to summarise the main differences in the nature of housing supply in the three countries. By 'nature' was implied in the introduction, the extent to which the state is an active participant in the systems of housing supply; alternatively, the extent to which the market sector is the main player. Although there are problems with 'state-market' frameworks, particularly where the two concepts are deliberately polarised (Barlow and Duncan, 1994, p.xi), any examination of the way in which a system is structured may be precursored from this conventional viewpoint. A note of caution however is first required.

Analyses of the role of the state and its relationship with the market are often enunciated in terms of the degree of intervention or regulation which government is responsible for. Unfortunately, however, concepts of 'intervention' and 'regulation' are very difficult to measure, mainly because 'state' and 'market' are inextricably linked. Arguably, the terms 'intervention' and 'regulation' are only different extents of government policy action. The terms are particularly problematical for comparative analysis. It is nevertheless possible by making a number of assumptions about events represented by 'state' action and events represented by the 'market', to differentiate between systems of housing supply. To this end, this summary looks at the systems of housing supply in terms of the divisions of labour between government (national and local) on the one side, and private sector parties (firms and individuals) on the other. In so far that the 'state' is represented by 'government' and the 'market' by private sector activity, then a 'state-market' analytical framework becomes broadly valid. The different facets of housing supply, of which there have been six introduced in Chapter 3, are now compared.

Housing production policy (Section 3.2)

Government housing production policies were examined in Section 3.2 in terms of the levels of investment devoted to housing and in terms of the subsidy programmes implemented since the early 1970s. This analysis mainly left aside the measurement of tenure outcomes which could be seen from the Introduction to differ very much between countries (Figures 1.2. 1.3 and 1.4). Rather the extent to which governments have been directly involved in promoting new housing was seen to be a function of different demographic pressures and the nature of housing stock developed during the immediate post-war period. Both different rates of household formation, as well as differences in policies aimed at renewal rather than new building, explain to some extent why levels of investment in housing also differ. For the period 1970 onwards, levels of investment by two measures at least, (Figure 3.1), show the Netherlands and Germany devoting more resources to housing than the United Kingdom.

Whether this means 'more government' or 'more intervention' in those two countries, can only be deduced by looking at investment levels in the light of the production outcomes themselves. That is to say, by knowing the level of government resources devoted directly to social housing, or perhaps to private rented housing through tax or other incentives. Such an exercise would be a separate empirical study, not least because of the intricate way in which governments have actually promoted different forms of housing in Europe. This is particularly the case in countries such as Germany and the Netherlands, where tenure is more complex and broad ranging than in the United Kingdom. Only really in the case of the United Kingdom, is it possible to tentatively suggest that governments have been less supportive. This is because not only levels of investment are lower than elsewhere (Figure 3.1), but also, levels of private sector production, particularly in the 1980s, have been higher.

The specific housing production programmes implemented also reflect on the nature of government intervention in housing. This is in the sense that, in particular, central governments overtly set out policies for alleviating crude housing shortages or particular forms of housing need. Where the policies are made open to a number of housing suppliers, such as in Germany through the Förderungswege, the notion of a 'state sponsored housing programme' can be gained. Where central government makes its subsidy arrangements privy only to a particular sector of supply, such as with local authorities and housing associations in the United Kingdom, then the ability to sustain a national production programme will always be subject to political decisions. In Germany, this has also been the case, although the encouragement of individuals to invest in the rented sector, has helped the mitigate the effects of reducing state expenditure in housing.

Other factors however, come into play. These relate to the nature of the subsidy programmes themselves. The more extensive use of 'conditional object' subsidies (Oxley, 1987, p.166) by Dutch and German governments to promote new housing reflect a different approach in production policies. This type of subsidy is evident in both the German Förderungswege and Sector A and B housing in the Netherlands. These approaches can be interpreted as being on the one hand, prescriptive and, on the other, paternalistic: not only is there a concern with directly addressing housing need, but also a concern that the implementational process will not fail housing consumers. In the United Kingdom, it would be wrong to say that housing need has not been addressed by local authorities and housing associations. Rather that the process of addressing need is indirect and more discretionary.

Land policy (Section 3.3)

As a facet of housing supply, land policy is more readily adaptable for analysis within a 'state-market' framework, than is the case for housing production policy. In so far that the ownership of development land represents a good measure of government or private sector influence, it is possible to quantify how much, or how little, the state is involved in land supply.

In these respects, land policy is more similar in the United Kingdom and Germany. The land policy in the Netherlands is shown to be significantly different with a much higher proportion of development land being held by municipalities; whereas in both the United Kingdom and Germany, development land is normally held by private interests. These may be original owners or development companies, and the extent of their ownership was compared with the Dutch at the stage at which land is ready to be built on.

Dutch land policy is also differentiated from the policies of Germany and the United Kingdom by the way Dutch central governments have intervened in the land market to regulate land prices. Whilst the price at which land is exchanged is ultimately a function of government *and* market, it is only in the case of the Netherlands, that central government has overtly fixed land prices in order to influence development outcomes. In both the United Kingdom and Germany, state intervention in the land market has been much more a function of other aspects of policy, notably physical planning, where betterment, for example, is dealt with through planning agreements or within the process of negotiating infrastructure. In the Dutch situation, the land prices stipulated by government are part of the betterment equation, giving municipalities the possibility to determine housing outcomes before releasing land to market builders or housing associations.

Planning policy (Section 3.4)

Planning was the third facet of the system of supply considered in Chapter 3. Discussing the extent to which this is a 'state', or 'market' sector responsibility in the three countries is a more difficult task than for other facets of housing supply such as land policy. Not least because planning policy provides few quantitative measures against which an evaluation of the role of government can be made. Differences in official definitions of 'planning' are evident, where concepts of planning in Germany and the Netherlands are more inclusive (Section 3.4). However, the selection of definition is of course a subjective exercise and hence not too much weight should be attached to the process.

One way of examining the role of government in planning housing development is to look for evidence of comprehensive national planning policy documents. If this is done, the Netherlands provides good continuity, where housing and other forms of development have been strategically programmed for certain areas over specific periods of time. In the other two countries, comprehensive state planning strategies are less in evidence. Rather specific local initiatives or urban renewal schemes are more in evidence: the German Städtebauliche Entwicklungmaßnahmen or the Urban Development Corporations in the United Kingdom, for example. Differences in approach between the Netherlands on the one hand and Germany and the United Kingdom, on the other, may be a function of several factors to do with the scale of planning, or differences in the emphasis given to regional or market dimensions.

Development plans were discussed as a planning policy issue in Section 3.4. In some respects, a prescriptive system of development control through legally binding plans evidences a strong intent to regulate land markets. Legally binding planning systems exist in the Netherlands and Germany at the local level through Bestemmingplannen and Bebauungspläne. On the other hand, discretionary or non-mandatory development plan systems leave open the question of the precise role of the state in development control. This has been the situation in the United Kingdom for much of the past twenty five years, where the private sector and the house building industry have been encouraged to influence the planning process in conjunction with local authority planners.

However, the precise consequences of the state's policy on development plans cannot be gauged solely on the basis of the status of the plans themselves. Section 3.4 showed how in the broader context of land supply, development plans have very different effects on land values. There are (Figure 3.5), prescriptive development plans in the Netherlands and Germany. However, the percentage increase in land value due to planning consent varies considerably, a function of different land ownership norms and different development processes. Thus, a similar stance with respect to a particular aspect of policy, can lead to very different outcomes in practice.

Land supply (Section 3.5)

Similarities in the way in which land is supplied reflects, perhaps not surprisingly, the policy adopted by the state on land. As a fourth facet of the system of housing supply, there is greater similarity in the systems of land supply in the United Kingdom and Germany. The system of land supply in the Netherlands is distinguished from the other two countries by the active role of the state at the local level. This is quantified in research, where traditionally around 75% of all land for housing development is supplied by the state. In the United Kingdom, this is not the case where generally private housing is built on land which is either supplied by the agency building the housing, or where land is purchased by the house builder directly from the farmer or other original owner. In Germany this model occurs in practice, specifically where private households purchase land for housing construction or where other Unternehmen wish to build ownership or rented housing. Land supplied by German municipalities for development is only around 10% of total land supply (Scholland, 1987).

As with other individual facets of the system, land supply should not be viewed in isolation when considering the consequences for housing development. The best case for an holistic analysis of the system is found in the role played by Dutch municipalities as both suppliers of land and physical planning authorities. Section 3.5 envisaged a number of scenarios or trade-offs, between land allocation and land availability issues, where in theory, state intervention in both planning and land policy fields is necessary to wholly regulate housing production.

Infrastructure provision (Section 3.6)

The second main stage in the process of housing development considered was infrastructure provision. Section 3.6 provided the details of this facet of housing supply. Research conducted by the German government into the land market in the 1980s (B.M.Bau 1993) provides a distinct overview of infrastructure provision in the three countries. This is helpful in quantifying the extent to which there is public sector participation at this stage of the development process.

At opposite ends of the public-private sector, 'continuum', are the United Kingdom and the Netherlands. In the Netherlands, 90% of development land has infrastructure provided by municipalities, whereas in the United Kingdom, private developers are largely responsible for providing infrastructure: around 75% of all development land is serviced by this sector. In Germany, however, the division between 'private' and 'public' sector is less distinct than in the other two countries. Figure 3.9 (Section 3.6) shows the modes or norms to be more varied. The only purely private sector modes are 'C' and 'D'; these do not rely either on municipal involvement or public legal procedures. Modes 'C' and 'D' comprise around 45% of all development land. Infrastructure schemes carried out entirely by municipalities (Mode 'A') on the other hand amount to around 20%. This leaves two other modes, 'B' and 'E', which involve some public sector input. These make up the remaining 35%.

The building process (Section 3.7)

In Section 3.7, the building process was considered in the three countries. Here the aim was to summarise the role of state intervention in the building process. However, whereas as with some facets of supply, the picture is quite uniform, with the 'building process' this is varied and determined entirely by the source of housing supply. It is clear that where the housing supplier is a local authority, then public sector involvement more significant, but where the housing supplier is a volume private house builder, then the reverse is true. Beyond this, however, there is not so much to gauge. To some extent, questions about the relevance to housing suppliers of a 'building' or 'development' process are valid. But only in the sense that the individual building processes are reliant on the previous stages of development, namely land supply and infrastructure provision.

In some cases, most notably, the Netherlands, the argument can be made that the operation of house building is strongly reliant upon the state. The control of land supply by municipalities is one factor which puts house builders in a very different situation to house builders in the other two countries. Control of land supply in the Netherlands is linked with planning and infrastructure control and design. Those who supply housing are, in the comparative context, involved in a 'building' rather than 'development' process. Conversely, in the United Kingdom, the term 'development process' is more applicable, particularly for the private sector, where the mode of housing production relies to a significant extent on volume house builders who are active in both land and housing markets. However, between these two extremes, the state influences new housing production in very varied ways. This is particularly the case in Germany, where it is more difficult to slice the discussion tidily between 'state' and 'market' or 'public' and 'private'; a consequence of the complex procedures for infrastructure, as well as the diversity of modes of housing development that occur.

Conclusion

In conclusion it may be helpful to briefly set out an impression of the different facets of housing supply considered in this chapter. It should be re-emphasised that the objective has been to consider the role of private and public sector parties in policy and process. Figure 3.12 attempts to answer the question by providing such an impression:

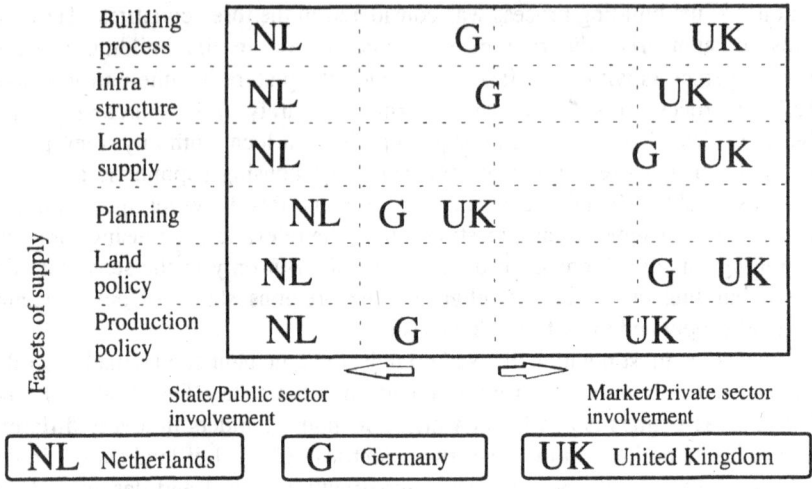

Figure 3.12 The role of state and market in housing supply

The subjective nature of this analysis cannot of course be understated. However, as will have been appreciated from the foregoing discussion, it is possible to quantify certain aspects of housing supply; this is the case for land policy, land supply and infrastructure provision. Other aspects such as planning and housing policy are less easy to quantify in terms of the role of particular agencies. One might nevertheless present some conclusions based on levels of housing investment, the nature and extent of housing subsidies and the effects of development plans on the uplift in land values.

4 Structure and agencies in housing supply

4.1. Introduction

This chapter aims to address an important aspect of the hypothesis, namely to examine the structure of systems of housing supply. Chapter 4 provides an important link between Chapter 3, which examined the systems of supply in the three countries from a 'state-market' perspective, and Chapter 5 which looks at housing production outcomes. This chapter aims to provide a discussion on the different ways in which the three housing systems can be conceptualised, paying specific attention in the conclusion to similarities and differences arising from each perspective. Conclusions from this and the previous chapter will be compared and contrasted in the light of the investigations of the following chapter.

The approach adopted in this chapter is strongly influenced by the framework of Chapter 2, which looked at comparative methodology and the scope for using different interpretations of structure to examine housing systems. At the beginning of each sub-section, there is a brief review of the assumptions underlying the models. The approach is first to look at the primary linkages in the system of housing supply; a key aspect of this focus is to look at the division of labour in each country within the housing development process. Then, to examine, the role that agencies play within these frameworks: central government, local government, private and social housing suppliers. The objectives are to evaluate the significance of particular agencies and to understand more about how they relate to each other. To do this, both concrete measures of housing outcome, as well as anecdotal and other empirical evidence are used. The final facet of this chapter examines the macroeconomies of the three countries. This is not an empirical exercise in itself, but an attempt to identify broad differences in the way the economies have been managed.

Chapter 4 aims to show where similarities exist, although it also attempts to provide different concepts for systems of housing supply. The purpose of the chapter will be to provide, above all, a basis for looking at housing output as examined in the following chapter.

4.2 Systems of housing supply: a functional approach

The potential contribution of the concept of the 'structure' was introduced in Chapter 2. One way of approaching the concept of a housing system is to look at the functional linkages between agencies. This approach (Chapter 2) owes much to a focus on the development process, where one main aim is to identify the nature of the key players and attempt to examine the extent to which they represent public or private sector housing provision. One aim, as followed in the following text in Section 4.2, is to ask questions of each of the three countries, about the divisions of labour between public and private sectors in the development process and the system of supply.

The focus on the functional aspects and divisions of labour can enable conclusions to be drawn about the extent to which systems of housing supply are seen to be complex or straightforward. Is it the case that therefore that:

> simple property-market systems function better than complicated ones (B.M.Bau 1993, p.xxxii).

and, if so, what systems are 'complex' and why?

To understand the main differences, Section 4.2 examines the three countries by asking a series of questions about the functional linkages between the agencies in housing supply. In particular, by examining the case for an 'integrated system' and by examining some of the main linkages between policy and the development process.

The United Kingdom

The case for an integrated system of housing supply
If a system of housing supply is to fully monitor housing production outcomes, then it needs to be integral. By this is meant that all facets, (policy and process aspects), should be interconnected in such a way that a change in policy direction can be efficiently effected through the whole system. In reality however, it is very difficult to evaluate the extent of 'integration', since only empirical tests would reveal or allow true comparisons between countries. Hence, it is practically necessary to rely on what is written about the relationships between policy and the development process in each of the three countries.

From this standpoint, the system of housing supply in the United Kingdom is very often remarked upon for the lack of integration between policy and development process. This is particularly the case where an overview is given of the relationships at the national level between the policy fields of housing, planning and land. Generally, the body of argument suggests a lack of co-ordination between these three main policy facets (Bramley, 1994; Carter and Brown, 1991; Chiddick and Dobson, 1986). The relationship between land use planning and land policy attracts the greatest interest and largest amount of criticism; and this is particularly the case since the beginning of the 1980s, when 'market solutions' and 'state policies' became increasingly seen as different, and often mutually exclusive, ways of tackling housing production issues. Mainly the challenge of integrating supply-side policies within the local development process has been frustrated by the inherent conflicts between the prescriptive approach of government on the one hand, and on the other, the market process itself. One example of this sort of conflict can be seen in government guidance on land availability in the 1980s, provided in Circulars 9/80 (D.o.E, 1980), 'Land for Private Housebuilding' and 15/84, 'Land for Housing' (D.o.E, 1984). In the latter, local authorities were urged to:

> ensure that at all times land is or will become available within the next five years which can be developed (or is being developed) within that period (D.o.E, 1984).

This directive proved, not surprisingly perhaps, to be problematical. What is 'developable' to the local authority has not necessarily been 'developable' to housing developers. 'Developability' hinges, not around statutory provisions, but on whether housing built in a certain area can be marketed and sold. It has generally not been enough that local authorities have set aside a five years supply of land. This land has to be both 'developable' and 'marketable' from a developers' point of view. The frustration caused by these sorts of problems led Chiddick and Dobson in 1986 to suggest that government should 'change the statutory basis in line with its advice by recognising the intrinsic linkage between economic and land use policies' (Chiddick and Dobson, 1986, p.13).

Attempts to bring about an integrated system of housing supply and housing production over the past twenty years, can be argued to be at best, sporadic. Where exceptions can be identified, their possible long term effects are unknown. Housing Investment Programmes (HIPs), for example, introduced in 1979 were one exceptional policy initiative which could have brought about closer integration in housing supply, particularly at the local level. HIPs, as introduced in Chapter 3, allowed local authorities to reconcile housing need with their planning objectives and to co-ordinate them within bids to the Department of the Environment. However, as was also argued in Section 3.1, HIPs were used by the Conservative governments of the 1980s, not as a mechanism to bring about greater policy integration, but simply to reduce the role of local authorities in council house building. Another more recent measure, introduced by the third Conservative government was the Planning and Compensation Act 1991, which allowed local authorities to build into development plans a provision for affordable housing. Here was a piece of legislation which had the potential to secure an ongoing place for social housing provision within a larger mixed housing production programme. In the initial inception phase there was much uncertainty as to the implied powers given to local authorities, an uncertainty which has been proved well founded in the light of the number of housing association completions since then.

Other commentaries on aspects relating to the system of housing supply equally appeal, albeit sometimes implicitly, for a more integrated approach. This can be traced to the work of Malpass and Murie (1991) who consider housing policy, or to Thornley (Thornley, 1993), who considers the planning system.

A simple or a complex system of housing supply?
The ideas underlying theoretical models of the development process or economic models of housing supply, could be applied, it is argued, within the context of a manufacturing system or process, where the concern is to minimise the number of disruptions or potential stoppages in the process. One way of doing this might be to bring many stages in the production system 'under one roof', so to speak. A firm might do this with the idea of 'vertically integrating' its production process (Clarke, 1985, p.6) so as to avoid relying upon specialist contract procedures for different stages of production. From this standpoint it could achieve its production objectives both in terms of volume and quality of product.

In the United Kingdom it is possible to speak of a single production 'channel' in respect of land acquisition, infrastructure provision and house building itself. This is evident in the private housing development process, particularly since 1979. Land, the raw material is made available for housing development via private owners or private developers. This can involve either the immediate sale of land with planning permission to house builders or can involve housing developers purchasing land without planning permission in the hope that eventually the land will be granted permission on which they can build. As was shown in Section 3.3, the state plays only a minor role, perhaps where land has been held by local authorities over a long period of time or where housing association development is involved.

The grant of planning permission, which is the next stage in the process, lies ultimately with the local planning authority. The provision of infrastructure, as a third stage in the development process lies largely with the private sector (Section 3.6). As was shown by the report of the German government (B.M.Bau, 1993) around 75% of all infrastructure is provided by private developers. Much of the way that infrastructure is achieved, is via planning agreements or more recently, planning obligations (Section 3.6). The procedure by which serviced building land is achieved relies then largely upon the private sector. The role of local authorities is confined mainly to a planning one.

Whilst the reliance on the private sector is very evident, it is perhaps more important to question the implications of the reliance on a single channel of land supply for housing production? Does this (reliance) in practice allow the system of housing supply in the United Kingdom to achieve its objectives in terms of fulfilling housing need and demand? More importantly in the comparative context, does it lead to similar outcomes where other systems have channels of land supply which are equally narrow, albeit from a different source? To answer these questions, it is necessary to look also at the other mechanisms controlling housing outcomes.

Mechanisms for determining and regulating new housing production
If the analogy of the firm and its production system is expanded, it may be suggested that not only ought the firm be able to produce in sufficient quantities, but it ought also to be able to change its type of product in response to factors causing changes in demand. In this research the focus is upon both private and social sector housing.

Since the end of the 1970s, and arguably also before this time, mechanisms for switching production neatly between tenures or sectors have been absent. Control over the tenure of new housing has to be referenced to the way in which the land market has operated. This can be argued to favour those housing suppliers who can bid the highest values for the land, a process in turn determined by residual costing methods. All other things equal, and in the absence of subsidy, these suppliers will come from the private sector because the private housing object realises a higher value in the main, than a dwelling built in the social sector. The ability of social housing suppliers to compete, is restricted by the market for land. An 'open' market in land might be described in terms of one which is free of controlled 'pricing', 'betterment', and 'taxation' (Section 3.3.). This is however not necessarily one which ensures variety of form and tenure in housing production. The open market can work against both sectors. The pricing mechanism may not only exclude social or affordable housing. It may also create obstacles or problems for private housing developers by virtue of land which is inordinately expensive at one moment whilst being inexpensive at another.

The case for seeing housing supply in the United Kingdom as a highly regulated and marshalled operation is questionable in the light of housing policy in the 1980s. Opportunities to provide forms of housing other than private sector owner occupied can be argued to be limited. Opportunities to expand the system to include different and innovative forms of new supply were not realised; the rented housing supply response was limited to increasing by a marginal amount, the number of private investors in rented market. In the 1990s there have been some further changes. Circular 7/91 (D.o.E, 1991) allows local authorities to require a percentage of 'affordable' housing in development schemes. Whether this signals a stronger link between planning and housing development in the social sector is yet to be seen. Whilst there is a consensus that more affordable housing is needed, what precisely 'affordable housing' is, has not yet been established. Perhaps more significant is the apparent inability of local authorities to relate this 'affordable housing' to any specific tenure (D.o.E, 1992).

The Netherlands

The case for an integrated system of housing supply
A conventional view of the process of housing policy making in the Netherlands, is that it is both well planned and well integrated. This is a viewpoint shared by experts within the Netherlands and commentators knowledgeable in the European policy fields. A detailed comparative study of planning control (Department of the Environment, 1989) suggests that the Netherlands is the most 'planned country in

Europe' (Davies, 1989, p.339). Needham et al (1993) re-inforce this viewpoint, although in a more light hearted way. There, it is suggested that 'planning' is promoted in such a pro-active way and to such an extent, that it has become a 'national joke' (ibid, p.86). Whether this anecdotal evidence enables significant distinctions to be made with, for example, the system of housing supply in the United Kingdom, is questionable. One can only say, that on the evidence of a research comparison such as this, it is necessary to look harder in making a case for a planned and integrated system in the United Kingdom, than in the Netherlands.

The case for a well planned and integrated system of supplying housing is made by an appeal to the broad principle of 'facet planning' (Brussaard, 1986). This is an attempt to bring together many different aspects of public policy, physical planning, land issues, environmental questions and housing objectives (ibid). Integration of policy facets is a key part of planning for housing at the national level. Questions relating to different facets are subject to the role of the Ministry of Housing, Physical Planning and Environment (MVROM). Governments have consistently introduced measures attempting to regulate housing production. The measures are most notable for their attempts to reconcile land use, economic and social policy issues. They are evident from the 1970s; in such documents as the Nota Huur en Subsidie Beleid (Directive on rents and subsidy policy), (MVROM, 1974), through to the 1980s where land prices were still regulated in most housing sectors (MVROM, 1991a); also in the Nota Volkshuisvesting in de Jaren Negentig (Memorandum on Housing on the 1990s) (MVROM, 1989), which is focused on a broad range of housing goals and policy instruments.

The integration of policies at the national level in different fields of land, housing and planning is important. However, equally important are the linkages between the central and local levels. Central government in the Netherlands has intervened consistently to allow municipalities to follow through their housing objectives. A quotation from a Housing Ministry study on land policy (MVROM, 1991) is a good starting point for understanding how these relationships operate:

> The direct link between municipality and central government ... is connected to the most important government steering: social rental houses with accompanying aid. The municipality commissioned or supervised the non-profit housing associations as to social rental housing: at the same time it supplied the required land that was prepared for building. Building land for social rental housing was not remunerative enough for private land exploiters so that a new task ...was entrusted (for the period 1901-1985) to municipalities ...municipal land exploitation (MVROM, 1991b, p.9).

There are some important points which are raised by this extract. First is the point about 'social rented houses with accompanying aid'. Second is the role of the municipality in land 'exploitation'. These issues are both significant in understanding housing outcomes. In what follows here, it is important to highlight that the quotation suggests social housing production should depend not simply upon central government housing subsidy, but upon an interaction of central government housing subsidy and municipal land policy. This also applies to housing in other sectors. These sectors could be (Figure 1.3) 'private rented', 'subsidised ownership', or could include, as is increasingly becoming the case, 'unsubsidised' private sector housing construction.

The link between central and local level extends to the fields of housing and land policy. This should not be overlooked as these facets are also coordinated with physical planning. As was shown in Section 3.5, municipalities are not only agencies of land supply, but also of land use planning. Physical plans, most evident in the bestemmingsplan, can be related closely to the financial provisions associated with central government subsidies as well as to the direct costs to the municipality of land preparation and infrastructure provision.

A simple or a complex system of housing supply?
If the Dutch system of supplying housing is analysed using the same framework as that for the United Kingdom, i.e. the 'firm' and its production process, it may be suggested to be a simple and vertically integrated one. This is initially by virtue of the fact that land supply is from a single (municipal) actor. Municipalities may be regarded as having virtual control over the production process where they filter land between a number of different house builders in the same way that a firm might change its production run in response to changes in demand for its products. The system may additionally be regarded as 'simple' because these house builders are not involved in the land market to any great extent. Problems associated with speculation, land holding or other obstacles to supply do not occur to the same extent as happens in other countries such as the United Kingdom.

An image is thus built up of a country in which the system of housing supply is both well integrated and uncomplicated, and where land supply is well coordinated with planning and housing policy. There are of course alternative viewpoints which might see the Dutch system as being more complicated. By contrast with the United Kingdom, where government has remained relatively distant from attempts to intervene or to integrate policy, Dutch governments have utilised an array of what might be seen to be complex policy instruments through which housing production outcomes may be controlled.

The broad policies are divided and sub-divided into smaller and more discrete ones, with intricate arrangements affecting the development process directly. One of the most important policy mechanisms are 'location' subsidies. These have been used extensively since the mid 1970s to influence both housing and commercial property development. Three main measures in use during the mid 1990s (Spaans et al, 1996, p.24) are the Locatiesubsidieregeling ('Location subsidy regulation'), the Subsidie grote bouwlocaties ('Subsidy regulation for large building sites') and the Hoofdinfrastructuurregeling ('Main infrastructure subsidy regulation'). Generally speaking, the provision of 'location' subsidies mean that housing production can be subsidised in two ways: both 'vertically' as well as 'horizontally' (Wigmans, 1993). It can be subsidised 'vertically' within the main channels of subsidy for housing production; that is to say, by tenure in particular; as well as 'horizontally' across specific locations. Therefore, the state potentially has not only control over the general numbers of each housing tenure, but also over the specific locations in which housing tenure is developed.

Mechanisms for determining and regulating new housing production
Chapter 3 and the previous two sections have aimed to describe the framework through which housing is supplied in the Netherlands. Production has been argued to rely to a significant extent upon the way in which central government subsidies and the municipal role in land supply and planning inter-relate. Policy instruments relate to planning, land pricing and housing subsidies. All taken together they effectively 'prescribe' the type of housing development that will take place. But how does this happen in practice? In particular how do municipalities determine how much social housing will be produced and how much housing in the market sector?

Municipalities, as the main planning agencies and initiators of development plans have been supported by central government land pricing policies, particularly for the social sector. The aims of the development plan are linked closely with the land pricing policy, particularly where a mix of housing development is envisaged. Land prices for housing in the social sector are fixed by central government on a yearly basis (Wigmans, 1992, p.24); the price, for example in 1992 for the Province of North Holland, in which Amsterdam is located, was Hfl 22,500 (£7,500 at current sterling rates) per plot. In order that municipalities do not charge housing associations or other house builders in the social sector so much that social housing becomes unviable, central government make a subsidy available, conditional upon the price of land being kept at the recommended level:

> as a condition of the subsidy it is also necessary that this maximum
> price does not become breached (Wigmans, 1992, p.23).

The subsidy for price lowering to build social housing is not always available in all areas (MVROM, 1991b, p.3), however. It is mainly used in locations in which it is desired to direct subsidised housing production. A distinction between areas in which subsidies apply and do not apply was made in a so-called 'Brown Booklet' introduced in the late 1960s and subsidy by location has been a guiding principle since that time. Where subsidies cannot be obtained, the municipality must attempt to cover its cost of land exploitation through the development scheme as a whole. Thus there is some element of risk taken on by the municipality.

Mainly two situations have occurred: one in which the municipality can develop social and other forms of subsidised housing with some form of subsidy guarantee, and the other where no subsidies apply. In the former situation, under which since 1985, subsidies come from one large urban renewal fund (MVROM 1991, p.27), municipalities do not need to increase the price of land for sale to the market sector since social housing land prices will be held down to the prescribed limit under the national scheme. Where, however, no subsidy is available and the municipality wishes for its own ends to provide social housing within the plan area, the limit on land prices for social housing may be higher than the maximum laid down by central government. Under these circumstances, the plot prices for land sold to the market sector may have to be raised. In other words, some form of cross-subsidisation may have to occur in order to cover the municipalities' land exploitation costs. These costs derive from land preparation as well as from the provision of infrastructure.

The 'exploitation' takes account of several variables. These can be divided into 'kosten' ('costs') and 'opbrengsten', ('benefits') (Wigmans, 1992). The costs relate to land acquisition, land preparation, provision of infrastructure, green space and areas for water settlement. The 'benefits' are seen in terms of the housing which results within the plan area or the value of the sale of the land. These variables are brought together in what is known as an 'exploitatierekening'. This is a financial statement for the proposed development. It includes the area (m^2) of the development, the number of dwellings in the scheme and other key financial variables. The exploitatierekening is accompanied by a bestemmingsplan. The exploitatierekening shows 'cost' elements of land acquisition, expropriation and site preparation costs as well as the contingencies of planning overheads and interest costs. The rekening shows also the 'opbrengsten' or 'benefits' which are in terms of dwellings produced. Also included amongst the benefits could be shops, industrial and commerce development. The exploitatierekening, along with the bestemmingsplan is normally forwarded to central government as a viability study for the area. It forms the basis for subsidy from central government, once the location subsidy element has been discounted.

It is important to note how outcomes are arrived at under this model of development. Both financial and land-use considerations are dovetailed together within the municipal land exploitation scheme. This is indicated in Figure 4.1.

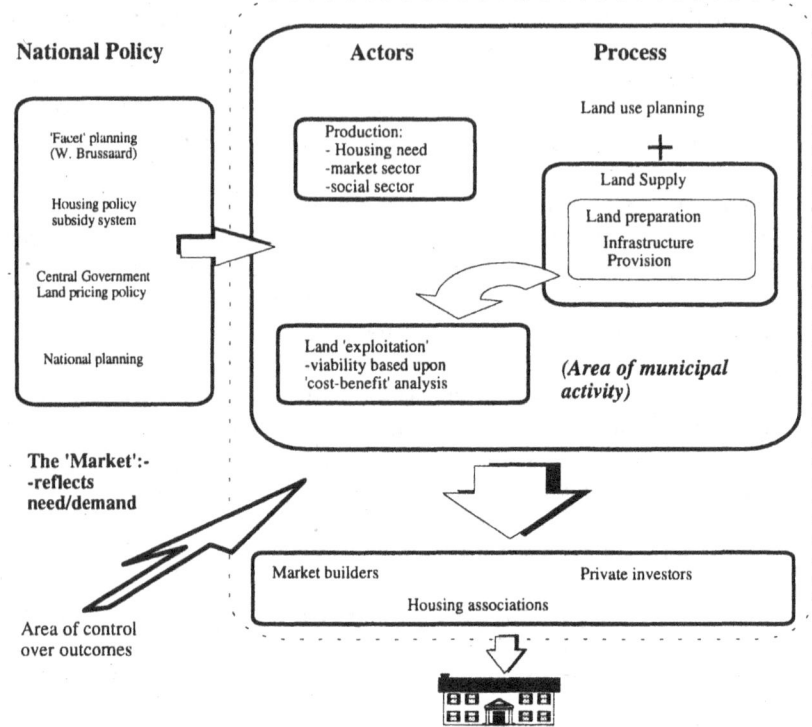

Figure 4.1   Linkages in housing supply in the Netherlands

Germany

The case for an integrated system of housing supply
The policy framework for housing in Germany is conventionally referenced to the role of the Länder (Dieterich et al, 1993, p.2; B.M.Bau, 1993, p.84; Hooper, 1989, p.256), the Federal states, of which there are sixteen since unification. This a constitutional structure which differs from the United Kingdom and the Netherlands, countries which are characterised by a unitary state (Williams and Wood, 1993, p.2; Needham et al, 1993, p.3). The Länder are to a significant extent financially autonomous of central government whereby a certain proportion of national taxation is passed directly on to the regional administrations. This provides the Länder with powers of self-governance in the important policy areas of education and housing. The mechanism which underpins the framework for central-regional relations was introduced in the late 1960s. Article 104a of the German constitution, sets out how financial burdens are to be shared (Bark and Gress, 1993). Article 104a gives:

the federal government the possibility...to grant individual states (Länder) financial assistance for especially important investments..., to equalise different economic power in the Federal Republic, or to promote economic growth. This general clause..... basically gives the federal government the task of establishing economic balance between the Länder (Bark and Gress, 1993, p.88).

The decentralised federal structure of the country, however, creates potential problems for the integration of housing, planning and land policy at the national level. Indeed, housing outcomes at this level should be seen in the context of differing policy stances of the Länder. Sometimes it is consistent with central government, other times less so. Different Länder promote differing housing policies. For example, owner-occupied housing is promoted more enthusiastically in the southern states of Bayern and Baden-Württemberg, whilst social housing is supported to a greater extent in the northern state of Nordrhein-Westphalen (Boelhouwer and Van der Heijden 1992, p.106). Getting a certain type of housing built therefore, depends to some extent upon *where* the supplier is trying to locate production. The importance of regional geography applies also to policies affecting the housing stock, where the funding of modernisation programmes varies very significantly between different Länder (Finanztest, 1996). The distribution of subsidies depends to a large extent upon the Länder:

The Länder are responsible for actually attributing the credits...the federal subsidies and those of the Länder constitute, all together, the fund of financial subsidies attributed to the construction of buildings for housing purposes. The Länder decide in which way the money is to be used: as capital aid, as a credit to the expenditures or, in a combined way, for both (Duvigneau and Schönefeld, 1989, p.10).

Despite the decentralised structure, central government have over time, been successful in setting the main policy perameters. Foremost examples of this are the housing production programmes which have been implemented since the Second World War. These originated in the First and Second Förderungswege, which have been very significant for housing supply (Figure 3.2). The state sponsored house building promotion schemes are still in evidence today in the form of the Third Förderungsweg, and in the Wohnungsbauerleicherungsgesetz 1990. The latter measure is a law to enable the production of social housing, which has been particularly important since unification.

A simple or complex system of housing supply?
The case for seeing the system of housing supply in Germany as a simple one is easily challenged not only because of the potential problems resulting from differing regional policies, but also because of the complexities involved in the housing development process itself. In a German government report (B.M.Bau 1993) these complexities are associated not least with the legal procedures involved with the

stage of infrastructure provision. This arrangement is not always seen to work smoothly. Where regional policies differ and the development process is shared amongst many different parties, the 'system' of supply cannot easily be anticipated to be unproblematic.

The various models of housing development are defined by the number of different housing suppliers who in turn, interact differently with the land market and the public and private bodies involved in infrastructure provision. Although the state has been reluctant to intervene in the land market, and hence land is mainly supplied by private interests, this is not the case in so far as the provision of infrastructure is concerned. Infrastructure provision in Germany (Section 3.6) does rely much more significantly than in the United Kingdom upon the Gemeinde, or local authority, although less so than in the Dutch case. The range of instruments lying within public law provides them with the opportunity to regulate infrastructure provision to an important extent. There is evidence (Figure 3.9) to suggest that they do this. However, it is at the stage at which roads, services, green space and other infrastructure must be provided, that the model of development can become most complex. This is probably most evident where the municipality exercises its public legal powers to alter property borders ('Grenzregelung') before prescribing how the new plots will appear ('Umlegung'). Figure 3.9 shows (Mode 'D') that this more complex arrangement is by no means uncommon, where around 20% of all development relies upon the procedures. Where municipal powers are used to influence plot layout on private land, there are a number of very complex questions to be resolved concerning levels of compensation, the timing of new construction and the viability of house building. Where the housing supplier is a company, then the issues are resolved between professional parties in public and private sectors. Where however, the supplier is a private household (both supplier and housing consumer), then the process may be more problematical.

Difficulties in developing housing in Germany are sometimes overcome by taking a more interventionist stance. Within the German system there are examples of housing development which are more similar to models in the Netherlands. There are examples of the comprehensive planning ideal. The Städtebauliches Entwicklungs maßnahmen (Duvigneau and Schönefeld, 1989, pp.40-1) are a case of a more integrated approach to development where Gemeinde have taken over an urban area with a view to re-development. In other cases a possibility arises for a municipality to grant planning and building permission to private owners on condition that part of the land is sold at a below market price. On this land, the municipality may build social housing. This was the case in the so-called 'Stuttgart model' of development (Golland et al, 1994). This example, and indeed that of the Städtebauliches Entwicklungs maßnahmen model of development, are exceptions rather than the rule.

Mechanisms for determining and regulating new housing production
The link between housing outcome, which can be reflected in production by different sectors and tenures, and the broader system of supply, is governed by a number of factors. In Germany these factors have more in common with the United

Kingdom than the Netherlands. In the Dutch case, it was shown that the type and tenure of housing produced was dependent very much upon the role of central government and municipality. This was most evidently achieved through the land market using land pricing and land ownership as a way of achieving housing objectives as well as reducing uncertainties in the housing market on behalf of house builders. Production in the Dutch market sector is thus closely linked with production in the social sector. In the United Kingdom the linkages between different sectors of supply have been argued to be weaker. This is likely also to be the case in Germany, when one considers that the market for development land is heavily influenced by private ownership. It is thus difficult for the state to regulate new building in a situation where the raw material for housing production can sometimes be unavailable or unaffordable, as can be understood from the following:

> The building land markets especially in the agglomerations of the Federal Republic of Germany are characterised by a situation in which land ready for building is not available to an adequate extent and that available building land is not coming on to the market on an adequate scale...a major cause of bottlenecks in supply, however, is that public and private sectors have not succeeded in making designated building land available...to eliminate bottlenecks in the supply of building land, it is necessary to both designate new building land and to make it available (B.M.Bau, 1993).

Land is a problem which is emphasised as a constraint to supply in all sectors. Governments, however in Germany, whilst recognising this, have provided subsidies on house building itself, as a method of stimulating production. The subsidies are available for a broad range of suppliers. Understanding the links between policy and outcome within the system of housing supply is probably best achieved therefore, by focusing not so much on the relationship between land and housing policy, but on the role played by building subsidies and the financial means available to private households, social housing producers and other Unternehmen. Finance for social housing production, for example, whilst relying to some extent on public subsidy, comes mainly from the private sector. This has been the case for some time now: Rosemann and Westra (1988) suggest that the 'financing of social housing construction was largely privatised by the beginning of the 1970s' and Kühne Büning (1991) highlights the independence of the sector in the following:

> In the context of the 'freely financed' or 'tax advantaged' house building sectors where there is an 'established interest-rate dependence', the relatively high significance of interest free or loans at marginal interest rates for the publicly funded housing construction, leads to a partial or distorted picture. Beyond that, it is to suppose that the construction of rented housing is more strongly dependent upon the interest rate than for owner-occupied housing construction (Kühne Büning, 1991, p.172).

The implications of this passage suggest that in sectors other than those which are wholly subsidised by the public sector (1-2% of all construction since the beginning of the 1980s (BDZ, 1993)), housing construction in the *rented sector as a whole* will be very much dependent upon what is happening in the economy at large. This will apply to construction in the social rented sector by private companies and individuals as well as to providers of private rented housing.

Independence of individual sectors is enhanced through the principle of 'Eigenwirtschaftlichkeit' which means 'own good management, thrift and husbandry'. This principle applies across all sectors including private households and is the idea that households who promote their own housing should do so on a self-governing basis. However, if the household is prepared to assume the risks for the development, then he or she will be aided by the state. This is conditional that the Bauherr:

> of his own account and risk builds, or has a building built and manages the building process. He must be reconciled to the risky nature of being a Bauherr and with it carry the typical risks associated with building costs, finance and building contracts which arise as a result of building on his plot. Other than this he must assume planning and execution (of building) as a matter of course (Schmitz, 1991, p.121).

This principle is exemplified in what has become known as the 'Bauherrenmodell', a model of supply which was particularly relevant under the CDU/FDP coalition government in the 1980s. The ability to qualify for subsidy in the form of tax reductions under the scheme depended upon both the nature of contracting, i.e. whether housing construction depends entirely upon the efforts of the household, as well as to some extent income considerations. The possibilities for tax deductions have been reduced rather during the 1990s, however (Schmitz, 1991, p.122).

4.3 Agencies in the system of housing supply

The focus on the linkages between the agencies in the systems of housing supply should be examined not only in terms of their position in the sequence of events in the development process, but also by reference to the nature of the agencies and the way in which they relate to each other and to housing outcomes.

Section 4.3 examines some of the most important agencies in the system of housing supply. These are central and local government, and private and social sector housing suppliers. The focus is also on the effects of changes in government and changes in attitude to towards local government, and on the nature of new housing production. Nevertheless, agency theory has an important role to play, particularly in prompting concrete questions about the economic position of specific housing providers. To some extent, these questions can be resolved through anecdotal evidence. This is used where appropriate in the following sub-sections of Section 4.3. The following headings are adopted:

'Central government: political parties and housing outcomes'
'Local government, central-local relations and housing outcomes'
'The private sector and its role in influencing housing output'
'Social sector housing suppliers, political change and housing output'

The United Kingdom

Central government: political parties and housing outcomes
Central government is the first agency to be considered for each of the three countries. At the outset, the motivation for central government involvement in housing supply in the United Kingdom may be argued to be no different to that in other countries. Government has intervened at various junctures since the Second World War in order to meet the general level of housing demand or need. There are aims of meeting overall housing production levels, of expanding owner-occupation (D.o.E, 1977; D.o.E, 1987) or of promoting the private rented sector (ibid). None of these policies are however particularly radical and do not of themselves say much about the particular consequences of having different political parties at the helm of housing policy.

To understand the significance of the role of central government as an agency in housing supply, it is necessary to link the changing political backcloth with housing outcomes themselves. As a step in this direction, Figure 4.2 provides an overview of governments in Britain for the period 1970 to 1993.

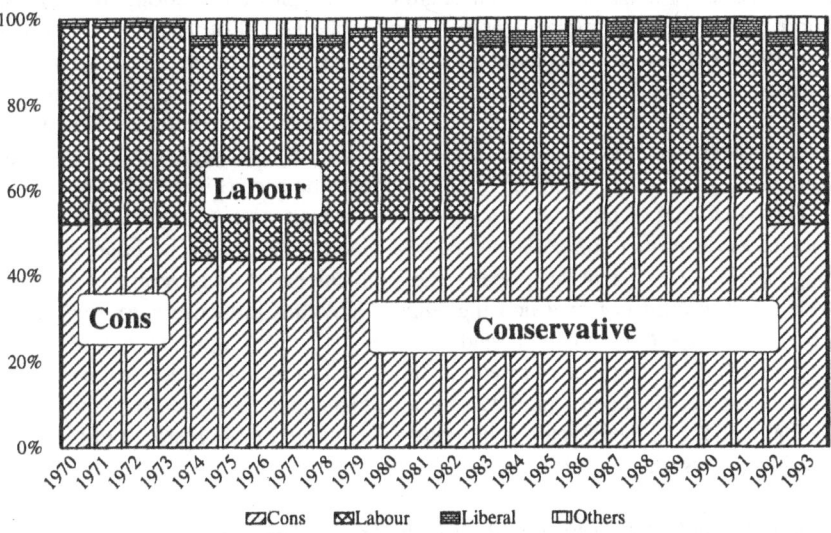

Source: Kavanagh and Butler (1992)

Figure 4.2 British governments, 1970-1993 (% of seats achieved)

111

Figure 4.2 shows the percentage of parliamentary seats held by the major political parties for each parliament. It is important to remark that central government reflects a single political party, rather than a coalition of interests. This situation is very different to that in the Netherlands and Germany, where a different system of voting occurs and where governments are normally represented by a coalition of political parties. The differences in these situations are explained by both the mechanics of the voting system and varying degrees of desire for political consensus. In the United Kingdom, the electoral system is run on the basis of 'first past the post' (Kavanagh, 1990, p.94). In this system the candidate with the most votes wins the constituency, whether or not he or she has a majority of votes (ibid). The government has traditionally been formed on the basis of the political party winning most parliamentary seats. The impact of this process in the United Kingdom has always drawn the attention of political commentators with an interest in the potential consequences of marginal changes in voting patterns.

Indeed, it does not need much investigation to show that in the U.K, marginal changes in the political constitution of parliament have lead to significant changes in housing policy. This is most evident in the tenure of new housing which has been produced since 1970. The relationship between the political party in government and housing tenure is not one dealt with in Chapter 5, (which looks mainly at outcomes), and thus some commentary on the relationship is felt to be warranted here. To do this, Figure 1.2, 'Housing Production in the United Kingdom' should be re-considered, alongside Figure 4.2, introduced above.

In making this comparison, it is evident that there is a strong association between the tenure of particular political parties and output from specific sectors of housing supply. The association between Conservative governments (Figure 4.2), for example, and private sector housing production (Figure 1.2) is consistently strong over the entire period 1970-1993. This is evident not only for the period of Thatcher governments since 1979, but is also transparent from the earlier period of the Heath government, between 1970 and 1974. The association between Conservative governments and private sector suppliers is to be contrasted with the period 1974 to 1979, when a Labour government was in power (Figure 4.2). During this period there was a quite distinct change of policy in favour of local authority housing (Figure 1.2).

This polarising of housing policy, whether through state or market means, is one which deserves further comparative analysis. Coles (1991, p.12) has concluded in the comparative context, that historically the political party of government in Britain exerts a strong influence over housing tenure. How this influence is exerted in terms of political connections, lobbying and so on, is not something which is researched to any great extent. One piece of research (Ball, 1983) looks at the political economy of owner-occupation and goes some way towards explaining the power relations between political parties and the development industry. However, more research of this kind is not easily accessible.

Local authorities, central-local relations and housing outcomes
The role played by local authorities in housing supply is determined to a large extent, by their relations with central government. In the comparative context, this

relationship can be argued to revolve around the constitutional position of local authorities as well as the extent of funding given by central government. In addition other factors, historical, geographical and physical, play a role in conditioning the relationship.

In the United Kingdom, the relationship between local authorities and central government can be discussed in terms of the weak constitutional position of the latter; as Williams and Wood point out (1994, p.4), local government has 'no right to exist' and can be abolished by an Act of Parliament. This situation was seen as an opportunity by the Conservative governments during the 1980s to rid themselves of political opponents; the clearest illustration being the abolition of the Greater London Council in 1985. As housing usually cannot be viewed in a political vacuum, it is perhaps not surprising that the role of local authorities in housing provision has changed over time in response to political changes at the central government level.

Before the 1980s, local authorities in the United Kingdom had a very important housing production role (Figure 1.2). By comparison with other European countries, their historical remit is very significant. Both Fuerst (1973) and Emms (1990) have remarked on the special place given to local authorities in the United Kingdom as suppliers of new housing. In both the Netherlands and Germany, municipalities have played a much more similar role to that played by local authorities in the United Kingdom *since* the mid 1980s. In the Dutch and German cases, housing associations or quasi-government organisations have been the traditional vehicle for social housing production. The reasons for these differences prior to the 1980s are manifold. Partially, they relate to historical factors, where in the United Kingdom, the decision to place the state at the forefront of the house building programme in 1945 did little to bring about a more flexible solution to housing shortages, as occurred particularly in Germany during the same period. The strong remit given to local authorities in the United Kingdom is thus explained to some extent by the lack of alternative sources of provision, in particular through the private rented sector which has been a more significant contributor in other countries. Equally important perhaps, as an explanation, was the assumption that the state should take ultimate responsibility for housing provision. It took until the mid 1970s before housing production was devolved to any significant extent to housing associations. Even then, prior to the 1980s, associations can be argued to have relied on high levels of government grant, and were not reliant on the private sector for funding to any great extent.

A number of changes occurred during the 1980s which altered the relationship between central and municipal levels. Some of the measures taken by central government are detailed in Section 3.2, which looked at aspects of housing investment. Of these, perhaps the most effective in reducing the power of local authorities in housing provision, were the Housing Investment Programmes. These were cut significantly on a year-by-year basis (Gibb and Munroe, 1991, p.75) to such a degree that authorities did not have sufficient funds to be able to supply new housing as they has done in the past. At the same time, their revenue base was reduced through the 'Right-to-Buy' scheme introduced in 1980. This transferred housing stock from municipal to private ownership, and further financial legislative provisions limited spending of the receipts from these transfers.

In addition to these measures there were clear indications that central government had a different role in mind for local authorities for the 1980s and beyond. In the White Paper 'Housing: The Government's Proposals', central government signalled the end of local authority house building programmes in setting out a municipal 'enabling' role:

> In the past building by local authorities was seen as the main way of meeting housing needs...However there will no longer be the same presumption that the local authority itself should take direct action to meet new or increasing demands. The future role of local authorities will essentially be a strategic one identifying housing needs and demands...In order to fulfil this strategic role they will have to work closely with housing associations; private landlords; developers; and building societies and other providers of finance (D.o.E, 1987, Paragraph 5.1).

The enabling role has changed the relationship between central government, local authorities and housing associations. It has brought the latter very much more to the forefront of social housing provision and it has arguably relegated local authorities to a supporting role. Malpass (1992, p.10) has described the 'enabling' role as a 'disabling' one because of the effect of the legislation, which has been to shift power back to the centre. In combination with a financial squeeze on local authority capital investment and ongoing expenditure, their role as new house builders has been significantly reduced. In place has grown up an arrangement whereby the local authority can assist housing association production targets through the planning process. Central government has been increasingly prepared to bolster this process, particularly during the 1990s, when questions have been increasingly asked about the sustainability of home ownership (Radley, 1996).

The private sector: the house building industry and its role in influencing housing output

The private house building sector in the United Kingdom is the most important agency in housing supply, at least in the sense that it has since the mid 1970s become the sector with the highest number of new housing completions (Figure 1.2). The 'private sector' in this research is defined in accordance with the Department of the Environment's Housing and Construction statistics annual publication. Although within this sector there are firms of different size and scope, (and hence the 'private sector' does not strictly present a homogenous source of supply), firms within this sector do share a number of operating norms. These were introduced in Section 3.7 as the speculative method of housing development involving the forward purchasing of land, the construction of housing and the eventual sale to an owner-occupier. Much of this development is carried out by a small number of 'volume' house builders (Section 3.7).

Figure 3.10 (Section 3.7) showed the contribution to total housing production made by the major house building firms in the United Kingdom. It showed the concentration of housing output to be in the hands of a relatively small number of firms. This concentration has however intensified since the mid 1970s. Smyth (1982) and Fleming (1984) provided early evidence of this trend and Ball (1996) has provided more recent data: from 1981 to 1994, those firms building 500 or more dwellings a year increased their market share from 39-51%. Additionally (ibid, p.30), there were 14 firms building over 2,000 having a third of the market. This concentration of housing supply in only relatively few hands has a number of consequences which can be considered within the frameworks of economic or social agency theory.

As large organisations, house building firms have access to capital funding based on operating profits and collateral base. All other things equal, the larger the firm, the greater the asset base and the ability to raise capital. For larger firms, exploiting this possibility can bring advantages not only in terms of purchasing land plots at favourable prices, but also in terms of ensuring that labour can be readily acquired throughout times of change in the housing market. Additionally, the speculative process of house building inherently demands some financial buffer whilst housing is completed but not yet sold. Although speculative house builders are seen to be 'conservative' (Ball, 1996, p.29) in aspects of housing design, they nevertheless are better placed to ride out troughs in the market if cash flow is good than where re-financing or equity input is required of the builder. Again, in these instances a large firm will be at an advantage.

If research findings are accurate, then it may be instructive to consider the trend towards increasingly larger firms in the context of an increasing proportion of output from the private sector since the 1970s (Figure 1.2). Such a comparison suggests a further conclusion at a national level: namely that increasing output from fewer firms, is associated with an increasing share of total national housing production from the private sector. This suggests not only that the private sector has expanded as a whole at the expense of the social and private rented sectors, but also that its production method is becoming increasingly monopolistic in nature. The economic theory underlying monopoly activity suggests that output of a commodity may not be maximised since the average revenue curve of the monopoly firm is the same as the demand curve of the industry (Hillebrandt, 1985, p.134). In other words, because it is the only supplier (and provided that the demand curve slopes downward), the monopoly firm receives less for each unit of output, as output increases. Furthermore, marginal revenue, the difference in revenue at different output and price trade-offs, falls at a faster rate than average revenue. This can have the result that it is more advantageous for the monopoly supplier to reduce capacity to the point where marginal costs equal marginal revenue and having the effect of maintaining prices at a higher level than they might otherwise be in a situation of perfect competition.

Applying this framework however, to the house building industry in the United Kingdom is potentially problematical. Although there is a movement towards consolidation, the industry remains rather more oligopolistic in nature, there being few firms with a large number of completions. The effect of this structure on output is not likely to be so restrictive as with a monopoly situation, since there is always the possibility that one supplier will try to undercut another. To maintain margins, this may mean increasing turnover and possibly also production. Supply-side competition thus reduces the likelihood that house builders can maintain artificially high price levels as would be the case in a purely monopolistic situation. Also, competition from the existing housing market in the United Kingdom is strong. Generally turnover in the existing stock is as significant to the ownership sector as new housing production. The level of housing construction in the United Kingdom, at an average (1970-1993) of 3 dwellings per 1000 inhabitants (United Nations) is low by European standards. Unless significantly greater amounts of land are released through the planning system, the role of the house building industry remains constrained.

The application of economic theory to the house building industry is further limited by the many different ways in which the large housing developers can maximise profits. Profit can come from housing construction, or from land dealing or from investments made by the company in other sectors. Supply-side frameworks using trade-offs between price and output are mainly applicable using house prices and new housing completions. The construction of detailed economic theory dealing with the factors influencing new and existing housing markets as well as land markets is a significant challenge. Oxley (1983) has suggested how these relationships might work, in a comparative thesis. Empirical analysis of output however, depends on many complex factors and further, large amounts of data. Whilst then a good case can be made for using monopoly or other economic frameworks to explain the role of the private sector in influencing output, there is a good deal more empirical work needed before concrete links are established.

Social housing suppliers, political change and housing output
Social housing in the United Kingdom is supplied from two sources: local authorities and housing associations. These sectors, or sources of supply, have traditionally been concerned with the provision of housing of an affordable nature. It is evident (Figure 1.2) that the role local authorities as social housing suppliers has declined since the mid 1970s and from a peak of around 50% of total production.

The supply of new social housing has, since the late 1970s, been mainly from housing associations, although the total volume of housing supplied may not be seen to be significant in the context of total housing production. Output by housing associations has always been relatively low and has fluctuated in accordance with central government policy. There are however no obvious linkages with either of the main political parties: absolute production levels were high under the Labour government of 1974 to 1979 (Figure 4.2); yet they were higher in absolute terms during the Fourth Conservative government during the early 1990s. Relative to total production, output by housing associations was also highest during this latter period, although social housing production as a whole is less significant than in the 1970s; a result of local authority completions falling off. As a consequence of the relatively low levels of housing association production, the housing stock is also relatively small, limiting the sector in its ability to expand. In 1987, housing association dwellings constituted only 3% of the total housing stock (D.o.E, 1987). In the European context, this can be contrasted with the Dutch housing association sector, which possesses a relatively larger housing stock (35% of all housing in 1987: Nationale Woningraad, 1995, p.4) and exerts a significant political influence.

The role of housing associations in the United Kingdom has traditionally been defined by their links with central government. These 'links' are seen to be twofold. First, in respect of levels of direct grant for new housing construction; a more concrete and financially 'measurable' relationship; and second, a relationship defined by central government's perception of housing associations as appropriate suppliers of new social housing.

The financial relationship can be explained in terms of central government's willingness to support local authorities and housing association estimates of housing need, as stated in the Housing Investment and Approved Development Programmes. As local authorities have withdrawn from direct housing supply, the bulk of capital funding for social housing has been shifted towards the association sector. This occurred most evidently during the early 1980s, although at a time when the absolute number of housing association completions were falling. In 1979/80, for example, the Housing Corporation programme accounted for only 15% of total net housing capital expenditure (Brown and Golland, 1995, p.29). By 1982/3 this had risen to 48%. Indeed, prior to the Housing Act of 1988 in the UK, levels of direct funding by central government were high. Housing Association Grant ran at on average 85% of all schemes (ibid), making new development very viable. Following the Act of 1988, however, levels of grant fell off significantly when policy changed in favour of giving associations more independence:

> Associations should....be given the opportunity to maximise the use of private funds to improve their effectiveness (D.o.E, 1987, p.12).

However, increased independence also meant increased responsibility and a new rental system:

> At present housing associations are heavily dependent on the Exchequer for financial support. This is because the 'fair rents' determined by the Rent Officer are only sufficient to cover a small part of the costs of new developments...some individual housing associations have been developing alternative financial possibilities with the encouragement of the Government (ibid).

These schemes involved two 'key elements'. The first was a deregulated system of rents and the second was a mixed funding regime. Since 1988, social housing development has utilised capital market funding to a much greater extent, even where schemes in the mid 1990s have been developed without any public subsidy.

The second defining factor in the political relationship between central government and the housing association sector relates to the perception of housing associations, particularly in contrast to local authorities. In the late 1980s, local authorities were seen to be large overbearing entities whose ability to deliver housing efficiently was seen to be limited. Local authority housing was associated with poor design and high levels of crime (ibid, p.2). They were also seen as being unable to filter subsidies in a sensitive manner between central government and tenants' needs within their housing stock. Housing associations by contrast, were seen as being a more flexible alternative better suited to the demands associated with mixed funding regimes and targeting housing need. Having their roots, as many do, in charitable organisations, and housing bodies directing their resources towards specific groups in society, they were seen as more appropriate long term solution to social housing:

> The housing association movement has shown that a bridge can be provided between the public and private sectors. The movement offers good quality rented accommodation for those with special needs or on low incomes (ibid, p.3).

Thus a specific government preference meant that housing associations became the main supplier of social housing in the late 1980s. The longer term trend in housing supply may however, also have had an impact on the promotion of housing associations at the expense of local authorities. That is to say, over time the nature of housing need has also changed; from the 1950s, 1960s and 1970s, where 'need' could be strongly argued to be to do with crude housing shortages; to the 1980s and beyond, where there were shortages, but of a much more discrete and focused nature. Housing associations are arguably better equipped to meet this new form of need.

The Netherlands

Central government: political parties and housing outcomes
The focus of the previous section on the role of central government in the United Kingdom, examined first the electoral system. To be consistent, this is also the initial context for understanding the way in which central government in the Netherlands can influence housing outcomes. The Dutch system of voting is, as in Germany, one of proportional representation. However, as with alternative systems such as 'first past the post' as operates in the UK, there are advantages and disadvantages. Proportional representation is a double-edged sword. On the one hand it represents a fairer and more democratic system, but on the other, situations can arise in which there is no privity of relationship between voter and member of parliament (Gladdish, 1991, p.100).

The electoral system explains to a significant extent, the nature of Dutch government, in which coalitions are the norm (Figure 4.3). No political party has ever succeeded in winning an electoral, or even a parliamentary, majority (Anderweg and Irwin, 1993, p.23). Figure 4.3 shows the percentage of votes gained by political parties. There are three main political parties: the CDA 'Christian Democrat', the PvdA, the 'Partei voor der Arbeid' (Labour) and the VVD 'Liberal' party. The way votes are cast however is not necessarily reflected in the nature of government. This is because coalitions are formed independently of the voting pattern (Gladdish, 1991, p.51).

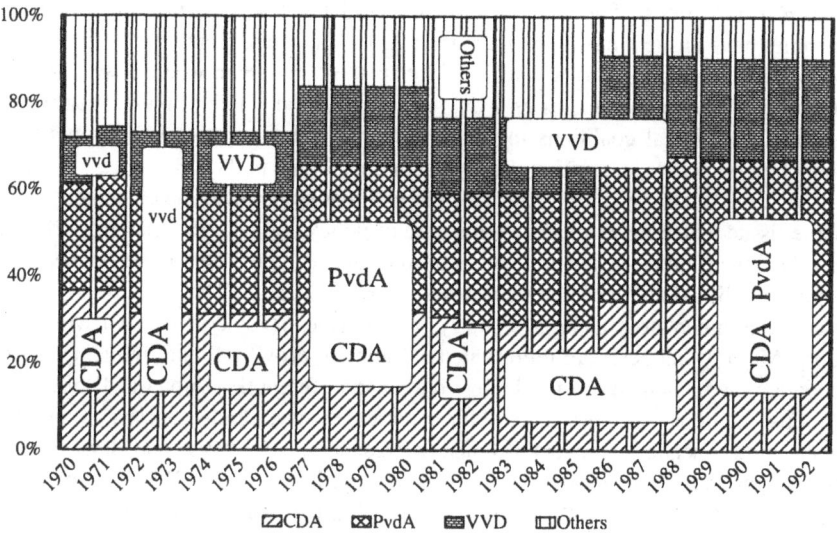

Source: Anderweg and Irwin (`1993)

Figure 4.3   Dutch governments, 1970-1992 (% of seats achieved)

In Figure 4.3, the parties constituting government are shown in the boxes. Over the period in question, the most common coalition has been between the Christian Democrats (CDA) and the Liberals (VVD). The effect of these coalitions has been to isolate the Labour PvdA party from the decision making process for significant periods of time (Figure 4.3). This is despite the fact that the PvdA has achieved a considerable number of votes in general elections.

In examining the relationship between the Dutch political and housing systems, it will be noted that there is only a very tenuous relationship, particularly in respect of changes in government and changes in production emphasis between tenures. This conclusion can be drawn by comparing Figures 1.3 and 4.3, above. By comparing these diagrams, it will be noted that the political colour of government does not appear to reconcile in any consistent way over time with particular tenures of housing supply. The electoral success of the CDA party, is one example. This party has been in every government over the entire period from 1970-1993 (Figure 4.3), during which housing policy has changed significantly. If a statistical correlation using proxy variables for political parties were to be provided, based on the association between the electoral success of the CDA and the tenure of new housing supply, only a weak relationship would be shown; the CDA have held around a consistent 40% of the total vote as part of various coalition governments (Figure 4.3), yet their lengthy period in office has been associated with very contrasting housing production policies.

The link between political parties and housing tenure is weak since where there have been coalitions of left and right (CDA and PvdA), very differing production outcomes have ensued; most notably in the late 1970s, where market sector production was collapsing (Figure 1.3) whilst in the latter, the late 1980s, where it was strongly promoted. A summary conclusion would suggest that the nature of the government, in the form of political coalitions in the Netherlands, does not correlate strongly with production outcomes; a situation wholly in contrast to that in the U.K.

Literature dealing with the nature of the political system and Dutch society details another issue which may influence the nature of policy and decision making and hence the relationship between government and housing outcome. This issue relates to the supposed political and social alliances within Dutch society. The Netherlands is seen by some commentators to be a 'country of minorities' (Anderweg and Irwin, 1993, p.23). Minority interests are represented at national, provincial and municipal levels. There are two main divisions, being 'class' and 'religion' (Lijphart, 1968). The religious factions are associated by political party, trade unions, employers organisations, schools, universities and newspapers; Anderweg and Irwin (1993) describe this sub-division as 'pillarisation', a translation of the Dutch *'Verzuiling'*. This interpretation of Dutch society and government raises questions about how decisions are actually made on housing production issues and how they are achieved. In a wholly pluralistic political system, it may be that the many splintered political interests operate beyond party politics. In this case, a deeper analysis of housing outcomes and the decision making process is required; one which does not simply focus on the parties in government. When governments are formed, parties with a significant amount of votes can be apparently excluded, but it is not certain in practice, what role they actually play.

Local authorities, central-local relations and housing outcomes
The principal role of municipalities in the Netherlands is not as a direct housing supplier, but as a facilitator of housing development. This has been the case for much of the post-war period. In this respect there are more similarities between the historic role of Dutch municipalities and the more recent enabling role of local authorities in the United Kingdom. Municipal housing production in the Netherlands has only accounted for around 5% of total annual housing completions since 1970 (Figure 1.3).

The Dutch municipal role is closely linked with the implementation of central government housing and planning objectives, but is perhaps most evident in the development process through the supply of land. The relationship between central and local government is finely balanced. Municipalities enjoy advantages as well as experiencing disadvantages. There is some degree of independence provided through the ownership of land, yet typically central government has indirectly influenced the timing of land supply through planning and subsidy regulations. Moreover, it is not entirely certain that municipalities would, in the absence of central government, choose to restrict land supply for their own ends. Needham (1992, p.684) has identified a quotation from the Rotterdam municipality which suggests a somewhat altruistic municipal attitude to land supply:

> As regards the making of profits, a municipal real estate department may in my opinion be compared to a department of public utility, such as for instance the municipal water works, where the primary consideration is to supply a good quality of drinking water at a reasonable price and not to make profits (Rotterdam municipality, 1959) (Needham, 1992, p.684).

Whether this assessment is still relevant today, is debatable. The view of one private sector developer interviewed for this research was that municipalities are often motivated to increase their land holdings by the opportunity for greater profit. This view may be supported, where it is stated that many municipalities 'set disposal prices that more than cover the costs of land development' (Needham et al, 1993, p.81). Indeed, the addendum to the quotation of the Rotterdam municipality states that although the intention is not profit related some profit at the end of the year 'may not be unwelcome'.

In the comparative context, Dutch municipalities can be argued to enjoy a higher degree of independence than their counterparts in the United Kingdom. Local government is incorporated within the Dutch constitution, whereby the Netherlands is called a 'decentralised, unitary state' (Needham et al, 1993, p.3). The emphasis is upon decentralised government. This has been particularly the case since the mid 1980s. Decentralisation is the method by which both land (MVROM, 1991) and housing policy (MVROM, 1989) objectives should be implemented. Decentralisation in one instance, involves a gradual relaxation of central government control over land prices, where municipalities are given greater freedom to anticipate the needs and demands for different types of housing. This has specific implications for housing suppliers which are discussed in the following two sections. Recent housing policy has also been aimed to give municipalities greater say in how they plan housing development. Yet at the same time, the financial position of municipalities has not improved significantly. In 1985, only 13% of municipal revenue came from local sources (property taxes and municipal property rents) (Needham et al, 1993, p.6), the rest being made up from central government grants. By the end of the 1980s, after which the process of decentralisation might have been expected to be well underway, this percentage had not altered (B.M.Bau, 1993, p.76). This situation can be compared with local authorities in the United Kingdom, where local authority revenue was 16% of the total required during the late 1980s.

The extent to which decentralisation of housing and land policy is actually occurring, is hence questionable. Fluerke and De Vries (1990, p.44) have suggested that 'decentralisation' is 'symbolic' only, there being little hard evidence of greater discretion at the local level. Also questionable is the broader historic relationship between the centre and the local level. Although, for example, municipalities are supported in constitutional law, their autonomy is only specified 'very loosely' (Needham et al, 1993, p.6), and they are also financially dependent upon central government for the major part of funding of their policy objectives.

The private sector: market builders and their role in influencing housing output
'Private sector' housing suppliers in the Netherlands are represented by the market builder sector. This sector builds mainly owner occupied housing (Figure 1.3). The role of market builders in the development process has been partially explored in Section 3.7. This is a house building sector which operates only to a limited extent in a speculative way (Vries, 1997). In many cases the house is 'pre-sold' to a client. Conijn and de Vries (1997, p.57) have shown that over 60% of dwellings were sold prior to the start of construction during the period 1992 to 1996.

There are significant differences between the Dutch market builder sector and the house building industry in the United Kingdom, especially in the extent to which the different sectors are involved in the land market. Dutch market builders rely very much on other agencies; for the greater part on municipalities for the supply of land. Historically, this has always been the case; in 1995 and 1996, municipalities supplied around 70% of all new land for housing (Conijn and de Vries, 1997, p.42). This situation has created an environment in which it is vital that state and market parties cooperate and it is accepted by builders in the market sector that municipal involvement in land supply is necessary (De Groot, 1995). This is particularly in view of the high risks associated with land preparation and infrastructure provision. Nevertheless, developers are increasingly concerned about how municipalities may exploit their role in the future, given greater autonomy. A developer interviewed in relation to this study, suggested that changes in the relationship between central and local government could be detrimental to the market sector, on the basis that many municipalities would seek to expand social housing production.

This research showed that market builder firms have to adapted to their role within the broader development process. Their ability to speculate in land is restricted, but this situation has to be balanced against the risks involved. Some developers more recently have taken initiative by purchasing agricultural land and then subsequently selling it back to the municipality once it has been granted planning permission. However, there are a number of disadvantages to this process. One likely outcome will be that the builder concerned will be ostracised in the future by the municipality. This means that the municipality will exclude the developer from future opportunities where land is released for new housing development schemes. The developer who is 'out to make a quick buck' risks being out of favour for some time. In a small country where housing networks are closely-knit, attempts to short-circuit the system are seen to be inadvisable. Whether market builders will attempt to take this risk in the future, is debatable. It is suggested that, as a result of the new Physical Planning Report, the 'VINEX', market builders will play a more active role in the land market (B&G, 1995). As they become more significant as a group of landholders, it is possible that municipalities will have to enter into partnerships or even support private sector land exploitation schemes (Spaans et al, 1996).

In the future it is possible that market builders in the Netherlands will become a more powerful sector in the development process. At the present time, however, production from the market sector generally does not involve the multi functional tasks of land purchase, house building and sale. The sector builds for a variety of end consumers, partially in a speculative way, but also to meet bespoke housing demand. As time passes, a concentration of production output may increase within the hands of fewer housing suppliers, as has done in the United Kingdom. Recent research into this area is inconclusive, although there is some evidence in research from the 1980s (Priemus, 1984) to show that the construction industry as a whole, is following a trend towards a small number of large firms. This trend can be identified particularly at the lower end of the scale, where the number of firms employing 5 or less people in 1960 was 60% of all firms, whilst in 1977, the figure had fallen to 51% (ibid, p.65).

Social housing suppliers, political change and housing output
Social housing is supplied primarily by housing associations in the Netherlands, with a very limited number of municipal housing completions (Figure 1.3). Over the period with which this research is concerned, over 90% of completions in the social sector resulted from housing associations. The influence of housing associations in the sphere of housing production is considerable by comparison with the United Kingdom. In contrast to their UK counterparts, Dutch housing associations have supplied up to 50% of total production in some years, and their contribution has never fallen below 30% of total completions (Figure 1.3). The Dutch housing association sector has historically served households on lower incomes although more recently a broader range of incomes is being catered for (Nationale Woningraad, 1995, p.7). Housing associations have a long history in the Netherlands and represent initiatives emanating from a broad cross-section of society:

> They are...founded over the last 90 years on the initiative of trade unions, the church, the social institutions, employers and individual citizens (B.M.Bau 1993a, p.9).

These groups are represented across the political spectrum in the Netherlands. A key relationship is that between municipality and housing association. Traditionally housing associations have been 'monitored primarily by the local authority in which they operate' (Boelhouwer and Van der Heijden, 1992, p.53). The perceptions of housing need projected by these groups to municipalities is a key issue in determining the pattern of social housing development across the country. However, the relationship between central government and housing associations is equally important, particularly since 'the associations stock was built with government support and the government sees to it that the associations' financial position develops soundly' (Nationale Woningraad, 1995, p.15).

In common with the United Kingdom, Dutch central government has seen fit to reduce the level of funding to the social sector. Under the slogan 'more market, less government' (ibid), social housing provision is undergoing a period of change. Since the mid 1980s, policy developments suggest a less easy going relationship between associations, local authorities and central government. This is for two main reasons which are largely inter-dependent. The first is the greater emphasis on unsubsidised production; new housing developments since 1990 are supposed to include only 30% subsidised housing. The second lies in the financial provisions supporting this policy. These provisions have been introduced in two main stages. The first stage, introduced in 1990 was linked to the theme of decentralisation, where a much more liberal remit was given to local authorities. The following extract summarises the changes:

> the most important difference between the new and the old financial schemes lies in the way in which central government controls housing quality, construction costs and the level of rents. In the past every individual project required the specific approval of central government...under the new scheme the guidance of central government is global and indirect in nature (Fleurke and De Vries, 1990, p.32).

The implication of the new system is that housing associations become even more dependent upon municipalities for housing allocations in new development schemes. Their concern is that municipalities will be bound by central government objectives of achieving 70% unsubsidised housing in every new development, thus reducing the role of housing associations in the future.

Social housing has come under attack, however, since 1995. Since April of that year, all object subsidies for the production of social housing were withdrawn under the BWS 'Dwelling-linked subsidies order'. This policy was fully in line with the emphasis in the Housing Memorandum (MVROM, 1989) on a greater role for the market and on a reduction in public spending. Potentially, the changes invoked have far-reaching consequences. Priemus (1995) has questioned whether the changes ultimately mean the 'abolition' of social housing.

Arguably, the need for alarm is not as great as might be expected. In keeping with much of what has gone before, there are a number of factors cushioning Dutch housing associations. The first is a very large lump-sum subsidy which housing associations have received from central government. This is in consideration of the future subsidies which they *would* have received on an annual basis, *were* the old system to have continued. Under a process known as 'grossing and balancing' (Priemus, 1995, p.150), central government and the housing associations have come to a compromise designed to suit both sides; associations have received money in one payment and government absolves itself of annual subsidies in the future.

Second, there is the issue of associations' financial reserves. These have been allowed to accumulate since the 1960s (Nationale Woningraad, 1995, p.5). In future, social housing construction can be funded from these resources in order to expand the stock. Further, it will be possible for housing associations to both sell existing stock to ownership households and also to construct new dwellings for 'private' rent in order to generate revenue (Inside Housing, 1995)

The future of social housing which emerges is perhaps therefore not as bleak as might be expected. In contrast with other countries where social housing producers are more evidently being sidelined, Dutch housing associations may survive the upheavals. Boelhouwer and Priemus (1990) have suggested that what is actually happening is:

> that the state's pretensions are scaled down, more scope offered for decentralised policy and for individual policy of the social landlord and other participants in the market. [There is] a continuation of the Dutch tradition in which central government continues to bear major responsibility for housing (Boelhouwer and Priemus, 1990, p.118).

This evaluation will no doubt be re-assessed as further changes become evident in the Dutch social sector.

Germany

Central government: political parties and housing outcomes
A main feature of the German political and electoral system, as in the Netherlands, is the system of proportional representation. This has the same benefits and disadvantages as elsewhere. Also in common with the Netherlands, and in contrast to the United Kingdom, coalitions have featured in an important way. In contrast to the Netherlands, however, political representation falls broadly between two main parties, the CDU (Christian Democratic Union), and the SDP (Social Democratic Party). Unlike in the Netherlands, where third parties make up a greater proportion of the vote (Figure 4.3), third parties in Germany, of the which the FDP (Free Democratic Party) is the main one, have typically gained a smaller number of votes. However, because the right of centre CDU, and the left of centre SDP have traditionally achieved a similar proportion of the vote (Figure 4.4), the political role of the liberal FDP party has been critical to the balance of power and to the formation of government.

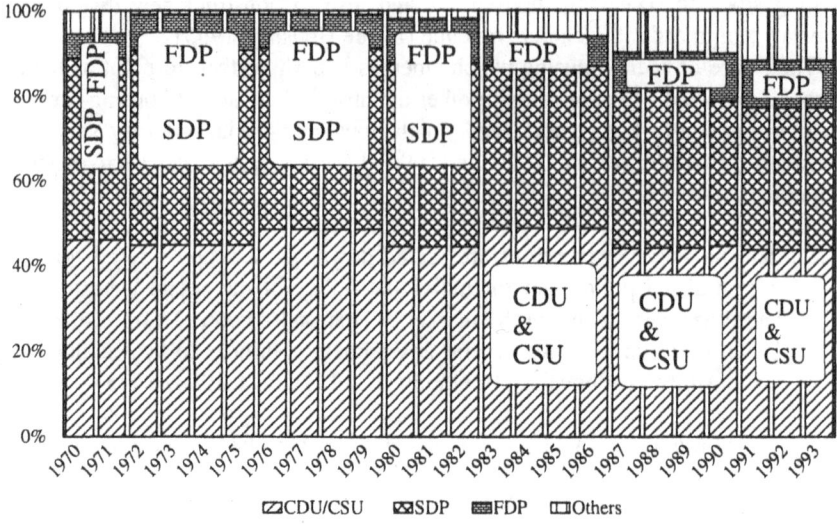

Figure 4.4   German governments, 1970-1993 (% of seats achieved)

Figure 4.4 shows how the political parties have formed coalitions over the period 1970 to 1993. There has only been one unbroken political alliance over the period; that between the CDU and the CSU (Christian Socialist Union). The former is a 'German' party (Lösche, 1993, p.122), represented throughout the country, whilst the CSU are represented mainly in the southern states of Bayern and Baden-Württemburg. The CSU represent a 'particular form of conservatism' (Lösche, 1993, p.122). The key to political balance of power, however, has lain elsewhere. The decision of the FDP to switch allegiance and to ally with the CDU/CSU prior to the 1983 election has proven to be a key issue in German politics throughout the 1980s.

To discuss the significance of central government as an agency in the system of housing supply, the relationship between changes in government and housing outcomes should be considered. As with the other two countries (Sections 4.3.1 and 4.3.2), we need to look again at the picture of housing production. For Germany, this is shown in Figure 1.4. The analysis of housing production in Germany requires some care, because of the complexities of the different tenures and methods of financing. A full attempt to unravel some of these complexities is not appropriate here but is made in Chapter 5. One or two points however can be made here about the relationship between housing tenure and the political constitution of government.

Production by private households, when considered in terms of the proportion of all production (Figure. 1.4) neither increases nor decreases significantly with the change of political power between the 1970s and 1990s (Ulbrich, 1996, p.329); hence the shift in the balance of power created by the FDP in the early 1980s appears to have had little influence on the longer term picture of housing production; at least in so far as the private household sector is concerned. This does not hold throughout however, where the shift from left to right has impacted significantly on the social sector. Social housing, as produced by the Gemeinnützige Wohnungsunternehmen ('GMN Untn') (Figure 1.4) does in fact decline as the political spectrum moves from 'left' (SDP/FDP coalition) in the 1970s to 'right' (CDU/CSU/FDP coalition) in the 1980s and 1990s. However, this relationship holds only until the late 1980s, whereafter social housing levels have been increased in response to the demands imposed by unification.

The relationship between the political constitution of government and housing tenure (or the lack of it), can be explained away to some extent by the greater priority given to housing volumes. Power (1993, p.160) has described housing policy in Germany as an 'all hands to the wheel' policy. Jaedicke and Wollman (1990, p.143) assert that the emphasis on 'volume' has tended to overlook the 'distributional effects'. The consistent proportion of output achieved by private households would seem to suggest that changes in government have little effect on that part of the housing system. However, in looking at the social sector, we can see comparisons with what has happened in other countries, such as the United Kingdom, when right of centre governments have come to power. The decline in the role of Gemeinnützige Wohnungsunternehmen as social housing providers in Germany has coincided with a period of power for the right and liberal governments of the 1980s and 1990s. A falling off in the level of completions is evident in that sector in Germany.

Local authorities, central-local relations and housing outcomes
The focus upon the municipality as an agency in the system of housing supply is intended to be a focus on an agency at the local level. In the United Kingdom and the Netherlands the 'local level' is reflected in the role of local authorities in the United Kingdom, and municipalities (Gemeenten) in the Netherlands. In Germany, however, the 'local level' is also reflected by the 'Kreis', which can be loosely equated with 'counties' in the United Kingdom (B.M.Bau, 1993, p.84). Mainly municipalities fall under the direction of a 'Kreis', 'Kreisangehörige Gemeinden', although sometimes larger towns undertake all municipal responsibilities; a situation in which a 'county tier' does not apply: the so called 'Kreisfreie Städte' ('county-free towns) (Dieterich et al, 1993).

The most important principle of local government is that of 'Kommunale Selbstverwaltung' (Saldern, von, 1993, p.2; Dieterich et al, 1993, p.3). This means that each municipality has its a right to be 'self-governing'. Municipalities each have their own elected council, and they are protected by law in the German constitution (Dieterich et al, 1993, p.3). In many respects they are the 'most important' level as far as the land and property market are concerned; this is exemplified well in their responsibility for the Bebauungsplan (Dieterich et al, 1993, p.3).

These are fairly recent views of German local government. To get an idea of the historical shifts in the balance of power between the central and local levels, we need to look further back in time. Saldern's analysis (1993), which examines municipal relations over the longer run suggests that although municipalities are now still relatively powerful political entities, their strength has been gradually eroded with time. Two periods of time can be identified with this shift. The first was during the period of political upheaval of the 1920s and 1930s and the second in the aftermath of the Second World War. The cause of the shifting in the balance of power is explained by the democratic process:

> As a result of the democratisation of the decision-making process of the state in the 20th Century, the meaning of local self-government has not become increased, rather significantly weakened (Saldern, von, 1993, p.15).

This has particular significance in relation to the establishment of the Federal Republic in 1946, which was seen to have resulted in making municipalities more accountable to the Länder (regional) and Bund (central) tiers of government (Saldern, von, 1993, p.16). However, the German municipalities are in the comparative context, still relatively independent. Their ability to achieve housing objectives is enhanced by a comparatively low subsidy requirement from central government and the Länder. Research indicates that during the late 1980s, German municipalities were on average drawing 56% of their income from their own sources (property taxes and other property revenue) (B.M.Bau, 1993, p.76). This can be compared with 13.4% in the Netherlands and 16% in the United Kingdom over the same period (ibid, p.76). This autonomy, however, has a price. As part of their enabling role, municipalities are expected to contribute to the national social housing programmes (Förderungswege). The lion's share of this funding comes from the Länder (around 70%) and central government (around 20%) (Kirchner and Sautter, 1993, p.518), whilst municipalities are expected to find the 'Spitzenfinanzierungsbedarf' ('top-up funding requirement'). The way this is used can enable particular projects to be achieved; either in specific locations or for a particular housing need (ibid, p.515).

Municipal policy needs to be considered in the light of policy relations with the Länder. Indeed, housing supply in Germany might well be best understood by reference to the regional level. If the nature of the housing stock is considered in different Länder, it can be shown that there are very large regional differences: there is, for example, a broad 'north-south' divide in terms of owner-occupation levels, where regions like Bayern (52.1% ownership) and Baden-Württemberg (33% ownership) differ from regions like Schleswig-Holstein (21% ownership) and Niedersachsen (22% ownership) (BDZ, 1993). And there are other measures which could focus upon levels of social house building and which would show interesting differences between the house building policy of the Länder. For example (BDZ, 1993) levels of building in the rented sector differ greatly. Within the 'Stadt - staaten', for example, which are the 'City states' of Hamburg, Bremen and Berlin, rented house building per 1000 inhabitants in 1992 was 1.9, 0.3 and 2.85 respectively.

The private sector: private households and their role in influencing housing output

'Private households' are considered to represent the 'private sector' for Germany, although it should be said they are not the only 'private' source of supply. Also included could be the number of developers who operate as 'Freie Unternehmen' (Figure 1.4), producing ownership as well as private rented housing. Additionally included could be a number of other organisations (Sonstige Unternehmen) who produce housing for the social sector using a significant amount of funding from the capital market.

Private households as a sector of supply, however, achieve the greatest number of annual housing completions. This sector has been the source of demand for around 60% of all production since 1970 (Figure 1.4). It is important however to highlight the diversity of this demand which comes in the form of individual 'Eigenheime' dwellings as well as in the form of owner-occupied housing within larger multi-family buildings; the so-called 'Eigentumswohnungen' (Ulbrich, 1996). Large regional as well as urban and rural differences make the demand for private housing even more differentiated. 'Private households' are hence not a uniform source of demand and their role as housing suppliers is not an easy one to quantify. Section 3.7 outlined the different ways in which private households develop housing. Two ways comprise varying degrees of self-involvement. By one route the household has a significant input, in the second, the household buys a dwelling which has been 'project managed'.

Understanding the relationship between the demand for housing created by private households and the source of supply itself, is not easy. Research (Ulbrich, 1996) suggests that no comprehensive studies are yet available. Some factors suggest however, that this source of supply exerts only a limited influence on land and housing markets. Perhaps the most significant of these factors is the individual nature of supply. The eventual housing consumer is, only in a limited number of cases, also the house builder (in 'self-build' schemes). Only therefore, on a few occasions do households operate as 'self-suppliers ' of housing. As individual purchasers they are unable to play a very influential role in the land market as a whole, since they purchase land on a plot-by-plot basis. They may not individually enjoy the benefit of lower land costs which may result from volume land acquisitions in the same way as might be the case for the larger house builders in the U.K. Another consequence of the individual nature of supply is that households lack knowledge of the way the land market operates; in effect households lack information which might otherwise be available to large firms with expertise in the field.

This research showed that the main obstacle for private households wishing to develop their own housing was land acquisition (Gee, 1994). In particular, the cost is an issue, and especially so in the southern Länder. Linked to the cost of land is the question of finance for self-promotion. Obtaining capital can be a long process (Gee, 1994) which requires would-be owners to deposit significant sums of money before a loan is granted. In addition households may have to contend with complicated procedures relating to the process of infrastructure provision (Section 3.6). This can involve the need to re-size plots or other municipal land management constraints. The process of house building can be as complex for the household itself as it is for the building contractor. A number of consumer organisations provide assistance for households wishing to build a house. The Haus und Garten journal (LBS, 1997), for example explains eight steps towards housing construction including objective setting, financial appraisal, identification of private sector funding, state subsidies, finding a plot, deciding on the design of the house, choosing a contractor and establishing a contract.

Social housing suppliers, political change and housing output
Social housing in Germany is supplied by a number of different sources, under the various methods of state housing promotion. In Chapter 5, the Gemeinnützige Wohnungsunternehmen are taken to be the most comparable sector to housing associations and local authorities in the United Kingdom and the Netherlands. This is largely because the Gemeinnützige sector aims to meet the housing needs of low income households on a non-profit making basis. It should be noted, however, that in the German context, social housing is defined by the method of financing, rather than by reference to the source of supply. 'Social housing', generally speaking is a function of any housing supplier or 'Bauherr' (Section 3.7) who utilises the public sector funding programmes. The most significant are the two Förderungswege (Section 3.2). No housing supplier is barred from utilising these pots of money, provided that the criteria is fulfilled for which the subsidy is made available. Social housing can be produced by housing associations, private households, or other housing organisations.

Social housing suppliers however, have a range of differing motivations. Housing can be supplied for owner-occupation, which is production mainly by private households. Or social housing can be housing on a non-profit basis, which is production mainly by Gemeinnützige Unternehmen. Or social housing can even be housing produced for profit, which is often production by Freie Unternehmen. Of these social housing suppliers, only the Gemeinnützige Unternehmen are registered institutions for the production of non-profit housing. The Gemeinütziges Wohnungsunternehmen, can be translated as 'housing association for the common weal' (Hallett, 1977, p.62). The associations can be seen, however, more in terms as 'enterprises' a term which reflects the nature of the 'professionally employed' people who work in them (ibid).

The Gemeinnützige Unternehmen have been a significant force in social housing supply since the Second World War. Their contribution has however declined since the early 1970s (Figure 1.4) and has been accompanied by a shift from left-of-centre to right-of-centre politics. The overall decline in social housing output, combined with the fact that social housing is produced by a broad, and rather ill defined spectrum of suppliers, makes it difficult to regard the sector as a particularly significant or cohesive one today. Historically, there has arguably only been one instance of an attempt to really institutionalise the production of social housing in Germany in the post-war period. This was a result of the activities of a company known as Neue Heimat. A short overview is necessary since the example of Neue

Heimat demonstrates some of the problems associated with the very flexible method of funding social housing in Germany.

Neue Heimat evolved in the post-war period from a non-profit housing organisation in Hamburg (Werner, 1974, p.70). It was in fact the 'largest non-profit housing organisation in all of Western Europe' (Power, 1993, p.132). Its contribution to social housing production was significant:

> in all, housing benefiting from public funds (which is called 'Social housing') constitutes about 227,000 units annually, or 40% of the total housing production in Germany. Neue Heimat provides about one sixth (Werner, 1974).

Neue Heimat produced large quantities of housing during the 1960s and 1970s. Much of this was on large peripheral estates (Power 1993:). The motive for production and involvement in housing seemed to be twofold. To:

> rais(e) the standards of home living', and by doing so to 'ensure that it remains in socially acceptable limits and thus operates in the public interest (Vietor: Präsident of Neue Heimat 1965, Hallett, 1977, p.69).

This was all to be done within the trade union's goals of making some profit, yet at the same time holding 'prices low' (Hallett, 1977:69). Neue Heimat, although it used public funding, was instrumental in 'pioneering the use of private funds from the capital market' (Hallett 1977, p.65). Therefore, although its aim in housing supply was similar to other social housing organisations in Europe, it was at the forefront of mixed funding schemes. In addition however, it was very entrepreneurial. The company became involved in land dealing, in the setting up of offshore construction companies and in other financial deals. The details of the companies activities are well documented by Power (1993, p.132-142), although that account confesses that the complexities of the financial activities are very difficult to analyse precisely. Eventually, what resulted was a financial scandal and ended in several employees being imprisoned on charges of financial corruption. The organisation was bankrupted in the mid 1980s.

The 'Neue Heimat' recount is an unfortunate one, but one in Germany which is identifiable with the potential consequences of having mixed funding systems and unregulated enterprise. Power writes:

> The very advantages of the German system, its public-private structure, its many channels of development and its flexibility, provided scope for possibly the most extraordinary social housing scandal of the post-war era (Power, 1993, p.132).

The production of social housing has throughout, and despite the Neue Heimat episode, continued to be produced by a range of suppliers. A more detailed description of the relationship between housing output from this sector, and changes in macroeconomic conditions is given in Chapter 5. This covers largely the period of the former West Germany. Since 1991, it should be pointed out, that social housing has been given a new emphasis. Just when central government were beginning to reduce the level of subsidy to the sector, political events overtook them. Re-unification has created a large new demand for affordable good quality housing in the eastern Länder, where housing conditions are poor. A new government ministry, the Kreditanstalt für Wiederaufbau (KfW) has been established to regulate development in the areas of the former German Democratic Republic.

4.4 The macroeconomies of the United Kingdom, the Netherlands and Germany: between Keynesian and Monetarist policies

Macroeconomic management and performance

Although this section does not provide a full empirical investigation of the relationship between macroeconomic variables and housing output in each country, it is nevertheless important to the analysis of housing supply to identify the main historical differences in the way the economies of the three countries have been managed. The discussion of the structure of the system of supply cannot be detached from the economic environment in which it takes place. In Section 4.4, the main differences in economic policy are identified using a trend showing how aspects of monetary and fiscal policy have differed between the three countries over time (Figure 4.5). All data is sourced from the European Commission and each variable is represented as an average for the period 1970-1993.

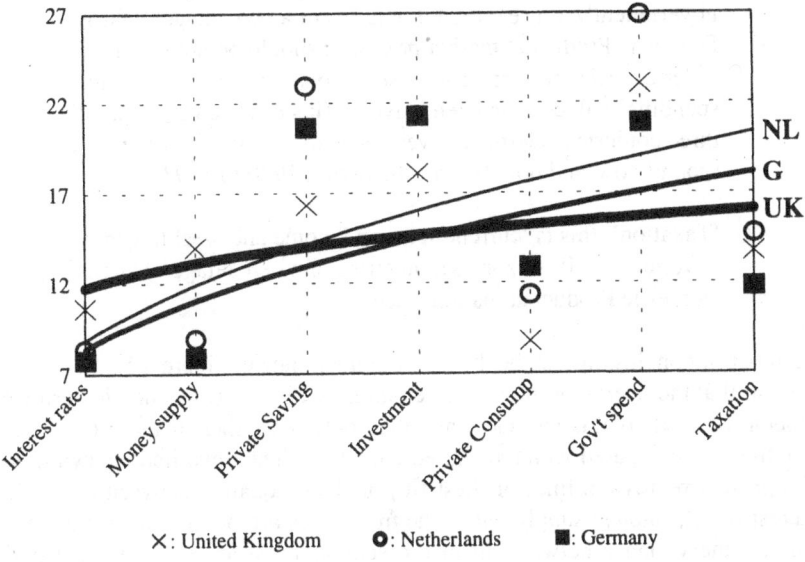

Figure 4.5 **The macroeconomies of the United Kingdom, the Netherlands and Germany**

Before discussing the main differences, it is important to establish precisely what is represented by the different variables shown in Figure 4.5:

1) 'Interest rates': these are the 'nominal long-term interest rates'. These are based on the long term bond rate.

2) 'Money supply': this is the money supply measure M2 or M3. The data provides a measure of the annual percentage change in the money supply.

3) 'Private saving': this is 'gross private saving' expressed as a percentage of Gross Domestic Product at market prices.

4) 'Investment': this is the 'gross fixed capital formation at current prices'. It relates to the total economy and is expressed in terms of a percentage of Gross Domestic Product at market prices.

5) 'Private consumption': this is 'private consumption at current prices per head of population' expressed in Ecu.

6) 'Government spending': this is 'total expenditure; general government'. It is expressed in terms of a percentage of Gross Domestic Product at market prices. It should be noted that in order to scale the graph for presentational purposes, 'government spending' values have been halved. This has been done for all three countries. German government spending, for example, is around 40% and not 20% for the period 1970 to 1993.

7) 'Taxation': this is 'current taxes on income and wealth; general government'. It is expressed in terms of a percentage of Gross Domestic Product at market prices.

A number of conclusions can be drawn from the trends in Figure 4.5.

First, that the overview shows greater similarity in macro-economic performance between the Netherlands and Germany than between either of these two countries when they are compared with the United Kingdom. The trend lines shown in Figure 4.5 represent regression lines of 'best fit', or 'least squares' between the variables, 'interest rates', 'money supply' etc. The trend lines are plotted in such a way as to minimise the variance between all macro-economic variables. The trend lines for the Netherlands and Germany are shown to be similar (Figure 4.5). This is particularly the case with variables such as interest rates and the money supply. A policy of keeping the money supply tight in those countries is associated with low nominal interest rates (Figure 4.5). In the United Kingdom, nominal interest rates have been significantly higher (a response to higher inflation), with the money supply increasing on average by 14% annually (Figure 4.5).

The monetary stance taken by German governments since the war has led commentators to suggest that the German economy has been distinctly 'anti-Keynesian' (Gruchy, 1977, p.146, Crouch, 1993, p.92), resisting government intervention to boost demand in the short run and maintaining a strong hold over inflation; 'Keynesian' and 'Monetarist' policy stances are explored below. Government spending in Germany as a proportion of GDP is at 40% on average, the lowest of the three countries. This contrasts strongly with the Netherlands which has on average government spending at over 50% of GDP for the period 1970 to 1993. It is towards the right hand side of the scale (Figure 4.5) where taxation and government spending are plotted, that the Dutch and German positions differ most. Whereas there are similarities in monetary policy, Dutch governments have spent more and taxed higher than their German counterparts.

The monetary and fiscal stances appear to have knock-on effects for the levels of private sector saving and consumption. Countries which have a slower changes in the rate of the money supply, namely Germany and Netherlands, also have considerably higher levels of savings as a proportion of total GDP. Savings, as a percentage of GDP, as well as private consumption as a percentage of GDP, are lowest in the United Kingdom (Figure 4.5). Total levels of investment, expressed in terms of gross fixed capital formation also shows the United Kingdom to be at the lowest level of the three countries (Section 3.1).

Between Keynesian and Monetarist policies: implications for housing supply in three economies

Two stances are generally distinguished in economic analysis to explain the way in which economies are managed: what is known on the one hand as the 'Keynesian' approach, after the economist Keynes, and on the other, the 'Monetarist' approach, promoted by not least Friedman. What distinguishes one approach from the other is by no means agreed upon by economists. A full discussion is given by Lipsey (1973). One main distinction, which is significant to the present comparison hinges on the importance governments attach to fluctuations in the money supply. Governments following wholly monetarist policies will attempt to deal with changes in economic demand by altering the money supply or by changing interest rates. History has shown strong links between changes in the money supply and levels of economic activity. These linkages work both ways; when the money supply increases, this is associated with increases in economic activity; conversely when the money supply falls, then economic activity also drops off. The latter scenario was observed during the 1920s and 1930s depressions. The monetarist solution to the problem of falling demand and a flat economy is to adjust the money supply or the interest rate to suit the strength of the economy. This is on the assumption that the economy is relatively self-regulating (Lipsey, 1973, p.758). Historically great importance was attached to keeping in balance the amount of gold reserves and the currency in circulation.

The main unresolved problem of monetary policy is that its precise relationship with economic activity is uncertain. Whilst specific empirical studies exist, showing links between levels of economic activity and the extent of money in circulation (ibid), there is no consistent historical relationship which shows that increases in the money supply lead per se, to increases in economic activity and increases in prices and demand. Governments during the 1980s and 1990s have turned more towards monetarist policies and had some success in regulating demand through interest rate changes and manipulating the money supply. However, this has largely been in situations where economies had already some momentum; in other words, demand was not significantly deficient. The problem of demand deficiency was seen by Keynes to be a problem which the natural economic cycle could not overcome, at least in the short to medium term. Where demand was low, as was the case in the 1930s, and unemployment was high, the solution was government intervention in the form of increased investment and changes in fiscal policy. This was needed because otherwise the economy could:

> come to rest with substantial unemployment and without any significant forces operating to push the economy back to full employment...creating a situation of permanent depression (Lipsey, 1973, p.761).

The response to economic problems of the past vary between the three countries examined in this study. As was suggested in the previous section, Germany's adopted stance following the Second World War, was an anti-Keynesian one. It looked to a central bank, the Bundesbank, to ensure that inflation was kept under control through interest rate and money supply policy. It rejected the demand management policies of Keynes, preferring instead the supply-side incentives which are evident not least in the housing production programmes since 1945. Mainly, with the exception of the period in the mid 1970s, during the oil-crisis (Dyker, 1992, p.36) government did not resort to potentially inflationary demand management.

The preference for the strongly monetarist stance adopted in Germany has had several implications for housing supply. Arguably, it has created a more certain economic environment, with low rates of interest and high levels of investment. These factors may help to explain, or have some bearing on the size and strength of the private rented sector today in Germany. Conversely, however, the policies followed may have worked against home ownership. Indeed, the relatively high levels of private savings (Figure 4.5) may have been created to some extent by conventional methods of financing home ownership.

The economy in the United Kingdom has been managed in a different way to that in Germany. Figure 4.5 provides all the economic indicators. These are most stark in terms of changes in the rate of money supply, the level of interest rates and level of private savings. These variables are to some extent interlinked. The economic stance adopted by governments in the United Kingdom has varied over time. Although the Thatcher governments adopted monetarist and supply-side policies, especially from the mid 1980s onwards, Keynesian thinking influenced economic policy from 1940 onwards (Jewell, 1993, p.55). A precursor to this, was the decision in 1946 by the Labour government to nationalise the Bank of England (ibid). Since then, monetary policy has always been in danger of being influenced by political parties from either end of the spectrum. The relationship between Bank and government has been at times 'top-down', especially where government has been caught up in crises abroad. In more recent times however, it has become more of a partnership, where monetary policy is set between the Chancellor and the Governor of the Bank.

The implications of the less rigid monetarist stance for housing supply in the United Kingdom are significant. Arguably, the inflationary conditions have assisted the growth of home ownership, where the demand for an asset which is both an investment and consumption good, has aided booms in speculative new house building. Also, the great economic advantages gained by home owners, have made other rented sectors uncompetitive in the long run. For tenants, the opportunity cost of ownership tends to rise proportionally with rises in house prices and the relatively low levels of housing production in other tenures may have much to do with high rents and housing shortages.

Figure 4.5 shows similarities in the way in which the Dutch and German economies have been managed; the only significant difference being in the extent of government spending and taxation. This difference may be attributed to differences in a number of factors, although perhaps one of the most important may be differences in levels of unemployment, which in the Netherlands have been high by western European standards (Jewell, 1993, p.204). The Dutch economy is however closely linked to the German, particularly through its export market; 28% of its total exports are purchased in Germany (ibid, p.203). Trade links and geographical proximity also appear to influence economic policy in line with that in Germany. Jewell (ibid) goes as far as to suggest:

> The link is so close that we can regard the Netherlands as part of the greater German economy. The two countries enjoy a monetary quasi-union in that the guilder is closely linked to the Deutschmark through the ERM (Jewell, 1993, p.203).

Close economic ties are also suggested by Crouch (1993, p.93):

> the German also.....Dutch economies.....combine exceptionally strong forms of corporatist co-ordination and co-operation among firms with a virtually neo-classical rigidity of central banking institutions.

Similarities in the way in which the economies of the two countries have been managed, may be expected to bring about similarities in the housing systems. Indeed, although it has been shown in Chapter 3, that the systems of supply differ greatly, it would be wrong to refute differences elsewhere. Particularly in so far as the tenure of the housing stock is concerned, where both the Netherlands and Germany share amongst the lowest levels of owner-occupation in Europe. Yet also, in so far that the housing stock in both countries has a much broader spread of housing types and tenures in the rented sector.

4.5 Conclusions: models of structure re-visited

An important objective of Chapter 4 was to examine the systems of housing supply from a number of different angles. From a theoretical aspect, a method of doing this is through models of structure. These models can take on various guises, as was outlined in Chapter 2. In this chapter, we have mainly looked at the functional linkages (Section 4.2), the role of agencies (Section 4.3) and the political economy in which these agencies function (Section 4.4). Loosely, these approaches straddle structure and agency theory as examined in Chapter 2.

In so far as substantive conclusions are to be made, there are clear differences in the way the systems of supply can be understood to operate. Where questions are asked about the potential for coordinating the process of supply between different (public and private) sector agencies, the Dutch system is favoured, largely because of the possibilities for changing the emphasis of production through municipal land ownership and planning powers. In the chain of events, the development process is driven significantly by the state at local level. This arguably makes it easier to envisage a 'simple' system, processing new housing in response to changes in demand.

Similarly, (albeit through private land ownership, infrastructure provision and construction activity), the system of supply in the United Kingdom, accords a division of labour heavily in favour of one side. This is different to the system in Germany, where public intervention is interspersed irregularly at junctures in the (private) land supply process and system of infrastructure provision.

When a different focus is given to understanding systems of housing supply, different conclusions arise. This is the case, when the nature and role of the agencies (central and local government, private and social housing suppliers) is examined. It is clear, for example, that central governments in Germany and the Netherlands have been less influential for the tenure of new housing that is produced, than has been the case in the United Kingdom. In the Netherlands, changes in the political colour of government have, for much of the post-war period, had negligible effects on the tenure of new housing. The same can broadly be said for German governments. However, the association between changes in government and changes in the tenure of new housing in the United Kingdom is very evident.

The role played by agencies other than central governments in housing supply, is influenced by a range of institutional, historical, economic and physical factors. Central-local government relations in Germany, for example are conditioned by a history of decentralised public policy, evident not least at a broader (Länder) level. German municipalities are, relative to the other two countries, more financially independent. In the Netherlands, despite the fact that municipalities rely more heavily on central government, there is greater independence than has been the case in the United Kingdom, particularly in terms of the development process. These differences undoubtedly go some way towards explaining the differing negotiating position of local authorities in so far as new housing development is concerned.

The different development processes create very particular roles for housing suppliers. It would not be accurate to see private or social housing suppliers of any two countries as being directly equivalent. Although private developers, market builders or private individuals may have some common motivations in producing new housing, they find themselves with different levels of responsibility for doing so, in each particular context. There is probably more similarity between Dutch and German private sector housing suppliers in their negotiating position with local authorities, than is the case in the United Kingdom. However, this can be to do with a number of factors ranging from the extent of land ownership in a particular locality, to the scale and size of the house building firm or provider. There are also few direct parallels across the countries between social sector housing providers and their relations with other agencies. In the Netherlands, this relationship is driven not least by the reliance on municipalities for land supply; in the United Kingdom, this has also been the case, although the sector as a whole is less significant and arguably has been more reliant on central government. In Germany, social housing, with the potential for many different sources of supply, might be argued to be less institutionalised in nature and reliant on both state and individual agencies.

Despite the diverse nature of housing supply in the three countries, there is a quite clear distinction that can be made in the way the economies have been managed over time (Section 4.4). This involves a similar macroeconomic policy having been pursued in the Netherlands and Germany, and which can be distinguished from that in the United Kingdom; macroeconomic policy in the mainland European countries having been characterised by lower interest rates, tighter control of the money supply and higher levels of saving and investment (Figure 4.5).

The precise consequences of these differing policies are not discussed here. Nevertheless, it is important to consider the potential implications of these differing scenarios in so far as the statistical investigations of Chapter 5 are concerned. For whereas good reasons can be offered as to why Germany and the Netherlands have pursued a similar monetary policy (Section 4.4), it is not immediately apparent how such a common economic policy impacts on housing outcomes, once it runs up against individual, political, institutional and development processes.

5 Housing production and housing systems: a statistical analysis

5.1. Introduction to the statistical analysis

The previous two chapters have described and presented the key facets of systems of housing supply in each country: the housing production policies, the land supply systems and the physical planning mechanisms which support them. It has been argued that there is a potential for different systems of housing supply with different emphases of state intervention, to lead to different housing outcomes.

It is the function of this chapter to identify ways in which the main hypothesis of the research can be addressed. In the following sections of this chapter, there will be a focus on some determinants of new housing output. In particular, on the total volume of output (Section 5.2); on output from the private sectors (Section 5.4) and on output from the social sector (Section 5.5). The particular questions are addressed by examining the role of demographics, profits (the relationship between house prices, land prices and building costs), and at the significance of changing rates of unemployment and GDP. These variables are not used in highly complex models of housing supply. The objective is to relate outcomes to the systems of supply from which they emanate.

The approach is in no small part determined by the availability of comparative data. The chapter attempts to outline and deal with these as it progresses. A full section (5.3) is dedicated to explaining the rationale behind the choice of sectors and the links between tenure, housing suppliers and modes of subsidy. Each sub-section is divided between the main theoretical standpoint, the data sources and statistical findings.

5.2 Housing production; total output, household formation and the housing stock

Thesis, rationale and model

There are a number of ways of examining, and hence explaining, total housing production output at a national level. Fluctuations in the level of housing investment play an important part, as well as changes in macroeconomic performance. In addition, demographic trends and the housing stock also play significant roles. To construct a model capable of predicting total housing output in the future, it might be necessary to include all these variables in a potentially complex regression equation. In this section, the focus is largely on the demographic aspects and the role that existing housing stock plays in determining new housing production.

The relationship between total housing output, demographic change and the housing stock is seen to be an essential function of the net increase in the number of households and the net decrease in the housing stock due to demolitions, discontinuance, and loss and change of use. These variables in combination, can be called upon to form a broad model of housing 'need'. This 'model' can be expressed:

$Tp = NHi + NSd$, where:

Tp = Total annual housing production
NHi = Net increase in the number of households
NSd = Net decrease in the housing stock

The model, it should be stated, is only applicable, however, where there is a general equilibrium, or balance in the relationship between the total housing stock and the total number of households. If there are historic housing shortages and the number of households exceeds the size of the housing stock, then it may be that the relationship between total housing production and housing 'need' (NHi + NSd) cannot be reconciled. Where historic housing shortages exist, annual housing production must exceed the annual 'need' (NHi + NSd) in order to catch up with the historic shortages. In a situation in which crude or broad housing surpluses exist, then total annual production may be less than NHi + NSd since the stock has capacity to absorb the increase in the number of households without the corresponding number of new dwellings being built. These assumptions follow the line (DETR, 1997, p.22) that annual housing need is the 'current balance between housing demand and housing supply', or 'the difference between the total number of households and the total number of dwellings at any point in time'. The assumptions are now discussed in the context of the three countries.

In the case of the United Kingdom and Germany, there are points in time which can be identified at which crude or broad housing shortages were overcome. In the United Kingdom this occurred around the year 1974 and in Germany 1975.

According to the official data for the Netherlands, however, there has been a consistent surplus of households over housing stock.

Data sources

Total housing production
The output trends in total housing production are given in Figure 1.2 (United Kingdom), Figure 1.3 (The Netherlands) and Figure 1.4 (Germany) along with the relevant sources. Output is shown in Table 5.1 below:

Table 5.1
Housing production: total output

Year	United Kingdom	Netherlands	Germany
1970	362226	128064	478000
1971	364475	152829	555000
1972	330936	171197	661000
1973	304637	172194	714000
1974	279472	158730	604000
1975	321936	126515	437000
1976	324839	109933	392000
1977	314093	114270	409000
1978	278603	108784	368000
1979	252086	115607	358000
1980	241986	118348	389000
1981	206625	124656	365000
1982	182863	132033	347000
1983	209033	113728	341000
1984	220561	117231	398000
1985	207656	103267	312000
1986	216132	107641	252000
1987	226157	114879	217000
1988	241931	121708	209000
1989	221425	113856	239000
1990	200272	100718	256000
1991	188584	82888	315000
1992	177225	86164	375000
1993	179527	86991	432000

Sources: Department of the Environment, Central Bureau of Statistics, Statistiches Bundesamt

Net household increase
The net increase in the number of households is the number of additional households which come into being each year as a result of the many factors which affect trends in the rate of household formation: births, marriages, deaths, divorces and so on. The data for net household increase is given in Table 5.2 for each of the three countries.

Table 5.2
Net household increase

Year	United Kingdom	Netherlands	Germany
1970	149000	96000	266000
1971	170000	108000	183000
1972	171000	117000	242000
1973	163000	126000	239000
1974	110000	117000	418000
1975	130000	107000	71000
1976	124000	99000	221000
1977	125000	92000	222000
1978	135000	87000	56000
1979	143000	72000	265000
1980	150000	95000	325000
1981	120000	97000	289000
1982	103000	136000	236000
1983	155000	128000	340000
1984	200000	127000	350000
1985	215000	119000	339000
1986	195000	98000	372000
1987	210000	103000	267000
1988	180000	71000	397000
1989	210000	76000	390000
1990	190000	100000	382000
1991	184000	102000	408000
1992	176000	88000	460000
1993	174000	93000	570000

Sources: Department of the Environment, Central Bureau of Statistics, Statistiches Bundesamt

A comprehensive data set for the United Kingdom on the number of households in existence was not identified. The data sets which do exist (Eurostat sources) are very general, giving household numbers only to the nearest 100,000 which is unsatisfactory for the purposes of analysis. A data set exists however for the 'net increase in the number of households' for England and Wales (King, 1993, p.109), which has been used.

The use of 'England and Wales' in proxy for the United Kingdom is argued not to affect the way the relationships investigated in Section 5.2.3, are viewed. Around 80% of household increase in the United Kingdom occurs due to the growth in the number of households in England and Wales (D.o.E, 1994). In the statistical investigation in Section 5.2.3, data for housing production in England and Wales has been used to maintain consistency.

Net household increase in the Netherlands is based on the data provided by the Dutch Housing Ministry (MVROM) for the 'total number of households' (Ligterink, 1993). The data for the 'net increase in the number of households' has been calculated by subtracting the number of households for a given year from the number in the following year. This figure is then used to represent the net increase in households for the following year.

The calculation of net household increase in Germany is based upon the data provided by the Statistiches Bundesamt (Eisel, 1993) for the total number of households. The data for the 'net increase in the number of households' has been calculated in the same way as for the Netherlands.

Decreases in the housing stock

Decreases in the stock affect the total need or demand for housing. A decrease in the stock can occur for a variety of reasons. It can occur due to demolitions or it can occur due to discontinuance orders where dwellings are unfit. Alternatively, decreases can occur due to changes of use. Table 5.3 provides data in a form which includes all reasons for stock decreases.

Table 5.3
Decreases in the housing stock

Year	United Kingdom	Netherlands	Germany
1970	71118	18544	26838
1971	74721	18590	32460
1972	70234	16641	33640
1973	69865	15321	32909
1974	64920	17079	30472
1975	42026	14667	28065
1976	53040	14724	27125
1977	46237	14189	25639
1978	40278	13468	29497
1979	33965	14008	26448
1980	30019	15002	24589
1981	28385	14229	25445
1982	23485	12572	20206
1983	17074	11304	19963
1984	11622	11590	17571
1985	10319	10121	15038
1986	9120	11524	15130
1987	7026	12445	15316
1988	6614	12673	15787
1989	5509	12953	14785
1990	6134	11548	14130
1991	3260	12754	14663
1992	2371	11659	15294
1993	2162	12984	15953

Sources: Department of the Environment, Central Bureau of Statistics, Statistiches Bundesamt

Data for the decrease in the housing stock in the United Kingdom is sourced from the Department of the Environment (Ellison, 1993). The data represents the total number of all dwellings 'demolished or closed'. The data relates to England and Wales. Data for the decrease in the Dutch housing stock is sourced from the Housing Ministry (Ligterink, 1993). The data represents the total number of all dwellings 'demolished, discontinued or closed for other purposes'. Data for the decrease in the housing stock in Germany is sourced from the Statistiches Bundesamt (Imming, 1993). The data represents the total number of all dwellings 'deducted' from the German housing stock.

The housing stock and number of households
Data sets on the size of the housing stock and the total number of households are given in Table 5.4. The rationale for using these data sets is given (Section 5.2).

Table 5.4
Housing stock and households ('000's)

Year	Stock (UK)	H'holds (UK)	Stock (NL)	H'holds (NL)	Stock (G)	H'holds (G)
1970	16892	17143	3657	3986	20807	22991
1971	17032	17313	3753	4094	21329	22752
1972	17376	17484	3873	4211	21957	22994
1973	17564	17647	4010	4377	22638	23233
1974	17759	17757	4151	4454	23212	23651
1975	17978	17887	4280	4561	23621	23722
1976	18203	18011	4387	4660	23986	23943
1977	18433	18136	4479	4752	24370	24165
1978	18578	18271	4577	4839	24708	24221
1979	18757	18414	4671	4911	25040	24486
1980	18932	18564	4747	5006	25406	24811
1981	19101	18684	4867	5103	25748	25100
1982	19249	18787	4957	5239	26076	25336
1983	19449	18942	5071	5367	26399	25679
1984	19637	19142	5178	5494	26782	26024
1985	19817	19537	5289	5613	27081	26367
1986	20010	19552	5384	5711	27694	26739
1987	20219	19762	5483	5814	27896	27006
1988	20432	19942	5558	5885	28102	27403
1989	20627	20152	5699	5961	28342	27793
1990	20803	20342	5802	6061	28907	28175
1991	20855	20526	5892	6163	28992	28583
1992	21178	20702	5965	6251	29308	29043
1993	21280	20876	6057	6329	29732	29368

Sources: Department of the Environment, Central Bureau of Statistics, Statistiches Bundesamt

Data for the housing stock is for England and Wales in order to be consistent with the other variables, 'decrease in the housing stock' and the 'net increase in the number of households'. The data for the housing stock is taken from Housing and

Construction Statistics (D.o.E). The data for the total number of households is taken from the increase in the number of households (Corner 1991, p.109) with a base year of 1990, at which there was 20,342,900 households in England and Wales (Local housing statistics 1992).

Data for both the Dutch housing stock and the total number of households in the Netherlands is sourced directly from information provided by the Dutch Housing Ministry (Ligterink, 1993).

Data for both the German housing stock and the number of households in Germany is sourced directly from information provided by the Statistiches Bundesamt in Wiesbaden (Eisel, 1993).

Outcomes: total housing output and annual housing need

Figures 5.1, 5.2 and 5.3 show the relationships between housing production, household increase and stock decrease for the three countries.

Generally, there is a convergence over time in the relationship between the total volume or level of housing production and the annual need (NHi + HSd) for housing in all three countries. The gap between the two variables can be seen to narrow, particularly since the late 1970s. These trends mean that when the two variables are correlated for the whole time period, it is unlikely that the coefficients of correlation will indicate a strong association. Nevertheless, this is not to say that the trends are unrelated and each country should be examined in turn.

The United Kingdom
Figure 5.1 shows the relationship between total housing production and annual housing need (NHi + NSd) for the United Kingdom (data: England and Wales). The coefficient of correlation for the period 1970-1993 is 0.395.

The statistical relationship between the two variables (Figure 2.1), however, for the years 1974 to 1993, provides a much lower correlation coefficient of -0.107. This period is considered, as it represents the time frame in which there has been a general equilibrium between the size of the housing stock and the number of households. The correlation coefficient for this period is however negative, suggesting that housing production falls as housing need increases, and vice-versa. This could explained by a number of events; in particular: high levels of production between 1974 and 1979, a period of local authority house building; and high rates of household growth during the mid 1980s, which was not matched by the rate of house building (Figure 5.1).

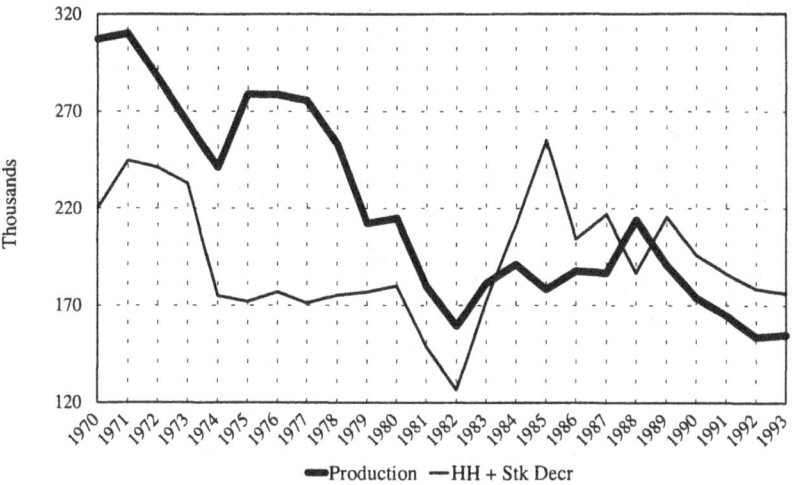

Source: Local Authority Housing Statistics, DoE Housing and Construction Statistics

Figure 5.1   Total housing production, household increase and housing stock decrease in the United Kingdom

The Netherlands

Figure 5.2 shows the relationship between total housing production and the annual housing need (NHi + NSd) in the Netherlands. The correlation coefficient for the two variables over the period 1970 to 1993 is 0.491.

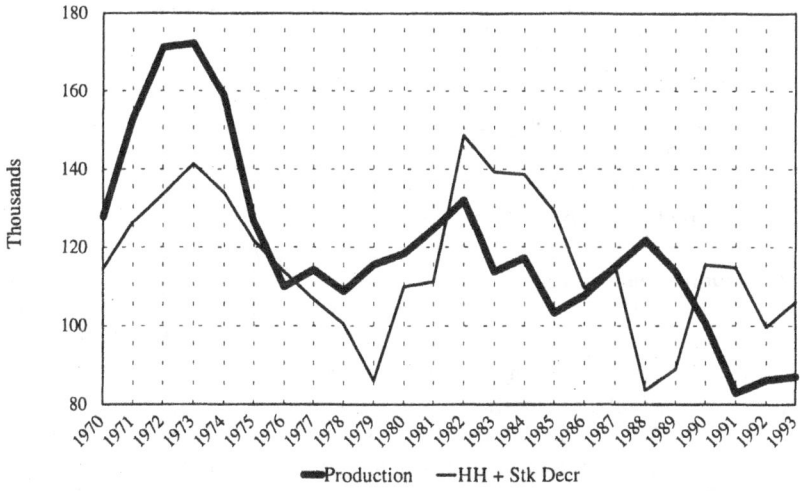

Source: Central Bureau of Statistics, Den Haag
Figure 5.2   Total housing production, household increase and housing stock decrease in the Netherlands

This is a significantly strong association over time and, as Figure 5.2 shows, the total volume of new housing production in the Netherlands responds quite robustly to demographic and housing stock changes. Given that the number of households in a country is difficult to assess and predict, a well integrated system of housing supply might be assumed or predicated. One explanation for the association given in Figure 5.2 is that, in aggregate, the municipal land supply system works effectively in reconciling housing need and demand with housing supply.

Germany

Figure 5.3 shows the relationship between total housing production and the annual housing need (NHi + NSd) for Germany. The correlation coefficient for the period 1970 to 1993 is -0.209.

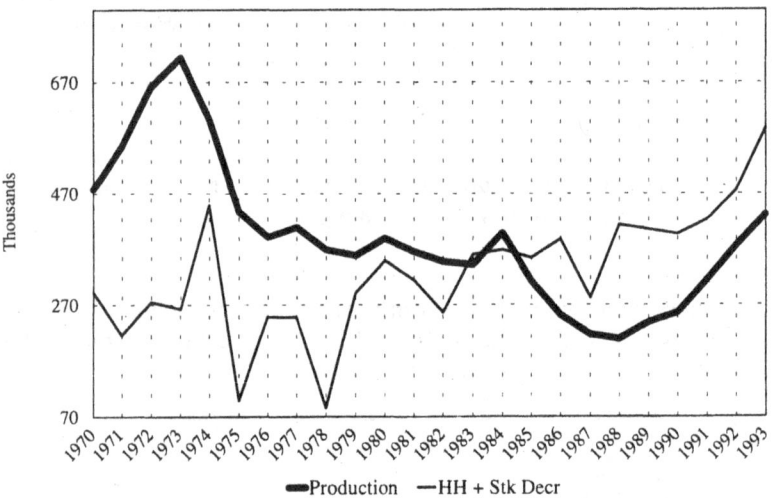

Source: Statistiches Bundesamt, B.M.Bau

Figure 5.3 Total housing production, household increase and housing stock decrease in Germany

This correlation is negative, indicating that as one variable rises, the other falls. This is perhaps an odd finding although it can be seen from Figure 5.3 that the trend in output is generally in a downward direction, whilst the broad trend in housing need is upward. From 1974, the German housing stock exceeded the number of households. The correlation coefficient for the period 1975 to 1993 is positive and more in line with the assumption that annual housing output responds positively to increases in housing need. However, at 0.0785 (correlation coefficient for the years 1975 to 1993), it is a weak relationship.

In addition to factors associated with the system of housing supply (Chapters 3 and 4), there are a number of other potential explanatory factors for the low statistical association in the case of Germany. One such, is the high level of in and out migration over German borders. Fluctuations in those variables are held to be particularly significant in Germany (Bucher, 1993, p.254). Research suggests (ibid) that very high fluctuations in the 1970s and the late 1980s in the total number of households (Figure 5.3) are associated with migration trends. This particular issue may make it difficult for the Länder and central government to reconcile production easily to changes in the number of households at any one time. It is also difficult to evaluate the effect that re-unification might have had on the relationship between output and housing need; since the late 1980s, housing production appears to run a deficit relative to the number of new households and decreases in the housing stock. This is a very different situation to the late 1970s and for most of the 1980s, where annual output was in excess of the general level of housing need. Thus two opposing trends are evident, making a high statistical association between the two factors over time, unlikely.

5.3 Private and social sector housing production: a comparative framework

Previous research

Forms of housing production are not easily compared. This is evident from Figures 1.2, 1.3 and 1.4. Official statistics do not immediately provide the comparative information and this means that a more detailed analysis is required. The question is how the task is undertaken.

Previous research indicates that there are significant problems in comparing housing in the sphere of supply and production. These are highlighted in distinctions between 'essentialist' and 'constructivist' approaches to housing tenure (Ruonavarra, 1993, pp.6-9), in pre-occupations with 'anglo-saxon' frameworks (Kemeny, 1994, p.14), and in difficulties in distinguishing tenures because of the ways in which housing is subsidised (Oxley, 1995).

In particular, comparative investigations which attempt to use tenures, rather than sectors, as a measure of housing production, may well run into problems. Kemeny (1994) makes a distinction between 'anglo-saxon' countries in which a 'feudal' approach to understanding tenure prevails, and those in which alternative forms of 'tenure' evaluation are promoted. Duncan and Barlow (1988) also allude to the problems associated with tenure. The preoccupation with an 'anglo-saxon' approach to understanding housing issues is criticised in what appears to be an appeal for researchers to look at problems from 'outside-in', rather than 'inside-out'. Problems of making comparisons could be hampered by the expectation that data will be readily available on 'owner-occupation', 'private renting' and 'social renting'. This is not always the case.

Ruonavarra (1993) provides housing researchers with a managed framework. From the 'messy real world of housing tenure' (Ruonavarra 1993, p.4) he shows how comparative questions can be looked under the headings of 'essentialist' and 'constructivist' paradigms. Those adopting the 'essentialist' approach might regard tenures as 'fixed entities with certain advantages and disadvantages from the point of view of the consumer', where in particular there is a preference for owner-occupation as a 'near universal attribute of mankind' (Ruonavarra, 1995, p.6). Those adopting the 'constructivist' viewpoint look to the 'structures of social relations' which are not 'immutable but develop through time'. Generally, within the 'constructivist' view:

> Any attempt to formulate a general, cross-nationally valid typology of housing tenure is bound to be futile, or, at least, of minor importance (Ruonavarra 1993, p.6).

Comparisons using tenure are very often frustrated by the question of how to reconcile subsidies. This problem is perhaps best illustrated by the case of Germany, where individual subsidy channels make possible social ownership, social renting and in some cases private renting. In other countries there is greater privity between subsidy schemes and particular housing suppliers. In both the United Kingdom and the Netherlands, social housing is often associated with the source of supply (housing associations and local authorities) rather than by its method of financing.

The potential complexities involved in attempting to make distinctions between tenures within the broader debate about subsidies and financial measures is analysed by Oxley (1995a). He forwards a framework revolving around issues of 'production', 'distribution', 'pricing', 'financing', 'subsidy' and 'profit'. Whilst some of these questions are pertinent to a discussion of the housing stock, issues such as the 'pricing of rents', 'public or private expenditure', 'nature of subsidy' and 'extent of profit' are also very significant for new housing production.

Formal definitions of social housing are given by Emms (1990) and Harloe (1988). Emms suggests 'social' housing to be:

> Housing whose construction and in consequence rents are subsidised from public funds (Emms 1990).

Harloe (1988) suggests that 'social housing' can be differentiated from other forms of housing in three major respects:

1) It is provided by landlords at a price which is not principally determined by considerations of profit.
2) It is administratively allocated according to some concept of need.
3) Political decision making has an important influence on the quantity, quality and terms of provision.

There is some common understanding in these two approaches, at least in the sense that state financial support has a significantly defining role in social housing production. Beyond this, however, the two attempts to define social housing leave open a number of questions, particularly in the comparative context. Here, great care needs to be exercised in ensuring that social housing is compared between 'non-profit' organisations. Furthermore, it should not be overlooked that other sectors of housing supply, including market and private sectors, can also benefit from state support through tax subsidies to consumers as well as by virtue of a government's stance on land and planning policy. Hence the distinctions between 'social' and 'private' sectors of housing supply are potentially greyer than might first be thought. It is easy to become swamped in a morass of definition problems. However, there is encouragement from some quarters. Duncan and Barlow, (1988, p.226), for example, have suggested that housing researchers might develop 'more adequate concepts' where problems of comparative analysis occur.

Establishing a framework

One way of establishing a comparative framework for the private and social sectors, is to examine how suppliers of new housing are related to their modes of financial support and the tenure of housing.

Figure 5.4 sets out the links between housing suppliers, financial support and tenure in the United Kingdom. These linkages are arguably more simple than in the case of the Netherlands or Germany (Figures 5.5 and 5.6). There are mainly two channels of housing supply (B.M.Bau, 1993, p.136): production by housing associations and local authorities for the social rented sector; and production by the speculative private house building industry for the owner-occupied market.

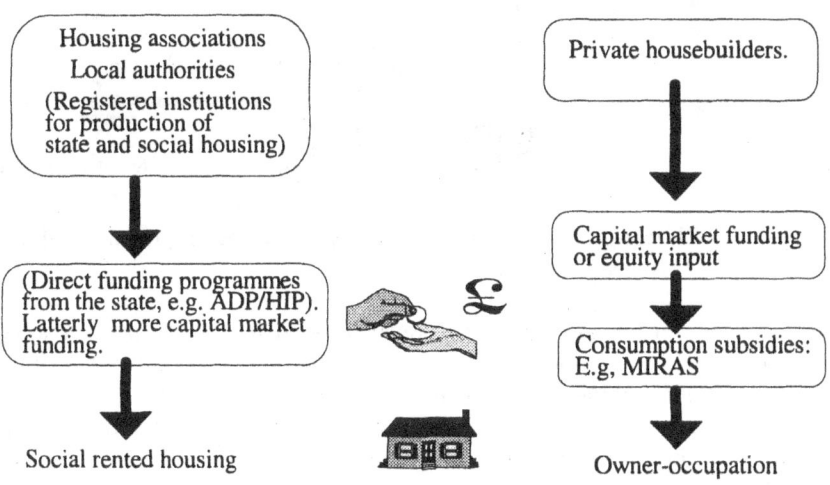

Figure 5.4   **Housing suppliers, housing finance and housing tenure in the United Kingdom**

The system in the United Kingdom is most remarkable in the comparative context for its lack of private rented housing supply. Housing associations and local authorities produce the bulk of rented housing. This has traditionally been considered 'social' in nature due to the significant amount of public funding: through Housing Investment Programmes (HIP) or Approved Development Programmes (ADP). However, (Figure 5.4), funding of social housing since the 1988 Housing Act, has relied much more upon the capital market. The private sector, is characterised by volume house builders operating speculatively. These firms build housing for owner occupation, largely in the absence of construction or object subsidies.

Figure 5.5 outlines the relationships between suppliers, means of finance and tenure in the Netherlands.

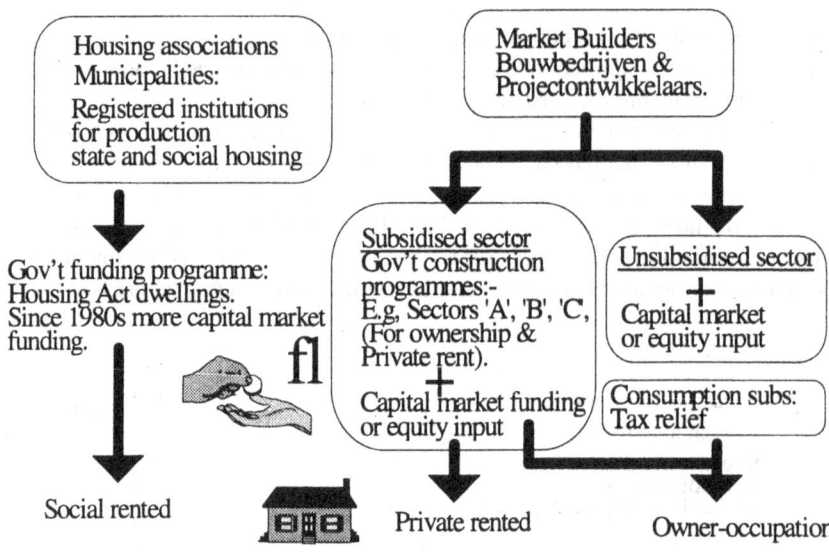

Figure 5.5 Housing suppliers, housing finance and housing tenure in the Netherlands

Although there are similarities to be drawn between the Dutch and UK systems (B.M.Bau, 1993, p.136), the linkages between supplier, financial support and tenure are arguably more complex in the Netherlands (Figure 5.5). This is particularly the case in the market or private sector. The social sector is provided for, mainly by housing associations (Figure 5.5).

In the market sector, there are the two main sources of housing supply, namely 'subsidised' and 'unsubsidised' (Figure 5.5). This refers to supply-side subsidies. Housing is subsidised through under various government programmes which support the construction of both housing for ownership and for private renting (Figure 5.5). Housing is also produced without subsidy for owner-occupation by market builders, although there is subsidy available to the occupier in the form of tax reliefs.

Figure 5.6 shows the more varied picture of housing supply in Germany. Due to the many possible modes of supply, *common routes* of producing new housing, as well as *possible routes* are suggested (Figure 5.6). 'Common' and 'possible' sources of supply are defined by reference to relative volumes of production as well as by commentary from authorities on the German housing system.

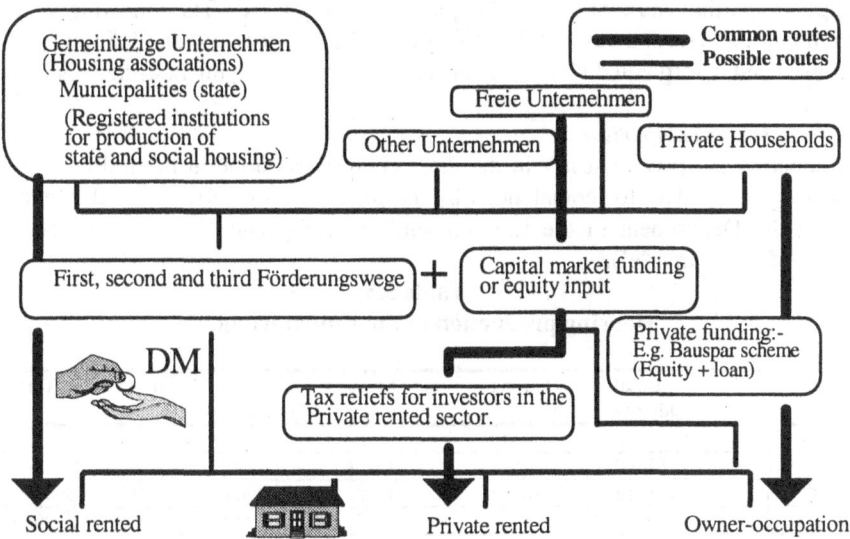

Figure 5.6 Housing suppliers, housing finance and housing tenure in Germany

Common routes of supplying housing are considered first. Of these, supply by the Gemeinützige Unternehmen via the government construction (Förderung) programmes is one of the most important. This is production by institutions with a registered interest in social housing and hence results in what might be termed 'social rented housing'. Another common route is housing supplied via the Freie Unternehmen. This is mainly private rented housing, often for institutional investors, or individuals with high incomes (Ulbrich, 1991, p.278). The motivation of this sector is largely related to profit (ibid) and hence its output in the comparative context is perhaps best termed 'private rented'. Another important source of housing supply is via private households for owner-occupation. The main method of financing is by a mortgage, although housing production via this route may also attract income tax relief over a limited period (B.M.Bau, 1993, p.133).

In addition, there are other *possible* routes for supplying housing. Private households for example, can take advantage of the flexibilities within the system to supply housing for a number of different tenures across the private and rented sectors: for owner-occupation, for investment and for social housing purposes. In the same way, the various Unternehmen sectors can produce housing for both the 'private' as well as the social housing rented sector.

Towards a comparative framework for analysing housing production

Figures 5.4, 5.5 and 5.6 are used as a framework for comparing private and social sectors. The way in which housing suppliers are related to the means of financial support and the tenure of housing supplied is the key issue. The following sections highlight the data sources and the main trends. In Sections 5.4 and 5.5, this data is utilised and incorporated in models and assumptions underlying housing supply.

Private sector comparison

Comparing the private sector in the three countries is done in the following way. First, by using data for completions by the private sector in the United Kingdom, using the Department of the Environment's Housing and Construction Statistics (Table 5.5, column 'e').

Table 5.5
Housing production in the United Kingdom

Year	Local Authority	Housing Assoc'ns	New Towns	Gov't Depart's	Private Sector	Total
	(a)	(b)	(c)	(d)	(e)	(f)
1970	163790	8511	13136	2447	174342	362226
1971	141512	10703	13382	2565	196313	364475
1972	110559	7780	9872	1970	200755	330936
1973	93816	8981	8788	1972	191080	304637
1974	108691	9968	12236	3420	145177	279492
1975	134768	14748	15758	2134	154528	321936
1976	135720	15770	16104	1946	155299	324839
1977	127320	25127	15930	1811	143905	314093
1978	101877	22779	10463	1318	142166	278603
1979	79009	18066	9746	1210	144055	252086
1980	79504	21422	8470	616	131974	241986
1981	57726	19479	10324	517	118579	206625
1982	36058	13532	3902	349	129022	182863
1983	36877	16777	2044	297	153038	209033
1984	35287	17308	2130	230	165606	220561
1985	29348	13734	985	119	163470	207656
1986	24128	13068	943	346	177647	216132
1987	20573	13117	542	738	191187	226157
1988	20714	13479	420	322	206996	241931
1989	18160	14598	467	696	187504	221425
1990	16908	17221	720	226	165197	200272
1991	10598	20500	550	77	156859	188584
1992	5134	25652	276	286	145877	177225
1993	2750	34409	176	42	142152	179527

Source: Department of the Environment, Housing and Construction Statistics

The private sector or market sectors supply housing primarily for owner-occupation, and largely in the absence of supply-side subsidies. The private sector in the United Kingdom is considered under the term 'private enterprise' (D.o.E, p.203), implying a production process involving a degree of initiative taking and speculation.

For the Netherlands, production by market builders is used in the comparison, where owner occupied housing without supply side subsidy is built. Data for this sector is sourced from Dutch Central Bureau of Statistics and is shown in Table 5.6, column 'e', ('Unsub'd').

Table 5.6
Housing production in the Netherlands

Year	State	Hsg Assn	Market Builders			Total
			Private rented	Ownership		
				Subsidised	Unsub'd	
	(a)	(b)	(c)	(d)	(e)	(f)
1970	19136	36993	28942	25698	17295	128064
1971	12214	54135	35328	30917	20235	152829
1972	9886	62494	43904	30325	24588	171197
1973	9042	63505	39818	30946	28883	172194
1974	6205	54608	33747	29896	34274	158730
1975	5188	40683	24231	31013	25400	126515
1976	3327	36213	17984	32080	20329	109933
1977	2856	35682	15856	33362	26514	114270
1978	2850	29339	12842	34233	29520	108784
1979	2578	23822	8148	27812	27966	115607
1980	5319	38154	11087	36049	27739	118348
1981	7340	54536	15812	30124	16844	124656
1982	8056	66256	23620	26020	8081	132033
1983	6419	48793	22368	30230	5918	113728
1984	6269	47463	20904	35116	7479	117231
1985	4658	35074	20210	40493	2832	103267
1986	3112	36969	18892	39624	9044	107641
1987	4866	35783	15861	39857	18512	114879
1988	3959	39500	11319	42250	24680	121708
1989	3786	34813	9741	36685	28831	113856
1990	2870	28952	8949	28632	31315	100718
1991	2733	21575	4732	24033	29815	82888
1992	1752	23312	5542	20976	34582	86164
1993	983	25726	5000	22782	32500	86991

Source: Central Bureau of Statistics, Maandstatistiek Bouwnijverheid

All data is sourced directly from the Central Bureau of Statistics' publication Maandstatistiek Bouwnijverheid (CBS). One point to note is that production of unsubsidised housing for ownership by market builders for the years 1984 to 1987 has been calculated by deducting production figures for 'Sector C' housing (with 'one off grants'), which relates in the private rented, as well as the owner-occupied sector (Boelhouwer and Van der Heijden, 1992). Data on ownership housing for these years does not directly distinguish between housing with 'one-off' grant status and unsubsidised production.

The private sector is now considered in Germany. Here, the comparative framework requires some scrutiny. The approach is by isolating production output from 'private households', which cannot be classified as being either 'social ownership' or 'social rented' production. Table 5.7 shows how the private household sector is divided into three sub-sectors. The column 'g' provides the data which is most comparative with the other two countries. The commentary following Table 5.7 explains how this, and other columns of data are sourced and calculated. It will be noted that more sources of data are required than for the other two countries.

Table 5.7
Housing production in Germany

Year	State	GMN Unt'n	Other Unt'n	Freie Unt'n	Private households			Total
					Social Owner ('Priv H/H 2')	Social rented ('Priv H/H 3')	'Neither' ('Priv H/H 1')	
	(a)	(b)	(c)	(d)	(e)	(f)	(g)	(h)
1970	9560	90820	33460	57360	67469	21631	197700	478000
1971	11100	99900	44400	72150	99333	23517	204600	555000
1972	13220	125590	59490	85930	83629	20111	273030	661000
1973	14280	129019	64760	10710	67412	12598	318830	714000
1974	18120	102680	42280	96640	83722	14198	246360	604000
1975	13110	65560	26210	61180	74721	13059	183160	437000
1976	15680	50960	23520	43120	71690	11390	175640	392000
1977	8180	53170	28630	53170	58704	7966	199180	409000
1978	3680	36800	22080	51520	70065	10935	172920	368000
1979	3580	32200	21500	50120	60386	9374	180840	358000
1980	1536	38900	27250	66130	54475	9545	191164	389000
1981	1095	36876	19334	76650	47895	10695	172455	365000
1982	1380	38170	17358	71482	41800	13200	163610	347000
1983	2387	35464	17050	73315	51137	11263	150384	341000
1984	1990	39800	19502	95520	41600	8000	191588	398000
1985	2184	28080	15600	74880	38474	6376	146406	312000
1986	1764	22680	10080	55440	33779	3661	124596	252000
1987	1519	18128	6510	50995	27769	2161	109918	217000
1988	1045	15675	8360	52459	25373	2317	103771	209000
1989	1195	16730	8365	62140	34320	6630	109620	239000
1990	2048	21248	8192	66560	41023	11757	105172	256000
1991	3938	29295	10080	80797	41022	11178	138690	315000
1992	4950	41245	13500	103800	39454	11876	160175	375000
1993	4320	51840	15120	114400	54883	15917	175440	432000

Source: Statistiches Bundesamt, B.M.Bau

Columns: method of sourcing and calculation:

'a': completions by the state, which is essentially production by municipalities. The data used is the percentage of all annual housing completions: for 1970-1988 (Ulbrich, 1991, p.279) and for 1989 - 1993, from BDZ (1993).

'b': completions by Gemeinützige Unternehmen. The data used is the percentage of all annual housing completions: for 1970-1988 (Ulbrich, 1991, p.279) and for 1989 - 1993, from BDZ (1993, p.62).

'c': completions by 'Other' Unternehmen. The data used is the percentage of all annual housing completions: for 1970-1988 (Ulbrich, 1991, p.279) and for 1989 - 1993, from BDZ (1993, p.62).

'd': completions by Freie Unternehmen. The data used is the percentage of all annual housing completions: for 1970-1988 (Ulbrich, 1991, p.279) and for 1989 - 1993, from BDZ (1993).

(For 'a' to 'd', all data on housing completions are calculated by using the percentages, based upon total levels of housing production in 'h').

'e': completions by private households in the 'social owner occupation sector'. This is achieved by taking the following two steps:

First, calculating the total number of completions by private households in the social sector. This is achieved by taking data for total 'social housing production' (B.M.Bau, 1994, p.66) and multiplying this by the percentages of completions by private households in the whole of the social sector (ibid).

Second, taking data from column 'f', below ('completions in the social rented sector by private households'). This is then subtracted from total production by private households in the social sector to give the number of completions by private households in the social ownership sector.

'f': completions by Private households in the 'social rented' sector. This is achieved by taking the following two steps:

First, calculating the total completions in the 'social rented sector' (B.M.Bau, 1994, p.66) and multiplying this data by the percentage of all social sector production produced for rent (ibid, p.65). This provides completions of rented housing in the social sector.

Second, by using data (Ulbrich, 1991, p.285) for the 'percentage of completions in the social rented sector by private households'. This then provides data for completions by private households in the social rented sector. These completions are shown in column 'f', (Table 5.7)

'g': completions by private households which can neither be said to be 'social rented', nor 'social' ownership'. This data set is achieved first by taking the total housing completions in Germany (column 'h', Table 5.7) and multiplying this by the percentage of total completions by private households (Ulbrich, 1991, p.62). To achieve the data set in column 'g' of Table 5.7, it is necessary to deduct from total production by private households, the addition of columns 'e' and 'f'. Doing this results in housing supply of private households which can be said to be neither 'social', nor 'rented'. This form of supply is shown in column 'g'(Table 5.7).

'h': total production completions. These are taken from the Bautätigkeitstatistik in the Haus und Wohnung publication of German housing ministry (B.M.Bau, 1994, p.44).

Social sector comparison
In order to define a 'social' sector which is comparable for the three countries, Figures 5.4, 5.5 and 5.6 should be re-visited. From these diagrams, links can be made between local authorities, housing associations, government subsidy programmes and the tenure of social rented housing. To make sense of these linkages, however, other research findings should assist. In particular, the discussion of the social sector should refer to the broader framework provided by Emms, Harloe and Oxley (Emms, 1990; Harloe 1988; Oxley 1995). Taken together, the 'social sector' is to do with notions of 'subsidy from public funds' (Emms 1990), 'non-profit', 'need', importance of 'political decision-making' (Harloe 1988), 'profit', and 'pricing' (Oxley, 1995). 'Social' sectors can be considered and compared according to this criteria.

On this basis, the Gemeinützige Unternehmen in Germany might best be selected to represent the social sector in Germany. These are non-profit making organisations who provide housing on the basis of social need (NWR, 1995; Ulbrich, 1991, p.278). They are also registered institutions for the production of social housing (Boelhouwer and Van der Heijden, 1992, p.116). Data for housing output by this sector is given in Table 5.7 (GMN Unt'n).

For the United Kingdom and the Netherlands, housing output by housing associations fits best perhaps the perception of social housing. Although since the early 1990s, these organisations have come to rely more on private finance for housing supply, their historic raison d'être lies in substantial levels of state support for capital expenditure programmes.

There is also however a case to be made for adding municipal or local authority housing output to that of housing associations. The importance of this sector varies considerably by country and over time. Although there are significant differences in the volume of output, supply of state housing is suggested to be worthy of inclusion. In the United Kingdom, for example, local authorities played a significant role in the 1970s, and looking simply at housing associations does not provide a representative picture of social housing supply over time. In Germany municipal housing is supplied on the basis of need (Ulbrich, 1991, p.278), and in the Netherlands it is supplied on a non-profit basis. (Boelhouwer and Van der Heijden 1992, p.48). In the comparative context, therefore, this is essentially, social housing.

5.4 Private sector housing supply and its relationship with profit

Thesis, rationale and model

In this section there is an investigation of the relationship between levels of housing output in the private sector, and profit. The underlying assumption is that changes in the level of 'profit' will determine changes in the levels of house building in the private sector. This expectation can be derived from microeconomic supply frameworks, although the assumption is more specifically identifiable in the housing field in the work of Ambrose and Barlow (1987, p.111), who have argued:

> that in most countries three factors are important in influencing the level of new house building: (1) direct capital investment by the state for public housing; (2) state support for production and consumption; and (3) changes in the profitability of house building within the private sector.

The term 'profitability' can therefore be used as a premise for explaining the level of house building in the private sector. Profitability, however, can be measured in several ways. It would be possible, for example, to take the profit and loss accounts of house building companies and correlate these figures in some way with house building levels of those companies. Alternatively the financial market position of a development or building firm may give an indication of its profitability. That is to say, the stock markets' valuation of a company. In some countries, particular approaches will work better in practice than others, although to manage a comparative analysis it will be helpful to begin by assuming a similar production function for all countries.

The approach adopted in this section to 'profitability' is a simple one. It relies on three variables, namely house prices, land prices and building costs. Data sets for these three variables can be combined to construct a simple model:

$\pi = HP - [LP+BC]$, where:

π = Profit.
HP = House prices.
LP = Land prices.
BC = Building costs.

This model can be linked to the assumptions of demand and supply in neo-classical economics, whereby supply of a commodity increases and decreases in line with increases and decreases in the price of that commodity (Begg et al, 1989, p.44). Translating this theoretical assumption to the relationship between housing supply in the private sector and levels of profit, it may be expected that as profit increases and decreases, housing supply will respond in an elastic way.

All other things being equal, it is possible that housing can be supplied in unlimited quantities, where profit levels are also unlimited. Equally, where profit is nil, housing output may also be nil. In practice, however, there are a number of factors which affect the assumptions of the model and which it is useful to outline before an analysis of the results is carried out.

Context and application of the framework
There is a likelihood that levels of housing production in any particular sector will be linked to the overall level of output. It is difficult to ignore this issue where demographic trends are seen to provide a lead in determining total housing output. New housing output will be linked to the total need or demand, however one views the particular roles of individual sectors of supply. There will be a ceiling at some point created by demographics trends and the stance taken by governments on housing renewal and levels of demolition. Governments may prioritise particular sectors of housing supply according to prevailing economic conditions (and particular sectors will find themselves residualised to a greater or lesser extent over time), although in the final analysis, there must be a broadly sufficient number of houses to meet household demand.

The assumption that private sector housing output will be based on changing levels of profitability as described in the framework above, makes it implicit that output will be influenced in the same way by the same combination of variables in each of the three countries. However, there is potentially some inequivalence in the significance of the particular variables (HP, LP and BC) within the framework as it applies across the three countries. The fact that there is state ownership of development land in the Netherlands, may mean, for example, that house prices alone influence output more than levels of 'profit'. On the same basis in Germany, output may be more influenced more by individual (consumer) decision making. In the United Kingdom, perhaps land prices are a better indicator of output. Other outcomes and influences are possible. The possibility that the production functions are different in each country, is real. However, to discover the extent to which there are different leading indicators it is helpful to start from common ground and this is the method which is followed.

The measurement of output: by absolute numbers or by percentages?
The different economic theories explaining output as well as the practical differences in state and market roles, determine that we should look carefully at the way housing output is measured. This can be done in two ways. The first way is to use absolute data. The second way is to measure output by sector, as a percentage of total housing production.

Finding specific reasons for using one method in preference to the other, is a difficult task. There are arguments for and against both methods, which apply equally whether the private or social sector is being measured. It might be assumed that housing output should be measured in absolute terms because individual sectors of supply are wholly independent of each other. On the other hand, it might be argued that one needs to look at output from individual sector in the context of all housing output on the premise that the proportionate measure of output gives a better indication of the connections between macroeconomy, government policy and the different housing suppliers.

Neither of these measures should be used to the exclusion of the other. The use of both measures provides a check as well as point of reference for conclusions about the role of government and market in each of the countries. In noting the correlation coefficients using both measures it may be instructive to note the consistencies and inconsistencies and this will be a focus of Section 5.4.

Data sources: house prices, land prices and building costs

This section provides data on house prices, land prices and building costs. The purpose of the section is to show which sources have been used, and how the data is collated for comparative analysis. The aim is to collate sufficient and consistent data to allow for a comparison between housing output within the framework described in the previous section. A further aim will be to present house prices, land prices and building costs per individual dwelling.

Consumer price indices
Consumer price indices are used to calculate real house prices as well as land and building costs in real terms. The indices are sourced from the United Nations Annual Bulletin of Housing and Construction Statistics (United Nations). Real values are calculated, based around an index of 100 for the year 1970. Nominal data for house prices, land prices and building costs are devalued in accordance with the indices.

The use of a deflator such as consumer prices can help to achieve greater stationarity in the data sets. Without some form of deflator, there is always the possibility that conclusions will be based simply on levels of inflation and not on the empirical relationships themselves.

Data sources for comparing house prices
Table 5.8 provides data for nominal and real house prices for the three countries. The sources and the method of compilation is given thereafter.

Table 5.8
Nominal and real house prices in the United Kingdom, the Netherlands and Germany

Year	Nominal house prices U.K (£)	Real house prices UK (£)	Nominal house prices NL (Hfl)	Real house prices NL (Hfl)	Nominal house prices G (DM)	Real house prices G (DM)
1970	4974	4974	76884	76884	138421	138421
1971	5632	5166	78346	73220	144836	137939
1972	7373	6301	84194	72581	170555	153653
1973	9941	7827	89354	71483	195789	164529
1974	10989	7425	98126	71624	202142	159167
1975	11786	6371	102598	67945	222000	164444
1976	12703	5881	131838	80389	216250	153369
1977	13649	5459	184126	105819	221745	150847
1978	15593	5733	198746	109805	220483	146989
1979	19924	6511	187222	99586	250370	159472
1980	23593	6609	171054	85527	272666	165253
1981	24187	6107	153424	72030	304558	174033
1982	25553	6012	138030	61600	321818	175857
1983	28592	6368	142072	62312	318793	168673
1984	30811	6560	139578	59648	308214	160528
1985	33187	6788	140094	58863	287241	145808
1986	38187	7659	146974	61754	291515	149495
1987	44220	8488	153930	65229	284428	145861
1988	54280	10222	160092	68416	289955	147185
1989	62135	10908	171570	72699	324102	162051
1990	66745	10888	174494	72105	360395	176664
1991	66825	10409	180400	71588	365369	173985
1992	63425	9595	194800	72417	393357	182109
1993	66158	9772	212400	74001	416309	185852

Sources: See Table 5.11

House prices in the United Kingdom
House prices are sourced from the Department of the Environments' Housing and Construction Statistics publication (D.o.E). The data represents the 'average price of all housing in the housing market'.

House prices in the Netherlands
House prices in the Netherlands are sourced from the Nederlandse Vereiniging van Makelaars (NVM), which is the Dutch umbrella organisation of Makelaars. The data represents the price of housing in the existing housing market and is published in Intern (NVM), a journal which provides data on house prices on an annual basis.

House prices in Germany
These are taken from the Ring Deutscher Maklers (RDM), who are also an umbrella organisation representing German Maklers. Data is published in the

Immobilienpreispeigel and represents the average price of detached owner-occupier housing. The data is representative of house prices across 45 'large cities under 500,000 inhabitants' and other 'middle sized cities'.

Data sources for comparing land prices

Table 5.9 provides data for nominal and real land prices for the three countries. The sources and the method of compilation is given thereafter.

Table 5.9
Nominal and real land plot prices in the United Kingdom, the Netherlands and Germany

Year	Nominal land prices U.K (£)	Real land prices UK (£)	Nominal land prices NL (Hfl)	Real land prices NL (Hfl)	Nominal land prices G (DM)	Real land prices G (DM)
1970	1228	1228	8190	8190	44464	44464
1971	1347	1236	9442	8824	48862	46535
1972	2102	1797	9485	8176	52928	47683
1973	2866	2257	11501	9200	61000	51765
1974	2987	2019	12265	8953	52750	14535
1975	2305	1246	14068	9317	53400	39555
1976	2338	1082	15617	9522	53857	38197
1977	2760	1104	17039	9793	57611	39192
1978	3600	1324	19288	10656	65142	43428
1979	4403	1439	23596	12551	77181	49160
1980	6475	1814	24381	12190	100173	60711
1981	7015	1772	26673	12522	101640	58080
1982	7740	1821	27204	12145	116172	63482
1983	8331	1855	35169	15425	127038	67216
1984	8788	1881	31878	13623	119000	61980
1985	12056	2466	35958	15109	111230	56462
1986	16583	3323	38916	16351	115551	59256
1987	21613	4148	37629	15945	104806	53747
1988	26346	4962	35645	15232	113742	57737
1989	27483	4822	42732	18107	122230	61115
1990	28602	4665	45993	19005	131571	64495
1991	23105	3599	46239	18349	138717	66056
1992	19134	2895	47852	17789	148097	68564
1993	17943	2651	51254	17859	157469	70298

Sources: See Table 5.11

The comparison of land prices between countries relies heavily on finding similar stages in the housing development process at which data is available. As has been discussed in previous chapters the development process varies considerably between countries. Government ministries and other agencies retain data according to the particular stages in the process which appear to be most relevant. For the United Kingdom, there are two stages at which consistent data sets are available. The first being for the price of agricultural land and the latter being for the price of land purchased by developers and builders for building. In the Netherlands, data on land prices is more comprehensive. The Housing Ministry provides data for price of land *sold to* municipalities as well the price of land *sold by* municipalities (MVROM, 1991c). Land prices are also classified according to the sector to which land is sold, by municipalities. For example, the social sector, where data is very detailed, or the market sector, which is used for this particular investigation. Prices of land in Germany are also detailed, although the level of detail relates to stages in the development process, rather than to sector of housing supply. In Germany, there are data sets provided by the government on the price of agricultural land, of Rohbauland (land zoned in the Flächenützungsplan), and also for Baureifesland which is building 'ready' land.

Towards a comparison of land prices

An objective of comparison will be to find a common 'stage' in the development process at which land prices can be compared. This is achieved in the Dutch and German cases in the following way: 'land sold by municipalities' in the Netherlands is sold in a serviced state and in Germany this situation is represented in Baureifes land. For the United Kingdom, however, land purchased by developers does not have infrastructure provision. This is a potential comparative problem which is recognised in B.M.Bau (1993, p.XXXIV).

To make the data sets more relevant for comparison, it is necessary to look at further research. In this respect, Conran Roche (1989) has been considered. Conran Roche has calculated that infrastructure costs add on average '45%' to land costs as they are discussed in the national statistics. This adjustment has been incorporated to the data sets in Table 5.9.

Land prices in the United Kingdom

Land prices are sourced from the Department of the Environments' Housing and Construction Statistics. The data relates to 'private sector purchase of sites for residential use with four or more plots where the value of the area of the sites are known' (D.o.E)

Plot prices are arrived at in Table 5.9 by taking the 'simple average price (of land) per hectare' and dividing it by the 'mean density' (of plots) for the given years. Plot sizes are of around $400m^2$.

Land prices in the Netherlands

Prices of land in the Netherlands are quoted per plot and per sector. In the market sector, plot prices for detached dwellings are available for the years 1982 onwards (MVROM, 1991). Prior to this, plot prices in the market sector have been calculated in accordance with the index of land prices in that sector (Klaren and Verpalen, 1989, p.69). The Dutch Housing Ministry report (MVROM, 1991c) shows plot size in the market sector (years 1982-1992) to average around $280m^2$, smaller than plots in the United Kingdom and Germany.

Land prices in Germany
German land prices are taken from the Ring Deutscher Maklers Immobilienpreispiegel (RDM). Land prices are for 'detached single and two family dwellings in an average location'. The data used considers 45 'large cities under 500,000 inhabitants' and other 'middle sized cities'. There is hence consistency with the sourcing of house prices. Prices in Table 5.9 are based upon plot sizes of 600m^2, a figure derived in combination with other research findings (B.M.Bau, 1993, p.198).

Data sources for comparing building costs
Table 5.10 provides data for nominal and real building costs for the three countries. The sources and the method of compilation is given thereafter.

Table 5.10
Nominal and real building costs per dwelling in the United Kingdom, the Netherlands and Germany

Year	Nominal building costs UK (£)	Real building costs UK (£)	Nominal building costs NL (Hfl)	Real building costs NL (Hfl)	Nominal building costs prices G (DM)	Real building costs G (DM)
1970	3079	3029	45619	45619	93348	98348
1971	3260	2990	51467	48100	106900	10189
1972	3442	2941	56146	48402	121500	109459
1973	3985	3137	63165	50508	136500	114706
1974	4936	3335	71353	52083	152300	119921
1975	6114	3304	77201	51127	157200	116444
1976	7155	3312	83050	50641	162500	115249
1977	8242	3297	91238	54436	169800	115510
1978	9258	3404	100596	55578	180100	120066
1979	10462	3418	109954	58487	198800	126624
1980	12545	3514	118142	59071	215200	130424
1981	13094	3511	121651	57113	235800	134743
1982	15126	3559	119311	53264	252900	138197
1983	16123	3591	118142	51817	255100	134974
1984	17119	3665	118422	50608	247100	128698
1985	18116	3707	116972	49148	247800	125787
1986	19021	3811	119311	50131	249400	127787
1987	19746	3791	123990	52539	258100	132356
1988	20883	3933	127500	54487	261700	132843
1989	22645	3973	129839	55016	271300	135650
1990	24094	3931	121907	50375	280900	137697
1991	25362	3951	136857	54309	298700	142239
1992	26086	3947	140374	52184	319900	148102
1993	27173	4014	144079	50302	336900	150402

Sources: See Table 5.11

Detailed data sets on house building costs are not readily identifiable. The use of building costs relies therefore also on indices which allow trends to be plotted over time. These trends can be used in combination with a reference to building costs at a given point in time.

'Building costs', however can account for a number of things. How comparable they are depends upon the basis upon which they are compiled. 'Costs' can be categorised by a number of operations. Most importantly these are 'site works, shell and finish', 'heating, ventilation and plumbing', 'electricity' and 'professional fees' (Contract Journal, 1994:12). The data sets used for the three countries have been scrutinised to ensure they include these major cost elements.

Building costs in the United Kingdom
Building costs in the United Kingdom are available from the Building Cost Information Service of the Royal Institution of Chartered Surveyors (RICS). This provides typical costs for the construction of housing. It also provides an index which has been used to calculate costs over time.

The source used in Table 5.10 is the cost of building a typical 'Estate' type house of size range $75m^2$ to $100m^2$. The building cost within this size category, when 1992 is used as a base year, is £ 282-00/m^2. The data set has been calculated by using the BCIS index applied to the base year of 1992.

Building costs in the Netherlands
Building costs in the Netherlands are provided in the publication Maandstatistiek Bouwnijverheid (CBS). Costs are provided for selected years and for selected forms of housing. These forms of housing are classified according to methods of subsidy rather than by the market or social sector.

The sector on which building costs are based is the 'non-subsidised'. The base year is 1988 and costs are quoted for the dwelling. The cost of a dwelling in 1988 in this sector was Hfl 127,500 (CBS). This reference point is used in conjunction with the general building cost index in Maandstatistiek Bouwnijverheid (CBS).

Building costs in Germany
Data sets for building costs are published by the German Housing and Planning Ministry (B.M.Bau, 1994, p.58). These are classified by Einfamilienhäuser (single family dwellings) and Mehrfamilienhäuser (dwellings for many families).

For the comparison, the data on the single family dwellings is used. This is then consistent with the classifications on house prices and land prices. There is no need to index the data as this is provided in absolute numbers for each year.

Summary of sources for house prices, land prices and building costs
Table 5.11 provides a summary of data, information and issues relating to house prices, land prices and building costs.

Table 5.11
House prices, land prices and building costs: data sources and definitions

Country	House Prices	Land Prices	Building Costs
UK	• Price of all housing in the housing market (Department of the Environment).	• Plot prices in the private sector, (Department of the Environment). • Addition for infrastructure provision (Conran Roche 1989) • Plot size c 400m².	• Average costs 'Estate type' housing (Royal Institution of Chartered Surveyors). • BCIS Index.
NL	• Price of housing in the existing housing market (Nederlandse Vereiniging van Makelaars).	• Serviced plots sold by municipalities to house builders in market sector.(VROM, Klaren & Verpalen). • Plot size c 280m².	• Building costs of non-subsidised housing (CBS, Maandstatistiek Bouwnijverheid). • Building cost index.
G	• Price of detached owner occupied houses in existing market (Ring Deutscher Maklers - RDM).	• Building plots for detached single and two family houses (RDM). • Baureifes ('building - ready' land). • Plot size c 600m².	• Average building costs for single family houses (B.M.Bau).

Comparing 'profit data' for private sector housing suppliers
The ability to draw conclusions in this part of the investigation is based upon the relationship between the private sector, as defined in Section 5.3, and 'profit'. The assumptions were explained in Section 5.4.1, 'Thesis and rationale'. 'Profit' is based upon the three variables house prices, land prices and building costs. The comparative issue is how closely are these variables related to the particular sectors of private housing supply.

For the United Kingdom, the possibility to tie private sector supply precisely with a specific set of house and land prices and building costs is not readily available. However, the significant influence of the private sector generally in the UK might suggest that trends in the variables affecting profit might substantially impact on the development process of private house building firms.

Elsewhere, it is possible to be more specific in linking the mode of supply with data on house, land and building costs. In the Netherlands, for example, it is possible to reconcile the market builder sector with land prices in the market sector. This is made possible through data sets provided by the Central Bureau of Statistics and the Housing Ministry. Building costs are also related to the way housing is financed, where the classification selected is 'non-subsidised'. This selection is reconciled with production by market builders supplying housing which is unsubsidised.

In Germany land prices and building costs are selected for single or two family homes. The link between this form of housing and the sector supplying it, namely private households can be established in the following:

> above all private households build single and two family houses. Their share (in this form of housing) is around 80%...indeed over time this (volume) has only altered marginally (Ulbrich, 1991:282).

Outcomes: private sector output and profit

Figures 5.7, 5.9 and 5.11 show the relationship between private sector production and profit, where output is expressed in absolute terms (see Section 5.4.1). Figures 5.8, 5.10 and 5.12 show the relationship between private sector production and profit, where output is expressed as a percentage of total production. In contrast to the relationships between total housing production and total housing need, as examined in Section 5.2, there is less commonality in so far as the private sector is concerned. Whereas similarities could be observed across the three countries in the previous focus, the relationships between private sector output and levels of profit (house prices, land prices and building costs), are very different in each of the three countries; a conclusion which holds for both (absolute and percentage) measures of private sector housing output. The specific country trends and relationships are now discussed.

The United Kingdom
Data on housing production in the private sector is derived from Table 5.5, column 'e' (Section 5.3.3) The data representing 'profit' is derived by utilising the data sets on house prices, land prices and building costs (Tables 5.8, 5.9 and 5.10) within the simple formula shown in Section 5.4.

For the United Kingdom, a coefficient of -0.058 results where data for private sector output and 'profit' is correlated. This conclusion is based on expressing the data for output in its absolute form. The time series are provided in Figure 5.7 for the period 1970 to 1993.

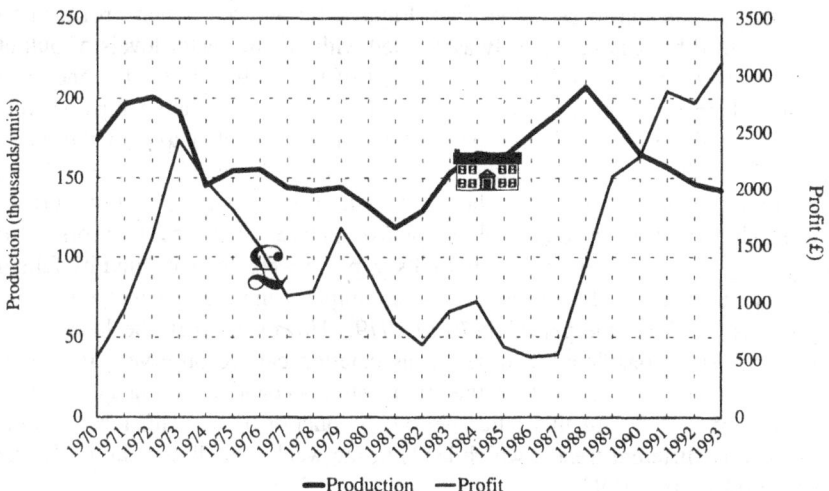

Source: D.o.E Housing and Construction Statistics; RICS Building Cost Information Services

Figure 5.7 Private sector housing production and profit in the United Kingdom (production as an absolute measure)

A coefficient of 0.219 results where data for private sector output and 'profit' is correlated (Figure 5.8). This conclusion is based on expressing the data for private sector output as a percentage of all production output (for the period 1970 to 1993).

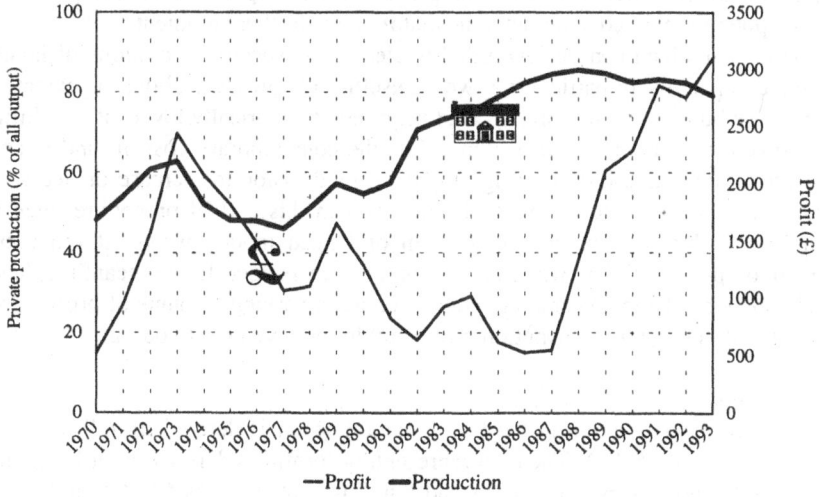

Source: D.o.E Housing and Construction Statistics; RICS Building Cost Information Services

Figure 5.8 Private sector housing production and profit in the United Kingdom (private output as a % of all output)

The general conclusion to be drawn from Figures 5.7 and 5.8 is that profit, in the way it is defined here, is very poorly associated with private sector levels of output. This is however, in so far as the whole period of time (1970-1993) is concerned. Otherwise, there is a clear distinction to be made between the relationships of profit and output in the 1970s and the relationships of profit and output in the 1980s (Figures 5.7 and 5.8). During the 1970s, arguably a period of greater state intervention in planning and land policy, the relationship between profit and private sector production was generally of a positive nature: increases in profit were accompanied by increases in output and falls in profit were accompanied by falls in output. The coefficient of correlation between output using the percentage measure and profit is 0.545 for the period 1970 to 1979. However, when the later period (1980 to 1988) is considered, a different association can be observed; instead of variables rising and falling together, the relationship is negative, giving a correlation co-efficient of -0.313. In this latter period, production rises, whilst profit falls. These are very different trends, which leads to the weak overall correlation for the longer period 1970 to 1993.

There are a number of potential explanations for the change in the basic relationship since the late 1970s. The political change of power at the beginning of the 1980s is an underlying explanation. The relaxation of land and planning policies following the change of government in 1979 appears to have significantly affected the relationship between input and output variables. One variable, namely land prices, is a key in explaining this changing situation. Land prices rose faster in real terms (Table 5.9), than house prices or building costs, meaning that 'profit' was, in real terms 'squeezed' during the 1980s. The effect of this reduction in profit appears however to have little effect on private sector output (Figures 5.7 and 5.8). This is a potentially interesting outcome that requires further comment.

One reason which can be forwarded relates to the specific operations of house building companies. In particular, it would useful to know more about the extent to which house building firms build on land acquired at historically low costs. If firms are involved in long term land banking, then the contemporary cost of land at any given time might have little bearing on the firm's decision to increase or decrease output. If all firms were known to be involved in this sort of procedure, then it might be possible to construct some form of lagged model, where, it might be assumed, output was linked with land prices some years ago. In the meantime, land is traded between large and small operators, creating varying amounts of profit, also potentially affecting the contribution of the builder or developer to output.

The Netherlands

Data on housing production in the Dutch market sector is derived from Table 5.6, column 'e' (Section 5.3.3) The data representing 'profit' is derived by utilising the data sets on house prices, land prices and building costs (Tables 5.8, 5.9 and 5.10) within the simple formula shown in Section 5.4.

For the Dutch market sector, a coefficient of 0.415 results where data on output and 'profit' are correlated. This conclusion is based on expressing the data for output in its absolute form. The time series are provided in Figure 5.9 for the period 1970 to 1993.

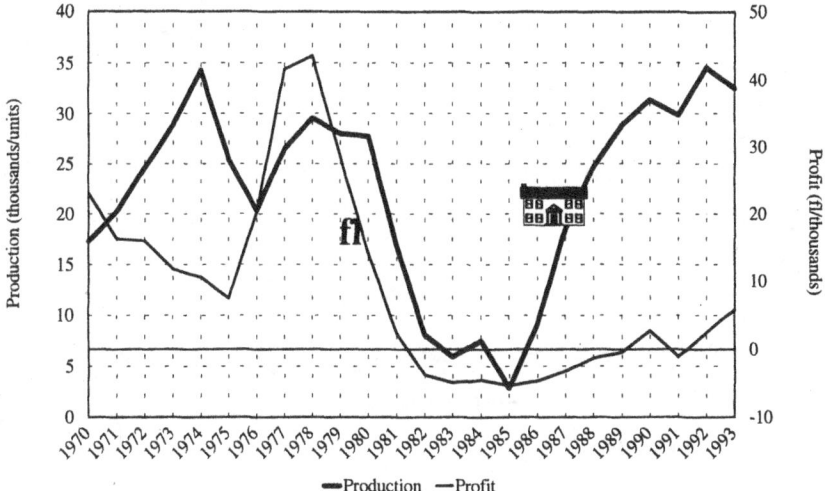

Source: CBS; NVM; VROM

Figure 5.9 Private sector housing production and profit in the Netherlands (production as an absolute measure)

A coefficient of 0.253 results where data for private sector output and 'profit' is correlated (Figure 5.10). This conclusion is based on expressing the data for the market sector output as a percentage of all production output. The time series are provided for the period 1970 to 1993.

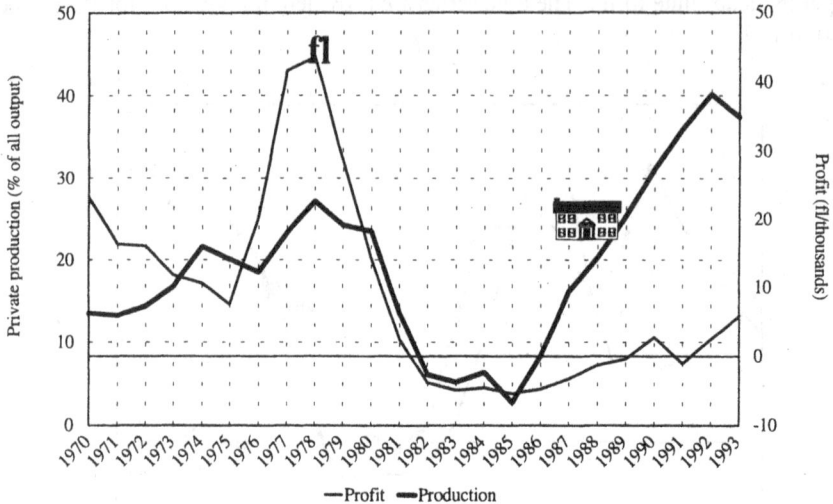

Source: CBS; NVM; VROM

Figure 5.10 Private sector housing production and profit in the Netherlands (private output as a % of all output)

The relationship between private sector output and profit in the Dutch case is stronger than in the United Kingdom. This is particularly the case when considering the absolute production measure (Figure 5.9), (correlation coefficient 0.415), but is also marginally (correlation coefficient 0.253) so, when using the percentage of total production as the dependent variable (Figure 5.10).

Perhaps the first outcome to comment upon is that the association between profit and market sector output in the Netherlands is positive in the case of both absolute and percentage measures (Figures 5.9 and 5.10). Although the associations are not by any means perfect, the graphs show, to a significant extent, that levels of profit and levels of output are associated; as one variable rises, so does the other, whilst the two variables fall together. The best example of this (Figure 5.9) is during the mid 1970s to the mid 1980s; a period of Dutch housing market 'boom and bust'.

The close associations over this period invite a re-examination of the political and economic context. Some reasons which might be offered to explain why changes in levels of profit are associated with changes in private sector output are as follows: the tenure neutral stance of governments, the relatively stable monetary climate, but above all, the land policy stance. In this latter aspect, it is possible that municipal land ownership results in a particular form of land rationing which allocates market housing in response to changing economic situations. This rationing process may be a more appropriate method of developing different forms of housing than exists in other countries, where the private sector is effectively the custodian of development land supply.

Germany

Data on housing production in the private sector is derived from Table 5.7, column 'g' (Section 5.3.3) The data representing 'profit' is derived by utilising the data sets on house prices, land prices and building costs (Tables 5.8, 5.9 and 5.10) within the simple formula shown in Section 5.4.1.

For Germany, a co-efficient of 0.721 results where data for private sector output and 'profit' is correlated. This conclusion is based on expressing the data for output in its absolute form. The time series are provided in Figure 5.11 for the period 1970 to 1993.

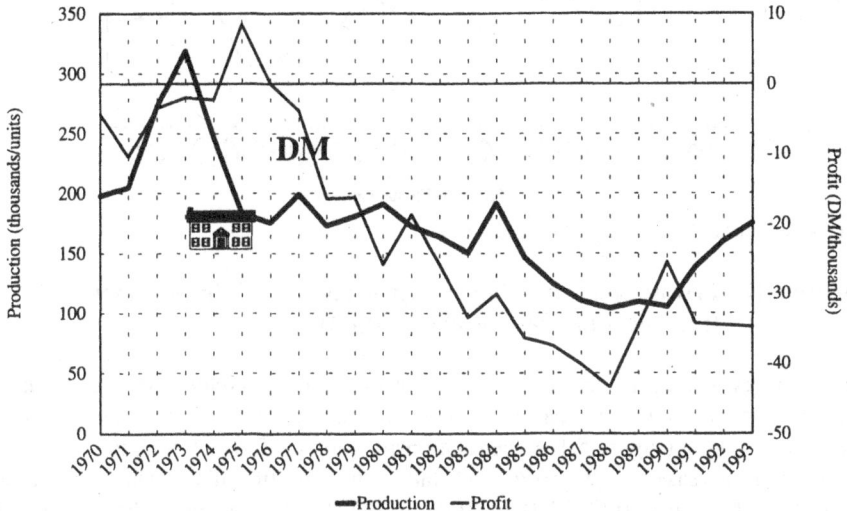

Source: Statistiches Bundesamt; RDM; BMBau

Figure 5.11 Private sector housing production and profit in Germany (production as an absolute measure)

A coefficient of -0.421 results where data for private sector output and 'profit' is correlated (Figure 5.12). This conclusion is based on expressing the data for private sector output as a percentage of all production output. The time series are provided for the period 1970 to 1993.

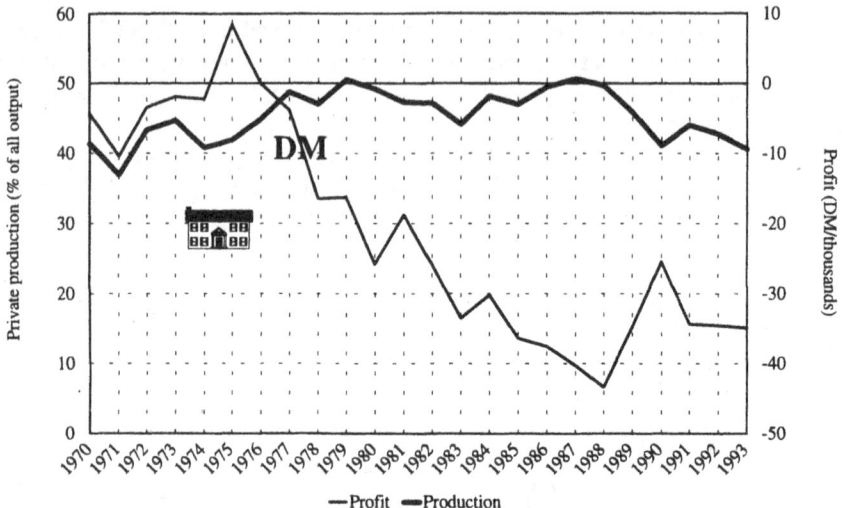

Figure 5.12 Private sector housing production and profit in Germany (private output as a % of all output)

The findings relating to private sector output in Germany, create a strong rationale for using more than one measure of housing output. When using the absolute measure of output (Figure 5.11), the relationship with profit is a strong positive one; production increases with profit, and falls when profit falls. The correlation coefficient for the period 1970 to 1993 is 0.721. When using the alternative percentage measure (Figure 5.12), however, the relationship is not only weaker (correlation coefficient 0.421) but also negative (-0.421); here production falls as profit increases and vice-versa. The two different results lead to different conclusions and it is a question of deciding which 'measure' to reject.

In deciding which might be the correct conclusion, a number of factors are to be considered. It is certainly clear that the high association in Figure 5.11 ('absolute output) must be questioned in the light of overall falling levels of production. That is to say, in the light of factors driving the general decline, of which demographic trends is a key issue. Thus it is important to know more about the links between demographic change and the production function in the German private household sector. If the other measure of production, namely proportionate output (Figure 5.12) is considered, then it is evident that private households as a sector maintain a constant share of overall output throughout times of political and economic change. There are few dramatic fluctuations in output from this sector which is in complete contrast with, for example, the United Kingdom, whose private sector share of total production almost doubled over the same period.

The arguments for drawing conclusions based on utilising the proportion of output as a measure go as follows in the case of private households in Germany: that the mode of housing provision for this sector is very particular and to some extent divorced from the rigours of broader economic change. In particular, the method of providing housing is not so speculative because housing is very often produced in a bespoke way. The system of housing finance for households is also arguably not as sophisticated and sensitive as elsewhere and the demands of the development process mean that housing production is not a reactive process. Rather it is proactive. In aggregate, the decisions of households are decisions about consumption as much as about production leading to the expectation that output will have a significant yet constant contribution to the total annual housing need.

5.5 Social sector housing: the relationship between output, Gross Domestic Product (GDP) and levels of unemployment

Theoretical standpoints

In Section 5.5, production in the social sector is examined in the context of two macroeconomic variables used as identities, or benchmarks, for examining the role played by new social housing supply in each of the three countries. These variables are changes in the levels of unemployment and changes in the level of gross domestic product (GDP). Changes in these two yardsticks can help to shed light on a number of issues to do with the prioritising of social sector production and the relations between social and other sectors of housing supply. Some further justification and explanation is now given.

Unemployment and new social housing supply
One assumption might be that changes in the level of unemployment lead to changes in the level of social housing production. This assertion could be made on the basis that as levels of unemployment rise, so there becomes an increased need for housing which is affordable. It may be assumed that social housing fulfils this particular need better than other forms of (market) housing. As levels of unemployment begin to fall, market forms of housing are demanded in greater quantity than before and thus the need for social housing falls. In a statistical time series investigation, we might expect the relationship to be a broadly positive one, where increases in levels of unemployment are accompanied by increases in social housing output, and vice-versa.

Caution is required however, in considering the nature of unemployment and the potential role of social housing in the economy. In particular, unemployment can take different forms and have a different significance to the economy at particular junctures in time. In terms of the demand for social housing, a different conclusion might be reached depending on the long or short term nature of job shortages. Long term or structural unemployment may demand particular social housing solutions. In the short run, social housing may provide solutions to housing need through the existing stock, rather than through large scale or long term building programmes. Above all, however, we should not lose sight of the possibility that very often, increasing the output of social housing is a response to both supply and demand factors; demand factors, in the form of the necessity to meet housing need; and supply factors, in the form a desire to combat directly levels of unemployment in the house building and construction industry.

GDP and new social housing supply

Another assumption about the social sector might be that levels of output are driven by the level of growth in the macroeconomy. Levels of gross domestic product might perhaps ultimately be used to help identify future trends in social housing output. The effects of increases in GDP might be twofold. An inverse relationship may be predicated on the basis that as the level of real GDP rises, so households devote increasing amounts of resources to forms of housing other than the social sector. Thus levels of social housing fall with increasing levels of economic growth; social housing, as in the previous section can be seen as a 'residual' element in the total picture of housing supply and is only needed when economic growth begins to slow or fall.

Another (opposite) assumption is that social housing output rises with increases in the level of GDP. This assumption might be predicated on the basis that as economies grow, so governments of those economies are increasingly able to devote more resources to the provision of new housing in the social sector. Thus, a positive association between economic growth and social housing output might be expected. As before, a number of cautions should be voiced before looking at the data and correlations.

Mainly, the problem lies in assumptions made about household's marginal benefits or costs. The process of deciding whether to have a dwelling in the social or private sector is not always straightforward. In many cases, the opportunity cost or relative affordability of a particular tenure is the deciding factor, although the question is really what tenure decisions households make, given increased levels of disposable income. The nature of the social sector and the client group it serves is also important in examining the links between output and trends in the macroeconomy. In some countries, the social sector is almost a 'market' or free standing sector, whilst in others there is heavy reliance on government. A clear differentiation of social sectors is needed in the comparative framework.

Data sources

European levels of unemployment

Table 5.12 shows the long run trend in levels of unemployment in the three countries. The source of data is European Economy which is published by the European Commission. The relevant measure used is the number of unemployed persons expressed as a percentage of the civilian labour force.

Table 5.12
Unemployment in the United Kingdom, the Netherlands and Germany

Year	United Kingdom (%)	Netherlands (%)	Germany (%)
1970	2.2	1	0.5
1971	2.7	1.3	0.6
1972	3.1	2.3	0.8
1973	2.2	2.4	0.8
1974	2	2.9	1.8
1975	3.2	5.5	3.3
1976	4.8	5.8	3.3
1977	5.1	5.6	3.2
1978	5	5.6	3.1
1979	4.6	5.7	2.7
1980	5.6	6.4	2.7
1981	8.9	8.9	3.9
1982	10.3	11.9	5.6
1983	11	12.1	6.9
1984	11	11.6	7.1
1985	11.4	10.5	7.1
1986	11.4	10.2	6.5
1987	10.4	10	6.3
1988	8.5	9.3	6.3
1989	7.1	8.5	5.6
1990	7	7.5	4.8
1991	8.9	7.1	4.2
1992	10.2	7.2	4.5
1993	10.5	8.8	5.6

Source: European Commission, European Economy

Table 5.12 shows, most evidently how levels of unemployment have risen throughout the 1970s and 1980s, with particularly steep increases in all three countries during the early to mid 1980s.

GDP in the three countries
Table 5.13 shows the long run trend in levels of GDP in the three countries. The source of data is European Economy. The table provides two measures of GDP, expressed at market prices. First, GDP is calculated in real terms using 1970 as a base year. Second, the (deflated) trend is then calculated in terms of annual percentage change. GDP, expressed in terms of 1970 prices, is calculated in accordance with the commentary below the table.

Table 5.13
GDP per head in the United Kingdom, the Netherlands and Germany

Year	UK (1970 real values £)	UK %'age change	NL (1970 real values Hfl)	NL %'age change	G (1970 real values DM)	G %'age change
1970	927	1.87	9458	2.62	11134	1.86
1971	947	2.12	9768	3.27	11385	2.25
1972	830	3.42	10015	2.53	11819	3.81
1973	1055	7.64	10443	4.27	12354	4.52
1974	1033	-2.02	10807	3.48	12359	0.04
1975	1033	0.00	10606	-1.85	12234	-1.01
1976	1071	3.62	11101	4.66	12975	6.06
1977	1140	6.42	11302	1.81	13389	3.19
1978	1248	9.34	11531	2.02	13819	3.21
1979	1284	3.04	11737	1.78	14415	4.31
1980	1249	-2.77	11744	0.05	14261	-1.06
1981	1230	-1.48	11578	-1.41	15121	6.03
1982	1253	1.88	11345	-2.01	14988	-0.88
1983	1300	3.71	11749	3.56	15321	2.22
1984	1331	2.42	12087	2.87	15819	3.25
1985	1377	3.45	12355	2.21	16180	2.28
1986	1437	4.32	12630	2.22	16557	2.33
1987	1572	9.41	12694	0.51	16800	1.47
1988	1651	4.99	12942	1.95	17333	3.17
1989	1685	2.06	13479	4.15	17800	2.69
1990	1687	0.16	13953	3.52	18811	5.67
1991	1644	-2.51	14162	1.49	19542	3.88
1992	1630	-0.88	14403	1.70	20939	7.14
1993	1667	2.25	14157	-1.70	20358	-2.77

Source: European Commission, European Economy

First, data is taken for GDP at current market prices in the national currencies, (European Commission, 1994, p.4). This data is then converted to annual percentage changes by multiplying the value for a given year by 100 and dividing by the value for the preceding year. This step provides a data set on nominal changes in GDP for each country. The 'price deflator GDP' (European Commission, 1994, p.26) is then subtracted from the nominal percentage annual change in GDP to arrive at annual real terms percentage increase (or decreases). Change in size of GDP is then calculated for each year, based upon the figure for GDP in 1970. This step gives a data set for each country for the annual size of GDP, but in real terms. These values are then calculated in terms of per head of population, again using data from the European Commission (1994, p.1)

The annual percentage change in GDP per head (Table 5.13) is calculated by multiplying the value for a given year by 100 and dividing by the value for the preceding year and continuing this procedure until all years are accounted for.

Outcomes: social sector output, unemployment and GDP

To investigate the volume of social housing output and its relationship with macroeconomic data, social sector production will be expressed both in absolute terms as well as a percentage of all output; as was the case for the private sectors.

Figures 5.13, 5.15 and 5.17 show the relationship between social sector output and unemployment, using the absolute measure of production. Figures 5.14, 5.16 and 5.18 show the relationship between social sector output and unemployment, where production is expressed as a percentage of total production.

Figures 5.19, 5.21 and 5.23 show the relationship between social sector output and changes in Gross Domestic Product, using the absolute measure of production. Figures 5.20, 5.22 and 5.24 show the relationship between social sector output and changes in Gross Domestic Product, where production is expressed as a percentage of total production.

Social housing production and unemployment

The United Kingdom
Figures 5.13 and 5.14 show the relationship between production of housing in the social sector and unemployment. The social sector is represented in housing association and local authority output (Table 5.5).

Both figures show a strong negative relationship over time where social housing production falls whilst unemployment (percentage of the civilian labour force) unemployed, rises.

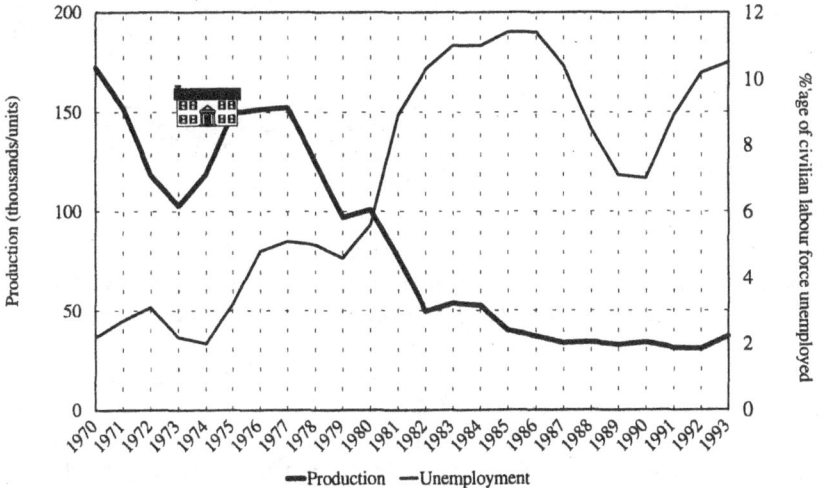

Source: D.o.E Housing and Construction Statistics, European Commmission

Figure 5.13 Social sector housing production and unemployment in the United Kingdom (production as an absolute measure)

Figure 5.13 shows social housing production and unemployment, where social housing is expressed in *absolute* terms. Over the entire period, the relationship is strongly negative or inverse, resulting in a correlation coefficient of -0.841. However, there is perhaps a worthwhile observation to be made about the period 1973 to 1979 in which the relationship is in fact positive; social housing production increasing and decreasing with unemployment. This period was one in which local authority production rose significantly. How much this was a response to unemployment or the prevailing economic climate is difficult to ascertain. The period (1973 to 1979) does however stand out as an exception to the overall trend. The trend in the social sector over the 1980s has been a downward one against an increasing rate of unemployment. The period 1986-1990 is the only exception, a time of increased economic growth during which the unemployment rate fell significantly.

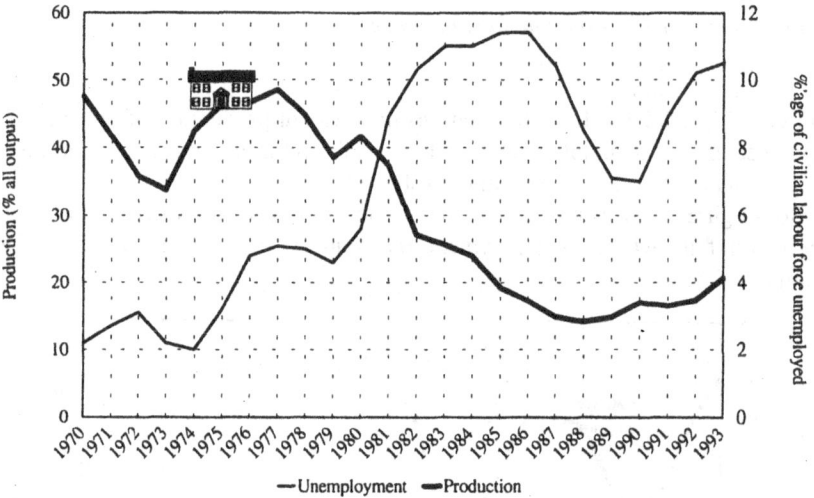

Source: D.o.E Housing and Construction Statistics, European Commmission

Figure 5.14 Social sector housing production and unemployment in the United Kingdom (social sector output as a % of all output)

The conclusion that the relationship between social housing production and unemployment is a negative one, is supported by the results shown using the percentage measure; social housing production as a percentage of total production (Figure 5.14). The correlation coefficient over the period is slightly weaker but is nevertheless significant at -0.765.

The Netherlands

Figures 5.15 and 5.16 show the relationship between production of housing in the social sector and unemployment in the Netherlands. The social sector is represented by housing association and local authority ('state') output (Table 5.6).

The Netherlands provides a very different set of relationships. Figure 5.15 shows that although the relationship between the two variables is negative (as for the UK), there is a weaker relationship; a coefficient of correlation of - 0.241 results for the period 1970 to 1993. Figure 5.15 expresses output in absolute terms.

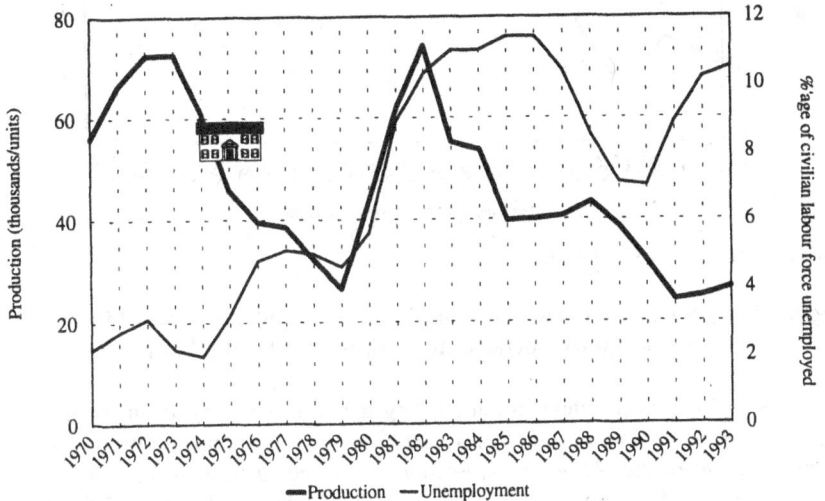

Source: CBS, European Commission

Figure 5.15   Social sector housing production and unemployment in the Netherlands (production as an absolute measure)

Figure 5.16, in which social housing production is expressed as a percentage of total production, evidences however a positive relationship between the two variables. A co-efficient of correlation of 0.183 results for the period 1970 to 1993.

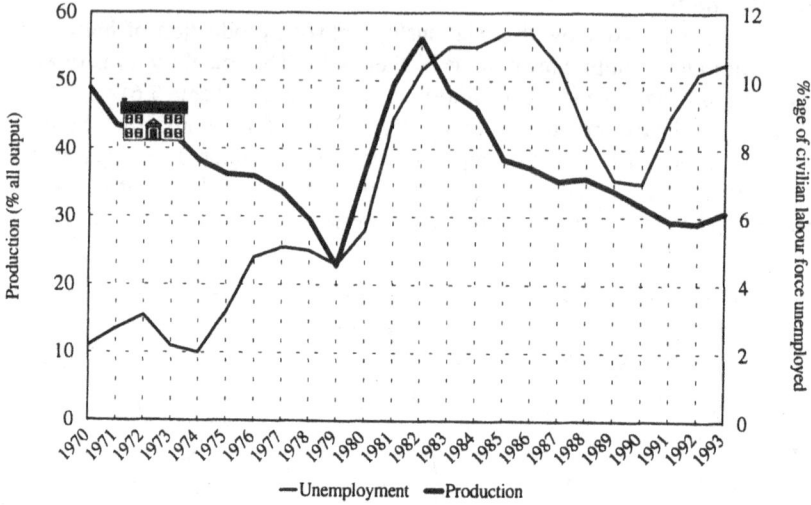

Source: CBS, European Commission

Figure 5.16 Social sector housing production and unemployment in the Netherlands (social sector output as a % of all output)

There is a potential problem in interpreting the results arising from the use of the two measures. The relationship between social housing production and unemployment in the Netherlands, however, is affected by two main trends. The period 1970 to 1978 shows an inverse relationship, whilst that from 1979 to 1993 shows a positive relationship. In the latter period the coefficients of correlation are 0.389 and 0.190 for absolute and percentage measures respectively.

These trends might be explained to some extent by changes in the market housing sector. It can be noted from Figures 5.9 and 5.10, how the level of profit rose from 1975 to 1978 and then fell dramatically between 1979 and 1982. This decline in private sector supply is compensated for by social housing supply during the early 1980s (Figures 5.15 and 5.16).

Germany

Figures 5.17 and 5.18 show the relationship between production of housing in the social sector and unemployment in Germany. The social sector is represented by the Gemeinnützige Unternehmen and a small amount of municipal and state housing (Table 5.7).

The relationship between social housing production and unemployment in Germany is more similar to that in the United Kingdom than in the Netherlands. There is in both countries a strong inverse correlation between the two variables. In Germany, the correlation coefficient for the relationship between the absolute volume of social housing production and unemployment is -0.803 (Figure 5.17), whilst the same relationship using the percentage of total production constituted by social housing (Figure 5.18) provides a correlation coefficient of -0.824, reinforcing the conclusion that as unemployment has risen, production of social housing has fallen.

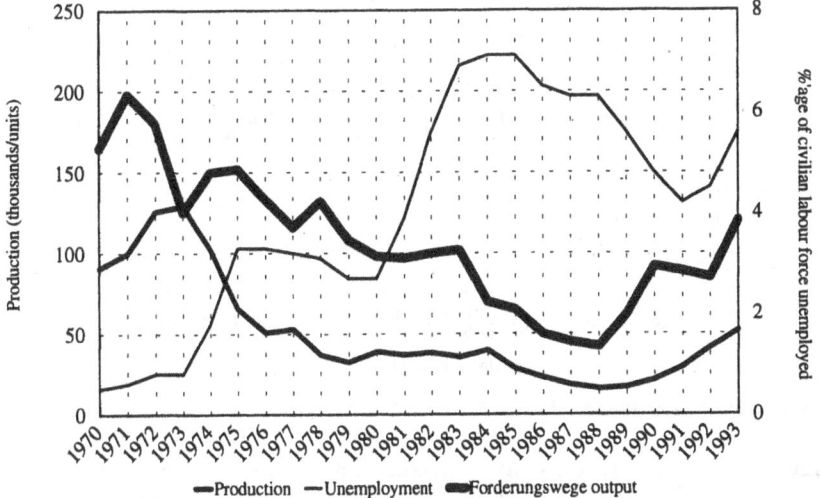

Source: Statistiches Bundesamt, BMBau, European Commission

Figure 5.17 Social sector housing production and unemployment in Germany (production as an absolute measure)

Figures 5.17 and 5.18, show that unlike in the Netherlands, the sharp rise in the percentage of the civilian labour force unemployed in Germany, which occurred in the early 1980s, created no increase in social housing supply, which continued to decline until the late 1980s.

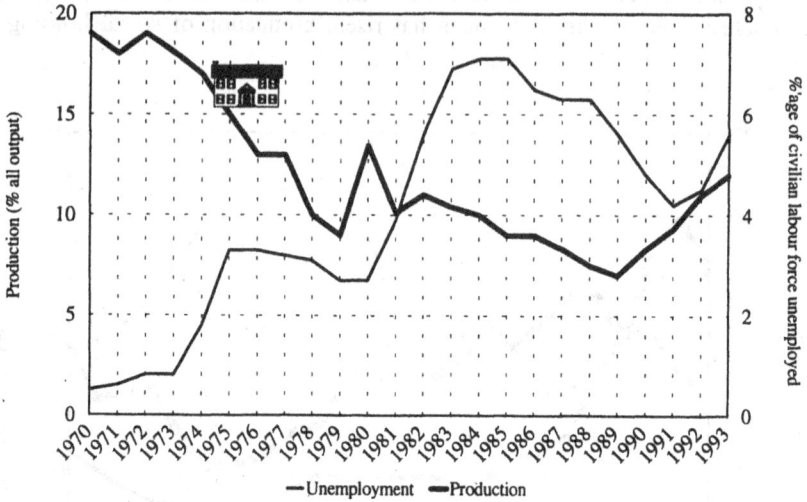

Source: Statistiches Bundesamt, BMBau, European Commission

Figure 5.18 Social sector housing production and unemployment in Germany (social sector output as a % of all output)

In some respects, the trend in output of German social housing is similar to that in the United Kingdom, with falls in production being accompanied by increases in the level of unemployment. There is a need, however, to refine the focus more in the case of Germany because the sources of housing supply in the social sector are more diverse. Although, as was suggested in Section 5.3.3, the Gemeinnützige Unternehmen sector is the best comparable with the United Kingdom, this is nevertheless a narrow way of defining social housing output. It should be recalled that social housing emanates from a number of different sources (Figure 5.6) and it may be instructive to see what happens when a different measure of social housing is utilised.

If the three Förderungswege, or methods of social housing promotion are used as a measure, the conclusions are not significantly different. Figure 5.17 shows the trend for social housing, when this is defined according to the Förderungswege. Using this alternative measure, however, does not alter the inverse relationship between social housing supply and unemployment (Figure 5.17).

Social housing production and GDP

The United Kingdom
Figures 5.19 and 5.20 show the relationship between production of housing in the social sector and gross domestic product (GDP) in the United Kingdom. The social sector is represented by housing association and local authority housing supply (Table 5.5).

The relationship between social housing production and gross domestic product, (price deflator at market prices, annual percentage change) is shown for the United Kingdom in Figure 5.19, where the absolute volume of social housing supply is considered. One assumption about this relationship (Section 5.5.1) was that as levels of GDP rise, social housing output falls.

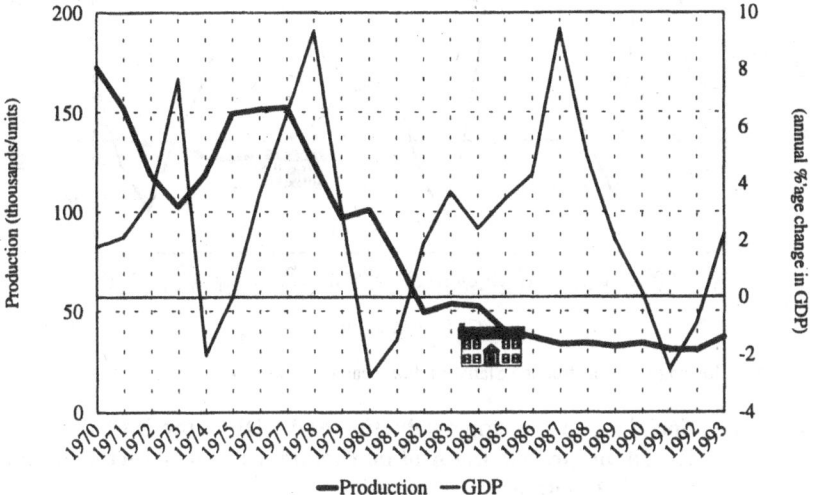

Source: D.o.E Housing and Construction Statistics, European Commission

Figure 5.19 Social sector housing production and GDP in the United Kingdom (price deflator at market prices) (production as an absolute measure)

Figure 5.19 shows that in the case of the United Kingdom, this assumption is not borne out. The coefficient of correlation for the period 1970 to 1993 is 0.108. This is positive, suggesting that the absolute volume of social housing production increases and decreases with line with changes in gross domestic product.

Figure 5.19 shows however the very tenuous and inconsistent nature of the relationship; there is essentially only one period, 1973-1977, which might fulfil the assumption about an inverse relation: from 1980 to 1991 there are significant fluctuations in the level of GDP (Figure 5.19), but with little response in terms of social housing output. Over the period 1991 to 1993, both GDP and social housing output are rising, although GDP at a faster rate.

A weak relationship is also observed when social housing production is expressed as a percentage of total housing production (Figure 5.20). The coefficient of correlation between the two variables for the period 1970 to 1993 is 0.0262.

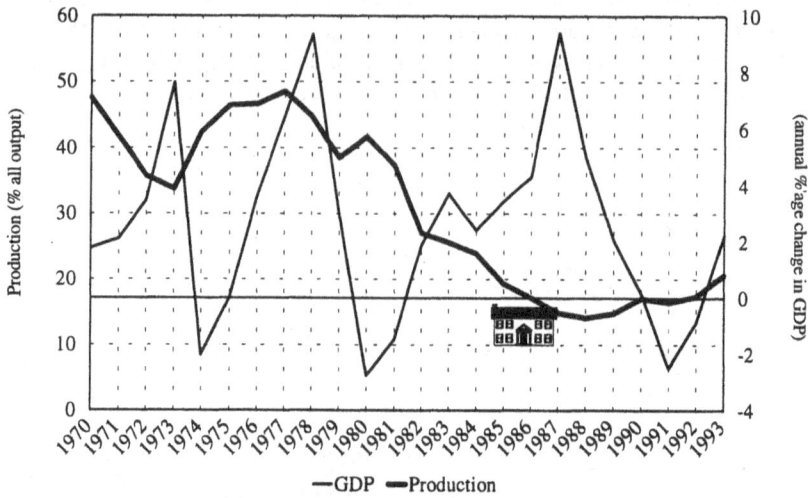

Source: DoE Housing and Construction Statistics, European Commission

Figure 5.20   Social sector housing production and GDP in the United Kingdom (price deflator at market prices) (social sector output as a % of all output)

The Netherlands
Figures 5.21 and 5.22 show the relationship between output of housing in the social sector and gross domestic product in the Netherlands. The social sector is represented by housing associations and municipalities. (Table 5.6).

Figure 5.21 shows the relationship between changes in GDP and social housing output, which is expressed in absolute terms. A coefficient of correlation of 0.375 results for the period 1970 to 1993. This is an entirely different relationship to that in the United Kingdom and one which appears to indicate different policy priorities. In the Netherlands, increases in GDP have been accompanied by increases in social housing output, whilst falls in GDP have also accompanied falls in social housing output.

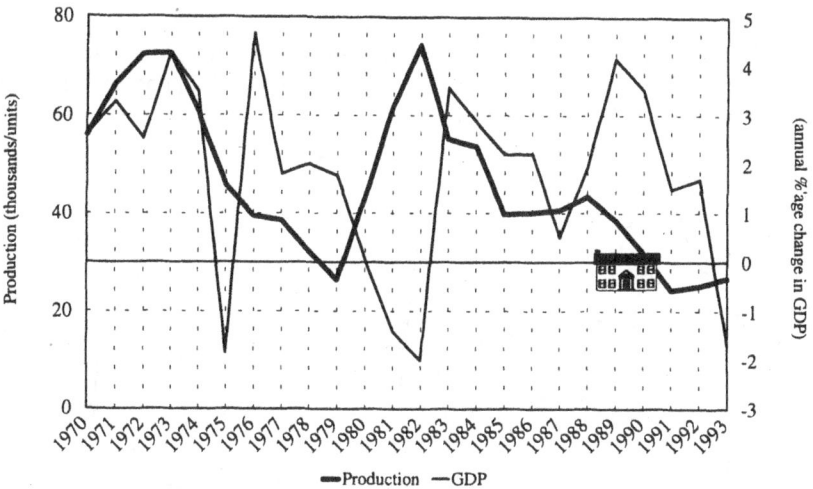

Source: CBS, European Commission

Figure 5.21 Social sector housing production and GDP in the Netherlands (price deflator at market prices) (production as an absolute measure)

Figure 5.22 shows the relationship between changes in GDP and social housing, which is expressed as a percentage of total production. A coefficient of correlation of 0.409 results for the period 1970 to 1993. This is a similar result to that shown in Figure 5.20, where output was measured in absolute terms.

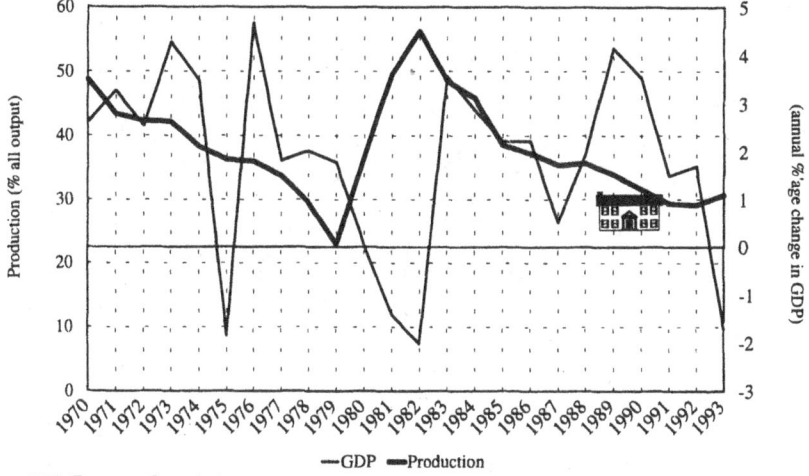

Source: CBS, European Commission

Figure 5.22 Social sector housing production and GDP in the Netherlands (price deflator at market prices) (social sector output as a % of all output)

Germany

Figures 5.23 and 5.24 show the relationship between production of housing in the social sector and GDP in Germany. The social sector is represented by the Gemeinnützige Unternehmen and local authority sectors (Table 5.7).

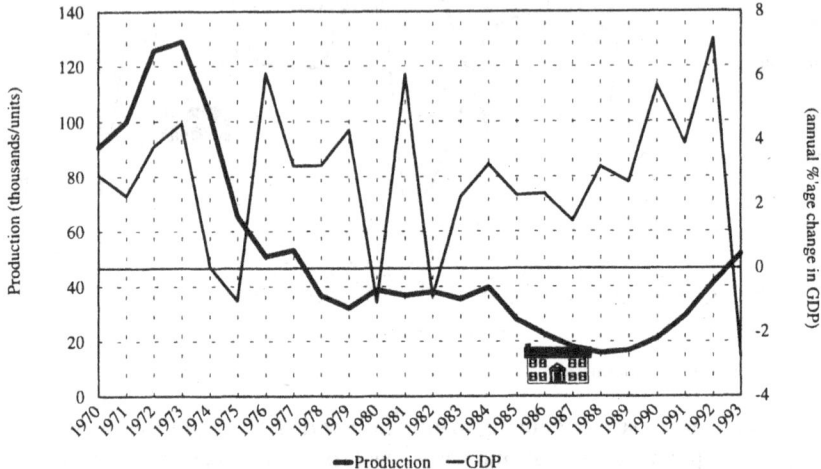

Source: Statistiches Bundesamt, European Commission

Figure 5.23 Social sector housing production and GDP in Germany (price deflator at market prices) (production as an absolute measure)

The relationship between social housing production and GDP is shown for Germany in Figure 5.23, where the absolute volume of social housing supply is considered.

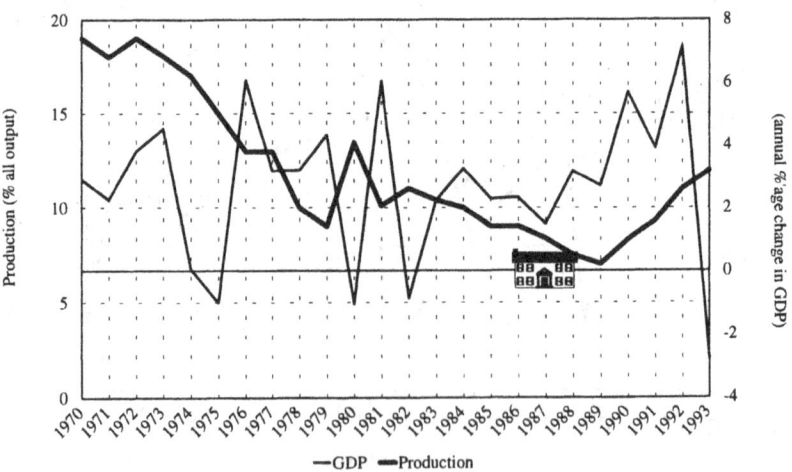

Source: Statistiches Bundesamt, European Commission

Figure 5.24 Social sector housing production and GDP in Germany (social sector output as % of all output)

The coefficient of correlation for the period 1970 to 1993 is a weak one, and one which is negative; at -0.110. Figure 5.24 shows that when social housing is expressed as a percentage of total housing production, the result is a marginally stronger (negative) coefficient of correlation; at -0.146.

Remarks on the relationship between social housing output and levels of GDP
The investigation of the relationship between social housing output and changes in the level of GDP provides one main conclusion. In neither the UK, nor Germany, has the level of social housing construction been particularly responsive to changes in the level of GDP. In the Netherlands, however, increases in the level of economic growth shown in GDP, have been accompanied to a significant extent by increases in the level of social housing construction, whilst falls in the one variable have been associated with falls in the other.

Differences between the countries in respect of the relationship between GDP and social housing output can be explained by reference to both the political and economic context. In particular, the way in which governments view the role of social housing is important. This can be a 'view' of social housing as an integral part of the housing production process. One could argue this approach to be the underlying policy in the Netherlands, where growth is accompanied by increases in social housing output. On the other hand, social housing can be regarded as a residual element in housing supply; one which is independent of changes in macroeconomic performance. It is possible, by looking at relationships between GDP and social housing output in the United Kingdom and Germany, to assume a very different underlying policy.

6 Conclusions

6.1 A review of objectives, methods and findings

Two main objectives were set for this research:

> To improve understanding of the way in which European systems of housing supply function and hence to explain better production outcomes.

and to:

> Identify different theoretical and methodological approaches to comparing housing systems and to consider their efficacy in the light of an empirical investigation.

In order to include both these objectives within a methodology for comparing housing systems, a hypothesis was devised based on the examples of the United Kingdom, the Netherlands and Germany:

> Systems of housing supply in which the state plays a very different role can produce similar housing production outcomes (and) this is, to a significant extent, due to the way in which the housing systems are structured.

The interest in this approach, as explained in Chapter 1, lay in comparing three housing systems which previous and contemporary research show to be significantly different, particularly in respect of the different ways governments intervene in housing production and associated land and planning policies. Two of these studies (B.M.Bau, 1993; Barlow and Duncan, 1994) bear a direct relation to the framework and the countries involved. In particular, the purpose of the study has been to consider the comparison of the United Kingdom and the Netherlands, two housing and land systems which stand, from a historical perspective, at different ends of the market-state continuum (B.M.Bau, 1993). Moreover, previous research provided evidence to show that the German system of housing supply had some elements or facets in common with both countries, although nevertheless retained its own identity. The state-market theme has been a focal point of research which tries to link housing systems and their outcomes with the context of the nature of the welfare states in which they operate (Barlow and Duncan, 1994). This particular framework is useful, although not entirely robust (as is explained in the foregoing), for looking at the three countries as examples of 'liberal', 'corporatist' and 'social-democratic' states (ibid).

To give further initial interest to the comparison, housing production outcomes were considered (Figures 1.1 to 1.4) by reference to the levels of output (overall and by each sector). It has been shown throughout how different these sectors are, and the way in which housing, land and land policies influence the overall picture that emerges. It was explained at the outset of the book, which particular facets of housing supply were to be examined. These included an analysis of policy and development processes in each country.

Having attempted to make a practical case for a study of the particular countries in question, a methodology was sought. A considerable discussion has been devoted to this aspect. This is necessary given the rather provisional nature of comparative analysis, the problems of data generation and the general social science context in which housing studies finds itself (Chapter 2). In these respects, it has been important to state whereabouts the approach to this comparison lies between empirical and rational methodologies. In the event, and without re-iterating the approach in full, a route has been taken which attempts to combine an empirical and statistical method with rational models and their interpretation. This can be stated to be a realistic way forward given that neither full bodied economic modelling, nor rational paradigms seem to have been successful in dealing with housing, or systems, or comparisons in the past. It was also important to link back to the hypothesis which placed a significant emphasis on the concept of 'structure' as a way of advancing understanding about housing systems and their outcomes.

The inclusion of 'structure' in the hypothesis provides both opportunities as well as constraints. The utility of 'structure' as a concept is that it is multi-faceted and ranges from ideas about technical or functional linkages between actors and policies, to interpretations about how these linkages are exploited, to frameworks reflecting value-based assumptions about society. The flexibility of the concept is potentially an advantage. However, as will also no doubt have been appreciated by reading this and other texts, there are great methodological challenges. The attempt to link the broader concepts of structure to housing and comparative housing systems has presented a main challenge. The main problem which has presented itself hinges on the extent to which it is possible to link the conceptual with the more concrete. In the comparative context it was important to try to spell out just how an approach which attempted to reconcile so many different theoretical and methodological aspects, might be forwarded.

In attempting to provide some conclusions which are useful to both practitioners as well as theorists, a significant amount of substantive evidence was gathered. Chapter 3 has described in some detail, the nature of the three systems of housing supply. Although there are problems presented by systems changing over time, there was found to be some consistent themes which allowed for meaningful comparisons.

Generally, the system of housing supply in the United Kingdom relies more heavily on market and private sector parties than in the Netherlands and Germany. This is however more the case by comparison with the former, than with the latter. There are more than a few instances where it is possible to make distinctions between particular facets of housing supply in the extent of state intervention. Distinctions are perhaps most evident in the different systems of land supply, where previous research has shown the Dutch land policy and hence land supply process, to be far more reliant on the state. Land supply in the United Kingdom and Germany, has, for the period under investigation here, been largely a function of private interests. The distribution of tasks between private and public sector bodies in land supply is generally repeated at the stage of infrastructure provision. In some respects, this is a logical consequence of the practicalities of the development process; in other ways, the responsibility for provision is explained by the trade-off inherent in externality benefits and planning consents. In the Netherlands, these complex relationships are addressed in practice by giving municipalities full control over infrastructure provision, where building firms take a back seat. In the United Kingdom, the opposite occurs with firms being more likely to be involved in the whole 'development' process. In Germany, there is a statutory responsibility on the municipalities to ensure the correct standards of provision. However, in practice the burden falls across many different parties (B.M.Bau, 1993).

Rather greyer, however, are the distinctions to be made between the extent of state intervention with housing production and planning policies. Some conclusions on this theme can be reached by examining levels of housing investment and the nature of housing production subsidies. In Section 3.2, it was concluded that on the basis of these parameters, production policies in Germany and the Netherlands were more similar, having higher relative levels of investment in housing and a broader range of object subsidies to new housing than in the United Kingdom. These differences are explained however as much by reactive as by pro-active or idealistic policies. Demographic factors as well as historic housing shortages contribute much to an explanation of different housing production policies.

Whilst Chapter 3 focused specifically on the role of state and market in housing supply, Chapter 4 looked at the way in which systems are structured. This meant that questions were asked about the complexities involved in systems of supply and the extent to which they could be argued to be integral. Systems of housing supply, such as those which are found in the Netherlands and the United Kingdom, and which rely more or less on one (public or private) sector, can be viewed as more simplistic: land, planning and housing policy roles in the Dutch case being mainly a function of municipalities. The role of agencies in housing supply was also considered in Chapter 4. It was shown, above all, that changes in the political constitution of central government in the U.K, have much further reaching consequences for housing than is the case in the other two countries In the Netherlands and Germany, the changing political scene has had much less effect on the tenure of new housing output. Likewise, development processes elevate and relegate agencies in particular ways. At the local level, municipalities, development companies and housing associations combine to provide new housing, but their relations are governed not only by financial perameters, but also by institutional and historic development arrangements. A key relationship governing housing development in the Netherlands is that between housing associations and municipalities. Historically, there has been strong understanding, usually giving associations full opportunity to develop new housing.

Some analysts of housing theory, most notably Healey and Barrett (1990) have attempted to draw together all the different strands needed to encapsulate a comparison of housing systems. One of the most important elements here is the 'dynamics of the economy'. The long-term performance of the macroeconomy, it is argued, can be viewed as a sort of 'structure' in itself. Comparisons can be made in this respect (Section 4.4) particularly where there is consistency in the way individual variables differ between countries across a time frame. It takes only a quite cursory investigation of some of the main macroeconomic variables in the three countries to note some consistent similarities and differences. Most notable is the similarity in monetary policies adopted by the Netherlands and Germany. Monetary policy, represented by decisions taken on the level of interest rates and the money supply, is quite different to that in the United Kingdom, where inflation has been higher over the past twenty five years. These differences help to explain levels of investment and private saving in the particular countries. Although the specific links between the macroeconomy and housing supply were not fully investigated, these distinctions are potentially helpful as a way of understanding differences in housing outcomes.

In Chapter 5, some outcomes of the different systems were investigated. To this end, it should be re-stated that the objective of the book has not been to build a model of the 'best' or most appropriate variables explaining housing production, but to look at the broad correlations between the make-up of housing systems and their outcomes. In considering how a number of measures help to explain the extent of similarity of outcome, demographics, house prices, land prices and building costs as well as selected macroeconomic variables were used. Chapter 5 sets out fully the findings and hence again a brief summary comment is required.

In terms of conforming to the expectations of the models and assumptions of Chapter 5, it was evident that the Dutch system of housing supply fitted best; in terms of understanding total output through variations in demographic variables and the housing stock; in terms of understanding private sector output through housing and land market variables; and in terms of understanding social sector output through measures of economic growth and levels of unemployment. When these measures were applied in the context of the United Kingdom, the correlations were generally low and often at odds with the assumptions made. When the assumptions were applied in German context, the different methods of measuring housing production gave very inconsistent results, particularly in the case of output from private households. The main conclusion to be drawn from this chapter is that there are different variables and lead indicators to focus on, depending on the country involved and irrespective of the assumption that particular sectors are 'similar'. In the following sections of this chapter there is a discussion which tries to meet up this point with the different structures of housing supply.

6.2   Policy implications

The implications of examining the relationship between systems of housing supply and the resulting housing outcomes, should not only be related to theory, but also to policy and practice.

In drawing any sort of conclusion about the efficacy or efficiency of one particular system (and hence the policy implications), it should be emphasised that conclusions should be based on a knowledge of the aims and objectives of the system.   Herein lies a potentially significant problem.   Following particularly, approaches which place emphasis on differences in welfare policy or differences in the role of the state in housing provision, it is a valid question which asks whether these differences imply different objectives for different systems.   On the other hand, more universal or convergence explanations might see the objectives as in some way fixed for individual countries (by common exogenous forces), and hence the objectives, whatever these might be, are less significant.

Unfortunately neither of these approaches fully deal with the problem, because each has weaknesses. To make some attempt to compare the efficacy of individual systems of housing supply, this analysis created hypotheses to explain levels of housing output, for which rationales were given in Chapter 5. The utility and justification for these will be judged independently. Other comparative texts do the same, sometimes considering their hypotheses as 'golden rules' (B.M.Bau, 1993) to be applied across all types of systems.

With these notes of caution, some comments can be offered on the policy implications arising from a comparison of the three different systems.

Achieving enough new housing: levels of total output

Ensuring that housing production levels are adequate to meet the total housing need in the economy may be considered a primary concern of housing policy. One of the stumbling blocks to the achievement of this objective is a technical inability to forecast precisely the housing requirement on an annual basis. This is something which demographers and others involved in the prognosis of social trends attempt to overcome.   The challenge for housing policy makers, however, is how best to regulate, by intervention or market solutions, the production of new housing.

It might be expected, and indeed the analysis shows it to be the case for the three countries examined, that changes in the number of households, as well as the relationship between the size of the housing stock and historic housing shortages, provide a broad indication of new housing need. However, this relationship differs to a significant extent between the three countries where the data is analysed. In so far that the data is robust and the comparative method sound, the results are instructive in suggesting how policy might be implemented to ensure that new housing supply reacts sensitively to changes in overall housing need. A few instances can be drawn out showing, for example, the relationship between changes in overall housing need and new output in the Dutch case. In the Netherlands, new output is by no means perfectly correlated with annual housing need. However, the relationship is considerably stronger than in the case of the other two countries.

The reasons for these differences are manifold. It should of course not be overlooked that the whole is the sum of the parts in so far as housing completions are concerned. In addition therefore to re-emphasising differences in the way planning, housing and land policy are integrated, it should be stressed that individual sectors of supply contribute to the total picture. In some cases, for example, in the United Kingdom, the relationship between these sectors is quite distant, a situation arguably exacerbated by leaving the market to sort out housing provision. Many different sources of development land and disparate land ownership patterns can lead to uncompetitive and even inequitable situations between different housing providers. In other cases, most notably the Netherlands, the different sectors are not so distant within the process from each other, because the nature of land policy is such that market builders and social sector suppliers rely on a common source of land supply. The level of total housing output is thus (potentially) easier to control. Whether this happens in practice depends on the wider system and the relationship between different political and planning hierarchies.

Market solutions to new housing demand: private sector output

The investigation of housing output by the private sector in Chapter 5, revealed a number of issues which are relevant to European housing policy makers today. Although all sectors were not perfectly comparable, a number of factors were identified to make the comparison meaningful.

In terms of understanding trends in private sector output, the extent of reliance on development rather than contract building is a critical factor. This issue opens up questions about the exposure of firms and households to land markets and participation in the land use planning process. The private sectors investigated were each a variation on the theme of output for owner-occupation, and largely in the absence of bricks and mortar subsidies. Key variations between the sectors concerned differences in land policy and the nature of housing suppliers: the private sector in the United Kingdom being seen as a speculative agency in the development process; the Dutch market sector being less active in the land market, but at the same time affected significantly by macroeconomic trends; and German sector being influenced more by a bespoke traditional of new housing provision.

Of these three models, the Dutch example was best fitted to the expectation that output should be a function of changes in the relationship between house prices on the one hand, and land prices and building costs on the other. In the other two countries, the relationship was much more disparate. Under these circumstances, further work is needed either using the same variables but in a different way, or, adding new variables to the equation. In terms of policy implications and how governments can influence private sector agencies, it is evident from the comparison that state intervention, particularly in the form of land ownership, can work to the mutual advantage of government and private firms. An arms length conclusion might suggest that such a situation would be welcomed elsewhere, for example in the United Kingdom and Germany. Indeed, this would be the case, were housing suppliers solely to be concerned with the relationship between output and levels of profit, as defined previously. In practice, this is not the case, probably because profit is derived in different ways according to the individual development processes. In the United Kingdom, profit from land deals plays a part. In Germany, changes in output from private households are not linked strongly to 'profit' as it has been considered, a fact which can be explained by reference to the particular development process, as has been outlined.

The advantage of convergence towards the Dutch mode of private sector housing in Europe would lie in reduced volatility in private sector output, relative to changes in market conditions. However, such a convergence would depend equally on the ability of different states to organise their housing and planning policies around a different form of land ownership. Part of the problem in previous attempts at state ownership of land in the United Kingdom, for example, has been a lack of an integrated approach to betterment and planning gain problems. A considerable shift, not only in ideology, but also towards workable policies therefore, would be needed to convince private developers of the benefits to be gained in letting the state take more of the responsibility for land supply.

Meeting housing need: policies for the social sector

The requirement for social housing is usually expressed in terms of a 'need'. In this research various measures of macroeconomic performance were compared in the light of social housing output. The aim was to see how changes in macroeconomic performance were absorbed by housing provided on the basis of need. Mainly it was shown that, using changes in GDP and levels of unemployment, output of social housing could not be easily predicted on the basis of the time period in question.

However, in the Dutch case, the relationships between social housing output and macroeconomic trends were very different to those in the United Kingdom and Germany. In the Netherlands, for the period in question, a positive relationship between social housing output and unemployment and GDP was shown. This can be contrasted with, in particular, the relationship between output and unemployment in the other two countries, which was strongly inverse.

Drawing lessons from this comparison, it might not be wrong to conclude that a different set of objectives are implicit in government policy making; it is interesting to note perhaps, that increases in the level of GDP are accompanied by increases in the level of social housing in the Netherlands. On this basis, it might be concluded that a different emphasis or economic focus is given to social housing in that country. In the United Kingdom and Germany, the associations are inconclusive. The policy lessons which can be drawn thus question initially the role of social housing in each economy.

To increase the output of social housing, which is a challenge for housing associations across Europe in the absence of declining levels of financial support, there needs to be a review not only of the financial framework, but also of the development context. In this latter respect, the Dutch case appears best equipped to deal with the future challenges. Although market disciplines are being absorbed into the sector of late, the structures for flexible forms of housing provision are still in place. Since the late 1970s and beyond, production by this sector has been very much a response to downturns in the economy. In these situations, municipal land ownership and land pricing mechanisms have been the cornerstone in the state's ability to turn around the emphasis of housing production.

The transferability of this system is again questionable in the light of the analysis of land policy in the previous section. It should also be stated that the market disciplines being introduced in the Netherlands since the beginning of the 1990s, have brought with them an increasing reluctance on the part of the state to subsidise land prices to the benefit of housing associations. This trend alone makes it difficult to foresee further intervention at the European level on behalf of social housing development. If social housing is to be further supported, then a stronger case needs perhaps to be made for the externality benefits for the macroeconomy, rather than relying on the case for social housing per se.

6.3   Theories and methods of housing analysis: the hypothesis revisited

The approach to comparing European systems of housing supply has been one which tries to look at housing production outcomes in the light of different interpretations of the concept of structure. 'Structure' as an integral part of the hypothesis, provides opportunities for looking at the individual systems of housing supply in different ways. As such, the concept can be used to explain why housing outcomes differ. Before doing this, however, it is important to consider again the question of whether housing systems (of supply) which are 'different in nature' lead to similar outcomes; as is posited in the first part of the research hypothesis.

Can systems of housing supply which are different in nature lead to similar outcomes?

The short answer to this question, based on evidence from the three countries investigated is 'no'. In so far that we are concerned with country cases representing very different forms of state intervention in housing, land and planning policy, these differences lead to different outcomes. By comparing outcomes from very opposite systems of housing supply, namely the United Kingdom and the Netherlands, it is not difficult to conclude that different forms of intervention lead to different outcomes. This conclusion is bolstered by the case of Germany, which is different again in the way its system of housing supply operates, the consequences of which are found in a very distinct set of outcomes.

Particular outcomes for particular systems are then to be anticipated. However, the comparative research interest lies not in proving that individual systems lead to individual outcomes, but in describing how this situation comes about. It is here that the concept of 'structure' has a part to play, particularly in showing *how* different systems are, in the light of different outcomes.

Different interpretations of structure as a means of explaining differences of outcome

The utility of the concept of structure as used in this approach, lay always in its potential to explain similar housing outcomes where simple state-market paradigms might fail. As the outcomes are in the first instance different, the utility of the concept lies more in looking at each of the different interpretations of the systems and trying to find occasions where some similarity of outcome might be expected.

The first interpretation of structure considered in Chapter 4, related to ideas of the way in which systems of supply are integrated. This included the concept of the development process as a sequence of events. A key theme was simplicity in the organisation of housing supply and also the division of labour between public and private sectors. This focus on coordination within the systems of housing supply might reasonably lead to the conclusion that housing outcomes are more controlled, or at least easier to control in the case of the Netherlands, particularly given the strong municipal role in the planning and development process. By comparison, it is less easy to make a case for a well integrated system of housing supply in the United Kingdom and Germany, where responsibilities for planning, land supply, infrastructure and house building are so various divided between public and private parties. Whether these conclusions lead further to the assumption that similarity of outcomes should be expected in UK and German cases, is another matter which is unlikely to be resolved without further detailed research into the policy making and development processes.

More immediately, the role of agencies in the system and structure of housing supply can be dealt with. In respect of the approach adopted in Chapter 4, a case can be made for some similarity, particularly in the role of central government in housing supply, between the Netherlands and Germany. In those countries, it would appear that a cooperative stance is taken at central government level, to ensure a steady flow of housing suitable for market conditions. Otherwise considered, this is a tenure-neutral policy which is uncharacteristic of housing supply in the United Kingdom. Examining the structuring of housing supply by reference to the relations between different agencies in the Netherlands and Germany strengthens the case for a corporatist interpretation of the state (Crouch, 1993; Barlow and Duncan, 1994). This is in the sense that there a reluctance to wholly let in the market in the way that has occurred with housing supply and housing policy in the United Kingdom. In the Netherlands, the reliance of housing suppliers on municipalities is significant, and there are historically strong links between the latter and housing associations. In

Germany, the process of housing development in most sectors brings in a broad range of parties and a complex system of infrastructure provision. In this sense, it is inclusive of state and market in a way which is different to say, the development process of volume house builders in the United Kingdom.

The third interpretation of 'structure' to be considered in Chapter 4 was the economic environment for housing supply. In the previous (agency) focus, similarities were drawn between the Netherlands and Germany. These similarities can also be argued to apply in so far as macroeconomic performance is concerned. Crouch (1993) describes the 'case of Germany' as one of 'co-operation and competition in an institutionalised economy', and this analysis could also be applied in the Dutch case in so far as political structures and economic policies are concerned. By comparison with the United Kingdom, economic policy in the other two countries has been characterised by a much tighter monetary stance. This is reflected in higher levels of investment and private saving. The Netherlands complements this with higher levels of government spending and higher levels of taxation, although German levels of taxation are generally lower, being accompanied by lower government spending. On the basis of these points, it may be suggested that the Netherlands and Germany reflect a similarly competitive economic strategy. The United Kingdom reflects a different economic strategy, which arguably has put domestic political interests before an economic stance aimed to promote competitiveness in the global sphere. The disciplines of the Maastricht criteria are now having an impact on the UK housing system, particularly in a more evenly balanced approach to housing tenure. In future years (Radley, 1996), home ownership is not expected to grow so fast.

The way housing systems are compared and contrasted according to different interpretations of their structure, is useful mainly by reference to the outcomes. In this respect, similarities between the Netherlands and Germany evident in macroeconomic and corporatist policy structures do not obviously bring about consistent housing production outcomes. Chapter 5 shows that there is no more consistency of outcome between these two countries than between any other two. Reasons for this are now commented on.

Holy alliances and unholy outcomes: towards improving the comparative method

One main finding of this book is that systems of housing supply are not easily reconciled with housing production outcomes. Systems exhibit similarities and degrees of overlap, but very often produce different housing outcomes. If comparative analysis is to remain a useful tool for learning about the relationship between a housing system and its outcomes, then it is evident, on the basis of this case study, that more sensitive methodologies will have to be adopted. In particular, the relationship between political and housing systems will have to be more precisely defined. At the present time, middle-range approaches attempt to bridge the gap and come in the form of theories of the state and their implications for housing. This relationship is however very loose and cannot be easily underpinned by the use of data which is often difficult to obtain, and sometimes incomparable.

As another methodological challenge, more concrete descriptions of housing systems are required, especially according to commonly agreed parameters.

Unfortunately however, this is only half of the challenge to the analysis of European and international housing systems. The systems are forever in motion and the speed of change can often only be gauged with hindsight. Although 'structure' paradigms can be used to discount for the state of flux, this is not a methodological challenge, but a conceptual one. In the European context, there are significant economic and political forces creating convergence. This 'convergence' is happening to varying degrees in housing systems and there is at present only a few isolated attempts to measure the direction and extent of change. To overcome this problem, much improved data sources are required. In addition, an increased ability on the part of housing researchers to monitor the situation is needed alongside resources enabling a wide dissemination of findings.

Bibliography and references

Adams, D and May, M (1990), Land Ownership and Land Use Planning, *The Planner*, 28th September 1990, Royal Town Planning Institute.

Adrian, H (1976), Konkurs der Planung - Zukunft oder Konzeption, *Der Architect*, 1/1976.

Alders, J (1991), *Vierde nota over de ruimtelijke ordening Extra*, deel III: kabinetsstandpunt, Tweede Kamer, vergaderjaar 1990-1991, 21.879, Nos. 5-6, 's-Gravenhage: SDU Uitgeverij.

Ambrose, P (1986), *Whatever happened to Planning?*, Methuen: London

Ambrose, P (1992), The Performance of National Housing Systems: a Three Nation Comparison, *Housing Studies*, Vol. 7, No.1, Longman.

Ambrose, P and Barlow, J (1987), Housing Provision and House Building in Western Europe: Increasing Expenditure, Declining Output? in van Vliet, W (ed.), *Housing Markets and Policies under Fiscal Austerity*, Greenwood Press: London.

Andeweg, R and Irwin, G (1993), *Dutch government and politics*, Macmillan: London.

B & G (1995), Consument verliezer in 'grond' rush VINEX gebieden, *Vereiniging Nederlandse Gemeenten*, 4th April 1995.

Balchin, P and Kieve, J (1988), *Urban Land Economics and Public Policy*, Macmillan: Basingstoke.

Ball, M (1983), *Housing and Economic Power; the Political Economy of Owner-Occupation*, Methuen: London.

Ball, M (1988), *Rebuilding Construction, Economic change and the British construction industry*, Routledge: London.

Ball, M (1996), *Housing and construction; A troubled relationship?* Joseph Rowntree Foundation: York.

Ball, M, Harloe, M and Martens, M (1988), *Housing and Social Change in Europe and the USA*, Routledge: London.

Ball, M, and Harloe, M (1992), Rhetorical Barriers to Understanding Housing Provision: What the 'Provision Thesis is and is not', *Housing Studies* Vol. 7, No.1, Longman.

Bark, G and Gress, J (1993), *Democracy and its Discontents: A History of West Germany*, Blackwell Publishers: Oxford.

Barlow, J and Duncan, S (1994), *Success and Failure in Housing Provision: European Systems compared*, Elsivier Science Ltd: Oxford.

Barlow, J (1993), Controlling the Housing Land market: some Examples from Europe, *Urban Studies*, Vol. 30, No.7.

Barlow, J (1994), *Affordable Housing - Unaffordable mistakes*, paper presented to the Housing Studies Association Conference, Bristol, September 1994.

BDZ (Bundesverband der Deutschen Zementindustrie e.v. (1993), *Statistiches Kompendium*, zum Kongress Zukunft Wohnen.

Begg, D, Fischer, S and Dornbusch (1989) *Economics*, McGraw-Hill: London.

B.M.Bau, (Bundesministerium für Raumordnung, Bauwesen und Städtebau) (1993), *Funktionsweise städtischer Bodenmärke in Mitgleidstaaten der Europäischen Gemeinschaft: ein Systemvergleich*, B.M.Bau: Bonn, Bad-Godesburg.

B.M.Bau, (Bundesministerium für Raumordnung, Bauwesen und Städtebau) (1993a), *Sozialwohnungsbau in den Niederlande*, B.M.Bau: Bonn, Bad-Godesburg.

B.M.Bau (Bundesministerium für Raumordnung, Bauwesen und Städtebau) (1994), *Haus und Wohnung: Im Spiegel der Statistik*, B.M.Bau: Bonn, Bad-Godesburg.

Boelhouwer, P and van der Heijden, H (1989), Vrije Sektor Woningsbouw; *Consequenties voor der Ruimtelijke Ordening de Volkshuisvesting en Bouwnijverheid, Volkshuisvesting en Bouwmarkt*, Delft University Press.

Boelhouwer, P and van der Heijden, H (1992), *Housing Systems in Europe: Part 1*, Delft University Press.

Boelhouwer, P and Priemus, H (1990), Dutch Housing Policy Realigned, *Netherlands Journal of Housing and Environmental Research*, Vol. 5, No.1, Delft University Press: Delft.

Bramley, G (1994), *The Housing and Planning Relationship*, paper presented to the Housing Studies Association Autumn Conference 1994.

Brindley, T, Rydin, Y and Stoker, G (1989), *Remaking Planning*, Unwin Hyman: London.

Brown, T, Findley, J, Hill, M, Joliffe, C, Oxley, M, Rydin, Y (1984), *Housing Land in Urban Areas*, Working Paper No.1, Department of Land Management, Leicester Polytechnic.

Brown, T and Golland, A (1995), *National Housing Policy*, School of the Built Environment, De Montfort University: Leicester.

Brussaard, W (1986), *The Rules of Physical Planning*, Ministerie van Volkshuisvesting, Ruimtelijke Ordening en Milieubeheer: Den Haag.

Bucher, H (1993), Die Außenwanderbeziehungen der Bundesrepublik Deutschland, *Raumforschung und Raumordnung*, Heft 5.

Buijs, S (1993) Urbanisation alternatives in the 4th Report on Physical Planning, *Netherlands Journal of Housing and the Built Environment*, Vol.7, No.2, Delft University Press.

Burns, L and Grebler, L (1967), *The Housing of Nations*, Macmillan:London.

Cadman, D and Austin-Crowe, L (1978), *Property Development*, Spon: London.

Carter, N, and Brown, T (1991), Local housing policies and plans in England, *Local Government Policy Making*, Vol. 17, No 4, Longman.

Carter, N, Brown, T and Hill, M (1986), *The Private Housing Development Process*, Department of Land Management, Leicester Polytechnic.

CBS (Central Bureau of Statistics), *Maandstatistiek Bouwnijverheid*, CBS: Voorburg, Den Haag.

Chiddick, D and Dobson, M (1986), Land for Housing - Circular Arguments, *The Planner*, March 1986, Royal Town Planning Institute: London.

Clarke, R (1985), *Industrial Economics*, Basil Blackwell.

Cole, G (1994), *Minder*, ITV Television.

Coles, A (1991), *Housing Finance*, August 1991.

Conijn, J and de Vries, P (1997), *Signaleringssysteem Nieubouw Koopwoningen*, OTB Research Institute, University of Delft.

Conran Roche (1989), *Costs of Residential Development: Final Report prepared for the Department of the Environment*, D.o.E: London.

Contract Journal (1994), The Cost of being British, *Contract Journal*, 14th July, 1994.

Corner, J (1991), Local Authority Housing Statistics, in Champion, T (ed.) *Population Matters*, Atheneum Press: Newcastle.

Crouch, C (1993), Co-operation and competition in an Institutionalized Economy: the case of Germany, in Crouch, C and Marquand, S (eds.) *Ethics and Markets*, Blackwell Publishers.

Dallmayr, F (1982), The Theory of Structuration: a Critique, in Giddens, A (ed.) *Profiles and Critiques in Social theory*, Macmillan Press : Basingstoke.

Davies, H (1989), The Netherlands, in Davies H (ed.) *Planning Control in Western Europe*, HMSO: London.

De Groot, (1995), *Interview*, 11th April 1995, De Groot and van Oome, Bouw en Aanehmingsbedrijf, Rotterdam, the Netherlands.

Der Spiegel (1994), *Karl. R. Popper; 1902 bis 1994; Nachruf*, Der Spiegel Vol 39.

Dieterich, H, Dransfeld, E and Voss, W (1993), *Germany: Urban Land and Property Markets*, U.C.L.Press: London.

D.o.E. (Department of the Environment) (1974), *Land, Cmnd 5730*, HMSO: London.

D.o.E. (Department of the Environment) (1975), *Community Land - Circular 1: General Introduction and Priorities*, paragraphs 11-14, Circular 121/75, HMSO: London.

D.o.E. (Department of the Environment) (1977), *Housing Policy: a consultative document Cmnd 6851*, HMSO: London.

D.o.E. (Department of the Environment) (1980), *Land for Private Housebuilding - Circular 9/80*, HMSO: London.

D.o.E. (Department of the Environment) (1980a), *Development Control Policy and Practice Circular 22/80*, HMSO: London.

D.o.E. (Department of the Environment) (1984), Land for Housing Circular 15/84, London: HMSO.

D.o.E. (Department of the Environment) (1984), *Memorandum on Structure and Local Plans - Circular 22/84*, HMSO: London.

D.o.E. (Department of the Environment) (1985), *Development and Employment Circular 14/85*, HMSO: London.

D.o.E. (Department of the Environment) (1987), *Housing: the Governments' Proposals, September 1987, Cmnd 214*, HMSO: London.

D.o.E. (Department of the Environment) (1989), *Planning control in Western Europe*, HMSO: London.

D.o.E. (Department of the Environment) (1991), *Planning and Affordable Housing, Circular 7/91*, HMSO: London.

D.o.E. (Department of the Environment) (1992), *Planning Policy Guidance Note 3, Paragraph 5-045*, HMSO: London.

D.o.E. (Department of the Environment) (1995), *Our Future Homes*, HMSO: London.

D.o.E. (Department of the Environment), (1997) *Housing and Construction Statistics*, HMSO; London.

Donnison, D and Ungerson, C (1982), *Housing Policy*, Harmondsworth Penguin: Middlesex.

Duncan, S. and Barlow, J (1988), The Use and Abuse of Housing Tenure, *Housing Studies*, Vol. 3, No.4, Longman:Harlow.

Dunsire, A (1978), *Implementing in a Bureaucracy*, Martin Robertson: Oxford.

Duvigneau, H and Schöneveld, B (1989), *Social housing policy, Federal Republic of Germany*, Brussels (c.o.f.a.c.e. document).

Dyker, D (1992), *The National Economies of Europe*, Longman: Harlow.

Easton, D (1965), *The Political System*, Knopf: New York.

Eisel, D (1993), *Household and housing stock data*, Statistiches Bundesamt: Wiesbaden.

Ellison, R (1993), *Housing stock data*, Department of the Environment: London.

Emms, P (1990), *Social housing in Europe: a European dilemma?*, SAUS: University of Bristol.

Epsing-Andersen, G (1990), *The Three Worlds of Welfare Capitalism*, Polity Press: Cambridge.

Ernst, W (1991), *Zur geschichtlichen Entwicklung der Raumordnung, Landes und Regionalplanung in der Bundesrepublik Deutschland*, Verlag der ARL: Hannover.

European Commission, (1994), *European Economy*, E.C.

Facione, P (1994), *The Students Guide to Philosophy*, Mayfield Publishing Company: USA.

Faludi, A (1989), Keeping the Netherlands in shape, *Built Environment* Vol. 15, No.1, Alexandrine Press: Newcastle.

Finanztest (1996), Hier hilft der Staat, *Stiftung Warentest*, 4/96.

Fleming, S (1984), *Housebuilders in an Area of Growth: Negotiation the Built Environment of Central Berkshire*, Geographical Papers, No. 84, University of Reading.

Fleurke, F and de Vries, P (1990), Decentralizing Public Housing in the Netherlands, *Netherlands Journal of Housing and Environmental Research*, Vol. 5, No.1, Delft University Press: Delft.

Form, W (1954), The Place of Social Structure in the Determination of Land Use in Stewart, M (ed.) *The City: problems of planning; selected readings*, The Open University: Penguin Education.

Forrest, R (1995), Editorial comment, *European Network for Housing Research Newsletter*, 3/95.

Frank, K (1978), Planungswörterbuch des Deutschen Verbandes für Wohnungswesen, Städtebau und Raumplanung; *Handlexicon für Bauherren, Hauskäufer und Wohnungseigentümer*, Goldmann Ratgeber.

Fuerst, J (1974), *Public Housing in Europe and America*, Croom Helm: London.

Fürst, D and Ritter, E (1993), *Landesentwicklungsplanung und Regional planung; ein verwaltungswissenschaftlicher Grundriß*, Werner Verlag.

Gee, C (1994) *Interview*, June 1994, University of Vaihingen, Baden Württemburg, Germany.

Gibb, K and Munro, M (1991), *Housing Finance in the UK: an Introduction*, Macmillan: Basingstoke.

Giddens, A (1979), *Central Problems in Social Theory: Action, Structure and Contradiction in Social Analysis*, Macmillan: London.

Giddens, A (1982), *Profiles and Critiques in Social Theory*, Macmillan: London.

Giddens, A (1984), *Capitalism and the modern social theory: an analysis of the writings of Marx, Durkheim and Max Weber*, Cambridge University Press: London.

Gillen, M (1994), Volume House Building Companies: Identification and Economic Influence, *paper presented to the European Network for Housing Research Conference*, Glasgow, Scotland 29th August - 2nd September 1994.

Gladdish, K (1991), *Governing from the Centre*, Routledge: London.

Golland, A, Carter, N and Oxley, M (1994), Stuttgart makes adjustment to regional planning machine, *Planning*, Vol 1078, Ambit Publishing Limited: Gloucester.

Golland, A (1996), Housing Supply, Profit and Housing Production: the case of the United Kingdom, the Netherlands and Germany, *Netherlands Journal of Housing and the Built Environment*, Vol. 11, No.1, Delft University Press.

Goodchild, R and Munton, R (1985), *Development and the Landowner*, Allen and Unwin: London.

Gruchy, C (1977), *Germany: comparing Economic systems: competing ways to stability, growth and welfare*, Mifflin Company: Houghton.

Hallett, G (1977), *Housing and Land Policies in West Germany and Britain*, Macmillan: London.

Ham, C and Hill, M (1984), *The Policy Process in the Modern Capitalist State*, Harvester Wheatsheaf: Hemel Hempstead.

Hands, D and Yendole, B (1992), Planning: Development still favoured - presumably?, *Estates Gazette*, Edition 9243, Reed Publishing: London.

Harloe, M (1978), in Brown, M and S. Baldwin (eds), The Year Book of Social Policy in Britain, 1977, Routledge and Kegan Paul.

Harloe, M (1988), The Changing role of Social Rented Housing, in Ball, M, Harloe, M and Martens, M (eds.), *Housing and Social Change in Europe and the USA*, Routledge: London.

Harvey, J (1987), *Urban Land Economics: the Economics of Real Property*, Macmillan: Basingstoke.

Hatim, B and Mason, I (1990), *Discourse and the Translator*, Longman:Harlow.

Healey, P and Barrett, S (1990), Structure and Agency in Land and Property Development Processes: some ideas for Research, *Urban Studies*, Vol. 27, No 1.

Healey, P (1991), Models of the Development process: a Review, *Journal of Property Research* Vol. 8, No.3, E.F. & N. Spon.

Healey, P (1992), Development Plans and Markets, *Planning Practice and Research*, Vol 7, No 2, Pion Limited: London.

Hillebrandt, P (1985), *Economic Theory and the Construction Industry*, Macmillan: London/Basingstoke.

Hogwood, B and Gunn, L (1984), *Policy Analysis for the Real World*, Oxford University Press.

Holmans, A (1987), *Housing Policy in Britain: a History*, Croom Helm: London.

Hooper, A (1989), Federal Republic of Germany, in Davies, H (ed.) *Planning Control in Western Europe*, HMSO.

Hooper, A (1992), The construction of theory: a comment, *Journal of Property Research*, Vol 9, E.and F.N.Spon: London.

Hospers, J (1970), *An Introduction to Philosophical Analysis*, Routledge and Kegan Paul Ltd.

Hughes, J (1990), *The Philosophy of Social Research*, Longman: Harlow.

Imming F (1993), *Housing stock data*, Statistiches Bundesamt: Wiesbaden.

Inside Housing (1994), *Dutch have courage to go it alone*, 27th May 1994, Inside Communications Limited: London.

Jaedicke, W and Wollmann, H (1990), in van Vliet, W. *The International handbook of housing policies and practice*, Greenwood Press: New York.

Jaffe, A (1989), Concepts of Property, Theories of Housing and the Choice of Housing Policy, *Netherlands Journal of Housing and Environmental Research*, Vol. 4, No. 4, Delft University Press.

Jenkis, H (1993), Die Wohnungsbaufinanzierung; Die Entwicklung der marktwirtschaftlichen Wohnungsbaufinanzierung bis heute, in Jenkis, H (ed.) *Kompendium der Wohnungwirtschaft*, 2nd Edition, Oldenbourg: Munich.

Jewell, B (1993), *The UK Economy and Europe*, Pitman Publishing.

Joseph Rowntree Foundation (1994), *Inquiry into Planning for Housing*, Joseph Rowntree Foundation: York.

Joseph Rowntree Foundation, (1995), *Housing demand and need in England 1991 - 2011* (Holmans A.), Findings No. 157, Joseph Rowntree Foundation: York.

Kaplan, A (1968), Positivism, *International Encyclopaedia of Social Sciences*, Volume 12, Crowell, Collier and Macmillan.

Kavanagh, D (1990), *British Politics - Continuities and Change*, Oxford University Press.

Keeble, L (1969), *Principles and Practice of Town and Country Planning*, Estates Gazette: Reed Publishing.

Kemeny, J (1987), Towards theorized housing studies: A counter-critique of the Provision Thesis, *Housing Studies*, Vol. 2, No.4, Longman.

Kemeny, J (1994), *Understanding European Rental Systems*, Working Paper, No 120, SAUS: Bristol.

Kimminich, O (1986), Town and Country Planning in the Federal Republic of Germany, in: Garner: *Planning law in Western Europe*, North Holland Publishing.

King, P (1995), *Introduction to Social Science Methods and Perspectives*, Department of Land Management, De Montfort University: Leicester.

King, D (1993), Demography and house building needs; a critique of the demographic bulldozer scenario in Champion, T (ed.) *Population Matters*, Athenaeum Press: Newcastle.

Kirchner, J and Sautter, H (1993), Kommunale Wohnungspolitik, in Roth. T and Wollmann, H (eds.) *Kommunalpolitik; Politisches Handeln in den Gemeinden*, Bundeszentrale für politische Bildung.

Klaren, H and Verpalen, J (1989), *Position Paper for the Netherlands*, Project Group on Urban Land Markets, Organization for Economic Co-operation and Development.

Kühne-Büning, L (1991), Wohnungswirtschaft und Konjunktur, in Jenkis, H *Kompendium der Wohnungwirtschaft*, Oldenbourg: Munich.

Kunzmann, K (1984), Germany, in Williams, R (ed.) *Planning in Western Europe*, Allen and Unwin.

Lauschmann, E (1991), Zur Bedeutung der Wohnungspolitik für die Regionalpolitik und Raumordnung, *Raumordnung und Raumplanung*, Heft 5.

LBS (Landesbausparkassen) (1997), *Schritte beim Hausbau*, LBS.

Leutner, B and Jensen, D (1988), German Federal Republic, in Kroes, H, Ymkers. F and Mulder, A (eds.) *Between owner-occupation and rented sector*.

Leutner, B (1990), *Wohnungspolitik nach dem 2. Weltkrieg*, B.M.Bau, (Bundesministerium für Raumordnung, Bauwesen und Städtebau), Bonn: Bad Godesburg.

Ligterink, R (1993), *Household and Housing stock data*, Ministerie van Volkshuisvesting, Ruimtelijke Ordening en Milieubeheer (MVROM): Den Haag.

Lijphart, J (1968), *The Politics of Accommodation, Pluralism and Democracy in the Netherlands*, University of Cardiff Press.

Lipsey, R (1973), *An Introduction to Positive Economics*, Weidenfeld and Nicolson: London.

Long, D (1994), *Household and Housing stock data*, Department of the Environment (D.o.E): London.

Lösche, P (1993), *Kleine Geschichte der Deutschen Partein*, Kohlhammer Verlag.

Maclennan, D (1993), A more flexible housing system: the case for private renting, *Housing and Planning Review* Oct/Nov 1993, N.H.T.P.C: London.

Malpass, P (1986), *The Housing Crisis*, Croom Helm: London.

Malpass, P (1992), in Birchall, J (ed.) *Housing Policy in the 1990s*, Routledge: London.

Malpass, P and Murie, A (1991), *Housing Policy and Practice*, Macmillan: Basingstoke.

Malpass, P and Murie, A (1994), *Housing Policy and Practice*, Macmillan: Basingstoke.

Massey, D and Catelano, A (1978), *Capital and Land*, Edward Arnold: London.

Matznetter, W (1995), *From Comparative Housing Policy to European Housing Research*, paper presented to the European Network for Housing Research Conference, Vienna.

Morgan, P and Nott, S (1988), *Development Control; Policy into Practice*, Butterworth.

MVROM, (Ministerie van Volkshuisvesting, Ruimtelijke Ordening en Milieubeheer) (1974), *Nota Huur en Subsidie Beleid*, SDU-Uitgeverij: Den Haag.

MVROM, (Ministerie van Volkshuisvesting, Ruimtelijke Ordening en Milieubeheer) (1989), *Nota Volkshuisvesting in de Jaren Negentig; van bouwen naar wonen*, SDU-Uitgeverij: Den Haag.

MVROM (Ministerie van Volkshuisvesting, Ruimtelijke Ordening en Milieubeheer) (1991a), *Foreign land policy in a Dutch perspective*, MVROM: Den Haag.

MVROM (Ministerie van Volkshuisvesting, Ruimtelijke Ordening en Milieubeheer) (1991b), Land *Policy of the central government for house production since 1900*, MVROM: Den Haag.

MVROM (Ministerie van Volkshuisvesting, Ruimtelijke Ordening en Milieubeheer) (1991c), *Grondprijzen en kavels 1991*, TAUW Infra Consult B.V.

Needham, B (1988), in Hallett, G (ed.) *Land and Housing policies in Europe and North America: a comparative analysis*, Routledge: London.

Needham, B (1992), A Theory of Land Prices when Land is Supplied Publicly: The Case of the Netherlands, *Urban Studies*: Carfax Publishing.

Needham, B, Kruijt, B and Koenders, P (1993), *Urban Land and Property Markets in the Netherlands*, UCL Press: London.

NVM (Nederlandse Vereiniging van Makelaars), *Intern*, NVM: Nieuwegein.

NWR (Nationale Woningraad) (1995), *Social Housing in the Netherlands*, NWR: Almere.

Oakeshott, P (1974), *Rationalism in Politics and other essays*, Methuen: London.

Oxley, M (1983), *Housing Policy in Europe*, PhD Thesis, Leicester University.

Oxley, M (1987), The Aims and Effects of Housing Allowances in Western Europe, in van Vliet, W (ed.) *Housing Markets and Policies under Fiscal Austerity*, Greenwood Press: London.

Oxley, M (1995), Book review, *Housing Studies*, Vol. 10, No.5, Longman.

Oxley, M (1995a), Private and Social Housing in Europe: Distinctions, Comparisons and Resource Allocation, *Scandanavian Housing and Planning Research*, Vol 12, Scandanavian University Press: Oslo.

Oxley, M (1991), The Aims and Methods of Comparative Housing Research, *Scandanavian Housing and Planning Research* No.8, Scandanavian University Press: Oslo.

Oxley, M, Golland, A and Carter, N (1995), The case for more housing in the UK, based on European comparisons, *Housing and Planning Review*, Vol. 50, No 1, February 1995, N.H.T.P.C: London.

Oxley, M and Smith, J (1995), Housing Investment, Macroeconomics and Demographics in Europe, *Netherlands Journal of Housing and the Built Environment*, Vol. 10, No. 3, Delft University Press.

Oxley, M. and J. Smith (1996), *Housing Investment in the UK: A European comparison*, Avebury: Aldershot.

Pahl, R (1977), *Managers, technical experts and the state*, in Harloe, M (ed.) Captive cities, John Wiley.

Papa, O (1992), *Housing systems in Europe, Part 2: a comparative study of housing finance*, Delft University Press.

Popper, K (1963), *Conjectures and Refutations*, Routledge: London.

Power, A (1993), *Hovels to High-Rise; state housing in Europe since 1850*, Routledge: London.

Prest, A (1981), *The taxation of urban land*, Manchester University Press.

Priemus, H (1984), *Bouwproces en Woningbouwmarkt*, Volkshuisvesting in theorie en praktijk 5: Delft University Press.

Priemus, H (1990), *Housing: Changing Roles of Government*, International Research Conference, Housing Debates - Urban Challenges, Paris.

Priemus, H (1991), Economic and Demographic Stagnation, Housing and Housing Policy; The Case of the Netherlands (1974-1984), *Housing Studies*, Vol. 2, No.1, Longman.

Priemus, H (1995), How to abolish social housing? The Dutch case, *International Journal of Urban and Regional Research*, Vol. 19, No. 1.

Purdue, M (1994), The Impact of Section 54A, *Journal of Planning and Environmental Law*, Sweet and Maxwell: London.

Radley, S (1996), *Sustainable Home Ownership: A New Concept*, The Henley Centre/Joseph Rowntree Foundation.

RDM (Ring Deutscher Maklers) (1995), *Preisspiegel*, Ring Deutscher Maklers: Hamburg.

Renier, F.G. (1992) *Dutch Dictionary*, Routledge: London.

Rosemann, J and Westra, H (1988), *'Neue Heimat' en de gevolgen*, Delft University Press.

Ross, A (1952), Design for a Brain: *The Origin of Adaptive Behavior*, Wiley: New York.

Royal Institution of Chartered Surveyors (RICS) (1994), *Building Cost Information Service*, RICS: London.

Ruonavarra, H (1993), Types and forms of Housing Tenure: Towards solving the Comparison/Translation Problem, *Scandanavian Housing and Planning Research* Vol. 10, Oslo: Scandanavian University Press: Oslo.

Saldern, von A (1993), Geschichte der kommunale Selbstverwaltung in Deutschland, in Roth and Wollmann (ed.) *Kommunalpolitik; Politisches Handeln in den Gemeinden*, Bundeszentrale für politische Bildung.

Saunders, P (1990), A *Nation of Home Owners*, Unwin Hyman.

Sayer, A (1995), *Radical political economy: a critique*, Blackwell Publishers: Oxford.

Schans, van der, J (1995), *Interview*, 12th April 1995, Rotterdam municipality, Netherlands.

Schar, van der J (1987), *Groei en bloei van het Nederlandse Volkhuisvestingsbelied*, Delft University Press.

Schmidt, S (1989), Convergence Theory, Labour Movements and Corporatism: the Case of Housing, *Scandanavian Housing and Planning Research* No.6, Scandanavian University Press, Oslo: Scandanavian University Press: Oslo.

Schmitz, W (1991), Der neue Bauherrenmodell-Erlaß in der Praxis, *Grundstückmarkt und Grundstückmarktwert* 3/91.

Scholland, R (1987), *Die Bedeutung der Funktionsweise des Bodensmarktes*, Allgemeines Vermessungsnachrichten.

Short, J (1982), *Housing in Britain: the post-war experience*, Methuen: London.

Simmie, J (1981), *Power, Property and Corporatism: the Political Sociology of Planning*, Macmillan Press: London.

Smyth, H (1982), *Land Banking, Land Availability and Planning for Private Housebuilding*, Working Paper 23 SAUS: University of Bristol.

Spaans, M, Golland, A and Carter, N (1996), Land Supply and Housing Development: a comparative analysis of Britain and the Netherlands 1970-1995, *International Planning Studies*, Vol. 1, No.3, Carfax Publishing.

Stevens, P (1994), Affordable Housing - DoE Policy under Threat, *Property Review*, March 1994, Eclipse Publishing Limited.

Thornley, A (1991), *Urban Planning under Thatcherism: the challenge of the Market*, Routledge: London.

Thornley, A (1993), Ideology and the By-passing of the Planning System: Case Studies of Canary Wharf and the Globe, Stockholm, *European Planning Studies*, Vol. 1, No.2.

Ulbrich, R (1991), Die Bauherren als Anbieter, in Ed: Jenkis H, *Kompendium der Wohnungswirtschaft*, 1st Edition, Oldenbourg: Munich.

Ulbrich, R (1996), Die Bauherren als Anbieter, in Ed: Jenkis H, *Kompendium der Wohnungswirtschaft*, 3rd Edition, Oldenbourg: Munich.

United Nations, *Annual Bulletin of Housing and Construction Statistics*, United Nations.

United Nations (1994), *Annual Bulletin of Housing and Construction Statistics*, United Nations.

Vries, O (1997), *Economisch Instituut voor de Bouwnijverheid*, Amsterdam.

Weber, M (1947), *The Theory of Social and Economic Organization*, Free Press: Glencoe.

Werner, J (1974), Trade Union Housing in Western Germany, in Ed: Fuerst, J.S. (1974) *Public Housing in Europe and America*, Croom Helm: London.

Wigmans, G (1992), *Uiteenzetting Grondexploitatiebegroting*, Faculteit Bouwkunde, Delft University.

Wigmans, G (1993) *Interview*, February 1993, Faculty of Bouwkunde, University of Delft, the Netherlands.

Williams, R and Wood, B (1994), *Urban Land and Property Markets: the UK*, University College Press: London.

Wittgenstein, L (1951), *Tractatus Logico-Philosophicus*, Routledge and Kegan Paul: London.